Human Growth and Development

Human Growth and Development

Chris Beckett

SAGE Publications
London ● Thousand Oaks ● New Delhi

SAGE Publications Ltd
1 Oliver's Yard
55 City Road
London EC1Y 1SP

SAGE Publications Inc
2455 Teller Road
Thousand Oaks
California 91320

SAGE Publications India Pvt. Ltd
B1/11 Mohan Cooperative Industrial Area
Mathura Road, New Delhi 110 044
India

SAGE Publications Asia-Pacific Pte Ltd
33 Pekin Street #02-01
Far East Square
Singapore 048763

British Library Cataloguing in Publication data
A catalogue record for this book is available from the British Library

ISBN 978-0-7619-7248-8
ISBN 978-0-7619-7249-5 (pbk)

Typeset by Keystroke, Jacaranda Lodge, Wolverhampton
Printed and bound in Great Britain by
Cromwell Press Limited, Trowbridge, Wiltshire

Contents

Introduction

This book is about how human beings grow and change over their lives, emotionally, psychologically, intellectually – and as social beings. Even a book twenty times this length could not hope to offer a comprehensive coverage of this question and this book does not claim to do so. I hope, however, that it will provide an introduction to some of the main ideas that emerged in this area during the last century – and to some of the objections to and limitations of those ideas.

Though this book is intended to be of interest to the general reader, it is aimed particularly at those working in, or studying for, the caring professions – professions such as social work, teaching, medicine, and nursing – for whom how human beings change is not just a matter of academic interest but one of practical concern. People in these professions have to draw on their understanding of what makes people grow and change in order to assess situations and decide on actions. In the absence of anything else, they have to rely on what they have learnt through their own experience. But I hope this book will add something to the 'tool-kit' of ideas which they use, and I have tried to illustrate the ideas with some practical examples such as might be encountered in the 'real world'.

There is no exact science of human growth and development. Not only is the subject too large to cover in one book, but even if you could read and remember everything about it that had ever been written, you would find that it would not add up to a single consensus. There would be gaps, contradictions and fundamental differences of opinion even about quite basic questions. But it is my own conviction that people working with people need an opportunity to test out their own ideas and try out different ideas and perspectives. So my aim has been not to write a detailed and up-to-the-minute account of academic debate in the various areas, but to provide a flavour of a range of contrasting approaches, for you to follow up on as you see fit.

Assumptions

In writing this book I have made certain assumptions about you as a reader. I have assumed that you live in what is loosely referred to as a 'Western' country, that is a country in the industrialised world. Naturally I hope the book will be of interest to readers living in the developing world too, but if I had written a book for them, my emphasis would have been different, and I would have wanted to do more research into the ideas and traditions that are important in those countries. All the ideas I present in this book, I would suggest, are in the Western scientific-rationalist tradition (even though there are considerable disagreements between the originators of these ideas, and some would question the right of others to call themselves 'scientific') I have, however, tried to acknowledge that there are other points of view to the 'Western' one, and that even within the so-called 'West' there are many millions of people with roots in other traditions, including no doubt some who will read this book.

I have also made the assumption that the reader is an adult. Children and teenagers are of course most welcome to read it, but if I had been writing a book specifically for them, again I would have chosen a different approach.

What I have tried *not* to do is to make assumptions about the gender, age or background of the reader, apart from these limitations. Some of the writers whom I quote have been guilty of gender bias and perhaps of making assumptions based on their particular social class. I have tried to avoid this, but no doubt have not always succeeded.

Except where it would cause confusion, I have used 'she' and 'her', to refer to a person of unspecified sex. This is to avoid the traditional practice of always using 'he' and 'him' in such circumstances, while at the same time avoiding the cumbersome 'his/her' and 'he/she'.

Viewpoint

There are many different perspectives from which you can look at human growth and development. You can look at it from a primarily biological viewpoint, looking at physical changes and chemistry, and some other books indeed do so. Or you can look at it from a psychological viewpoint, looking at what goes on in people's minds. Or you can look at it from the sociological point of view, which tends to see individual thoughts and feelings and beliefs as being 'socially constructed', the products of forces in society as a whole. (There are probably other ways of approaching the question too: a literary approach, perhaps, or a theological one, for example.)

In this book I will be looking at human growth and development mainly from a *psychosocial* and *pragmatic* point of view.

I say 'psychosocial' because my emphasis has been on the way an individual grows and develops through interaction with those around her. Although I allude to biological and wider sociological factors, I have not arranged the book around them (which is not to say that either the biological or sociological points of view are any less valid).

I say 'pragmatic' because, as I have already said, the bias of this book is towards the practical implications of different ideas, rather than towards the finer points of academic debate.

A limitation of this book is that I have not been able to go into much detail about the methodology used to arrive at the various ideas presented in this book, though this is clearly important for any detailed consideration of an idea or theory. Another limitation is that I have not, except in passing, gone into the various therapeutic approaches that flow out of the various different theoretical models.

Grand Theories and Dead White Men

The first part of the twentieth century was characterised by several 'grand theories' associated with famous names, such as Freud, Piaget and Bowlby. And they are mainly male famous names and white ones too, though there are influential women as well, such as Melanie Klein and Mary Ainsworth (whom I discuss in Chapters 2 and 3).

During the latter part of the twentieth century, these grand theories were modified and their boundaries blurred. The development of attachment theory (the subject of Chapter 3) is a good example of this: ideas which came originally from the Freudian tradition have been modified by empirical research on humans and animals. Likewise, 'cognitive psychology' and 'learning theory' (the subjects of Chapters 4 and 5), which were once very separate fields, now overlap in many areas. So things have moved on, but an introduction to this subject would be difficult to do without looking at the 'grand theories' which were the starting point for so much subsequent thinking. I appreciate however that some may dislike the apparent emphasis on the thinking of 'dead, white men'.

How this Book is Arranged

The chapter headings are, I hope, self-explanatory. The book begins with a birth and ends with a death; the first few chapters look mainly at childhood; the latter part moves on through ideas about adolescence, adulthood and old age. So the book's structure very roughly corresponds to the course of a human life. But some chapters are focused on a particular theoretical approach, others simply on a particular topic (Chapter 6 deals with the topic of adolescence, for example).

At the beginning of each chapter you will find a box listing the topics covered. This is followed by an introduction to the subject matter of the chapter and the various topics to be covered then follow under headings and sub-headings. At the end of each chapter is another box giving a summary of the chapter.

Activities

In each chapter you will find some 'activities' in numbered boxes, indicated with the symbol ✷. These are intended to provide you with opportunities to reflect on what you have been reading and to relate it to your own experience. I will sometimes ask you to reflect on your own life experience, partly because our own life experience is inevitably the most vivid source of information that we have about human growth and development – and partly because I think it is important to be aware of 'where you are coming from' yourself when you get involved in other people's lives. (Such reflections can occasionally be unexpectedly distressing, and if you find them so, I do hope that the distress involved is outweighed by the benefit.)

After each activity, I discuss the implications of the activity and sometimes suggest answers to questions where appropriate.

Although it is obviously up to you how much time you give to the activities – and I realise that some people dislike such devices, or do not find them useful – you do need at least to read them through because I will refer to them in the subsequent text.

From time to time, I have also inserted boxes in the text covering particular topics or providing additional commentary to the main text. These are marked with the symbol 📖.

References and suggested reading

Where I quote someone in the text, I give the name of the author (or of the first author in the case of texts with more than two authors) and the date of publication. A more detailed, comprehensive list of these references appears at the end of the book, listed by chapters.

At the end of each chapter, under the heading 'Suggested Reading', I suggest some books that you might want to look at if you want to pursue a subject further. Of course this is not in any way a comprehensive list, but hopefully it will be a useful starting point.

1 The Birth of a Human Being

What makes us who we are?

In a delivery room in a maternity hospital, a mother is about to give birth after an eight-hour labour. There are four people present: the mother herself, the baby's father, a midwife and a doctor. Everyone is trying to encourage the exhausted mother ('Keep pushing!' 'You're almost there!' 'Don't forget your breathing!').

Then the father shouts out excitedly 'I can see its head!'

Suddenly a fifth human being is in the room, a stranger, a new being that no one has ever seen before (though across the world four new babies are born every second).

'It's a girl!' says the midwife.

It's about the only thing they can tell about her at this stage, though soon they will weigh her and then there will be another fact to tell the relatives over the phone. If she had some obvious physical abnormality – a missing limb, a harelip, a spinal deformity – that would of course be another thing that they could see, and something that might drastically alter their initial response (see Chapter 9). *But apart from that, what else can they know about her?*

Even her future appearance can't really be discerned from the wizened ancient-looking little face (however much they may tell themselves she has her father's eyes, her mother's chin . . .), let alone her future personality, her future abilities, her future life story.

What will she become? Will she be the prime minister or an office cleaner? Will she be happy? Will she be healthy? Will she be loved? Will she win honours or commit crimes? Will she one day be in a place like this bringing her own baby into the world?

It is impossible to tell.

What is it that determines what sort of person we become? Is a child's future personality already determined at birth, or is a newborn baby like a blank sheet, waiting to be written on by life? Or perhaps both of those perspectives are too passive? Perhaps we somehow choose for ourselves who we are, create ourselves out of nothing? But if so, why do we make such different choices? These are important questions not only from an academic point of view, but also from a very practical one, because our views on these questions radically affect the way we see the world, our attitudes to other people and way we work with other people.

In this chapter I want to provide an overview of the sorts of questions that I will be looking at later in the book and at the sorts of answers, limited and debatable as they are, that are available for those questions. To begin with, I will ask you to look at your own ideas and assumptions about what makes people who they are, as it is really those ideas and assumptions which will either be validated or called into question by what you read in this book.

Then I want to offer a 'health warning' about theories. Fortunately or unfortunately, no theory about human life can ever be completely objective or value-free. Trying to look at ourselves completely objectively is perhaps a bit like trying to catch your mirror image when it's not looking at you. So I will suggest that you adopt a critical stance not only to your own existing ideas, but also to the ideas that I will present here – including of course my own.

I will then look at the ancient question of 'nature versus nurture'. Is who we are determined at birth, or are we shaped by the environment? And I will discuss the factors, both inherited and environmental, that contribute to human development, and consider how these factors interact.

In conclusion I will ask you to consider another very ancient philosophical question: that of 'free will' versus 'predetermination'. Can we choose our own lives, or are our lives determined by outside factors?

Ideas, Theories and Prejudices

Theories about people are not confined to psychologists and philosophers. All of us have been studying other people all our lives – if for no other reason than to work out how best to deal with them. All our lives we are also exposed to the ideas of others and the 'accepted wisdom' of the society in which we live. So we all have an enormous store of ideas, theories, information and, undoubtedly, misinformation in our heads about what makes people what they are.

The following activity may draw to your attention some of your own ideas and assumptions about what shapes people's lives.

✷ Activity 1.1 ✷

The following are some types of anti-social behaviour which you might encounter, either directly, or in the news. Why do people behave in these ways? Jot down a few thoughts for each.

- parents spending all their family income on heroin
- women violently assaulting men
- a man who attacks strangers with a sword, believing he is doing God's will
- adults injuring children in uncontrolled outbursts of rage
- obtaining money by threats of violence
- adults deliberately tormenting children
- men violently assaulting women
- shoplifting
- politicians accepting bribes
- children tormenting animals
- adults sexually abusing children

Comments on Activity 1.1

If you look at your answers you may find that they fall into a number of different categories. In some cases your answer may constitute a moral judgement: 'greed', 'selfishness' and so on. (A lot of people might describe corrupt politicians as greedy, for example, and regard that as sufficient explanation for their behaviour.) In other cases you may have explained the behaviour in quasi-medical terms, without any moral judgement. (You might describe the swordsman as suffering from a mental illness which has distorted his thinking, or perhaps the drug-abusing parents as having their thinking distorted by addiction.) Or in some cases you may use past events to account for behaviour. (You may have thought that a child who torments animals has probably been mistreated in some way herself.)

In short, in some cases you will have been inclined to say that there is a reason which accounts for the behaviour and to some extent 'excuses' it, whereas in other cases you will have been more inclined to say that the behaviour is simply 'bad'.

Actually which behaviour we choose to view in purely moral terms, and which behaviour we choose to understand in terms of external or internal causes is probably quite an arbitrary distinction which is as much to do with our own personal circumstances as anything else. If you are a smoker, or if you use or have used illegal drugs, you may find drug addiction relatively easy to understand. Whether you are a man or a woman may well affect your attitude to several of the behaviours described. Parents are often more understanding than non-parents, of people who injure their children in a rage, because most parents have experienced such rages, even if they have not acted on them. Most of us are more tolerant of 'crimes of passion' than of premeditated crimes, such as sexually abusing children or accepting bribes. And yet if we have experience of compulsive behaviour of some sort (even if it is only, say, a compulsion to buy cigarettes or play computer games) we may understand that a person who appears to act coldly and rationally may in fact be driven in some way. A corrupt politician who accepts bribes is greedy, yes, but why are some greedy in that way and others not at all? If it is sufficient explanation to describe the corrupt politician as 'greedy', why is it not sufficient explanation to describe the child who torments animals as simply 'wicked'?

I would suggest that our own theories and ideas about why people are as they are and behave as they behave, are usually quite inconsistent and arbitrary, based on our own experience and on our own needs.

A 'health warning' about theories

One of the implications of we have just been looking at is that our own personal interests influence the way we see the world. We are more likely to condemn behaviour which we ourselves are not guilty of, and excuse behaviour which we understand from our own personal experience. And this is true not just on an individual level but on a much wider level too.

We use ideas and theories to help us understand what makes us become what we are. But ideas and theories themselves grow and change and are shaped by circumstances. No theory about human beings, whether it is one we made up ourselves or one that is in a textbook, can be value-free. Things look different depending on our perspective, and on the dominant ideology of the society in which we live. For example Sigmund Freud, who I discuss in the next chapter, is sometimes criticised for basing a theory largely on the neuroses of middle-class Austrian Jewish women at a particular point in history, seen from the perspective of a middle-class Austrian Jewish man.

All the ideas I am going to discuss in this book, including of course my own comments, contain assumptions which can be challenged. Among the assumptions you will notice and may wish to question, you will find:

- assumptions about the roles of men and women
- assumptions that North American/European society is somehow the norm for the whole world (what are called 'Eurocentric' assumptions)
- assumptions that ideas derived from the study of prosperous middle-class people are necessarily relevant to people from different backgrounds

Many ideas have been widely accepted in the past, which we now would regard as obviously untrue. For instance, well into the twentieth century there was a wide consensus among men in Britain, America and most other countries that it would be a bad thing if women got the vote, that it would not be appropriate, in other words, for women to be involved in choosing the government of their own country. This formed part of a much wider ideological system that we now refer to as sexism, which is still with us. But there must be very few people now in Britain who would seriously argue that women should not have the vote, even though less than a century ago this was seen by many as a perfectly sensible and reasonable position to take.

Similarly, the idea that black people were inferior to white people was widely accepted, respectable, and even seen as 'common sense' during the heyday of slavery and empire building, presumably because it made things like buying and selling black people, or annexing territories inhabited by black people, seem somehow 'all right'. This ideology of racism – like sexism – became extremely pervasive. It is not surprising that racist ideas are still all around us and, whether we like it or not, within us.

Questionable assumptions will be present in many of the ideas we discuss in this book. When I notice them, I will point them out. You will probably spot others. If you would like to see a more rigorous critique of developmental theories than I will give here, you could look, for example, at Burman (1994).

But more generally you should bear in mind that just because an idea is widely accepted does not mean that it is 'true'. *Any* idea serves a purpose and we should consider what that purpose might be – and whose purpose it is. This applies to ordinary and everyday ideas, including your own, as well as to big ideological systems.

The so-called 'nature versus nurture' question, which we will now consider, demonstrates very well how ideas can be used to serve such purposes – and it provides some examples of how different ideas have been used for political ends, as well as of how ideas may be used by individuals on a day-to-day basis to justify their own position.

Nature versus Nurture

Which is more important in determining who we are and what we become? Biological inheritance ('nature')? Or the environment ('nurture')? As well as being a philosophical and scientific question since classical times, this is also a *highly* political question. 'Nature' or 'nurture' theories can both be used by vested interests – at the level of society at large and at the individual level – to justify their position or their actions.

But before I go on, here is an exercise to explore where you yourself stand on the nature–nurture question.

⚒ Activity 1.2 ⚒

At the beginning of this chapter I described the birth of a (fictional) child, and wondered what kind of person she would become: prime minister or office cleaner?

1 Suppose her parents were Mr and Mrs Smith. One was an office cleaner, and the other was long-term unemployed. Neither has any educational qualifications. What does that make you think about her chances of becoming prime minister?
2 Suppose her parents were Mr and Mrs Jones. Both came from distinguished, wealthy families. One is a world famous economist, the other a TV personality. How likely is it that she will become an office cleaner?
3 Suppose her parents were Mr and Mrs Smith, but both died in a tragic accident straight after her birth – and she was then adopted and brought up as their own by Mr and Mrs Jones. How do you see her future prospects?

Comments on Activity 1.2

You will probably agree that – in our society at least – the child of Mr and Mrs Smith is likely, on average, to have rather more modest career prospects than the child of Mr and Mrs Jones. There are many exceptions of course but, by and large, successful people are the children of other successful people, poor people are the children of other poor people. But why is this? Is it because successful people are born with above-average abilities – and pass these abilities on to their children through their genes? (That would be a 'nature' theory.) Or is it just because successful people are able to provide their children with a better education, a more stimulating environment, better contacts and so on? (That would be a 'nurture' theory.)

Where you stand on these questions will be indicated by your answer to question 3. Do you think that the child of Mr and Mrs Smith, if adopted by Mr and Mrs Jones, will perform just as well, in terms of career achievements, as a natural child of Mr and Mrs Jones would do? (If so, you take a 'nurture' view on the question of career success.) Or do you think that the child of Mr and Mrs Smith, even if exposed to all the advantages that Mr and Mrs Jones can offer, will still probably not be a high-flyer, because her natural parents were of limited ability? (If so, you lean towards a 'nature' view on this question.)

Of course career success is only one of a vast number of things that distinguish one person from another, of which some are clearly the products of genetic inheritance, while others are undoubtedly the products of environment. Few would dispute that hair colour is the result of genetic inheritance, or that the ability to speak Slovenian is a product of environment. No one is born with the ability to speak Slovenian. The ability is acquired either by growing up in a Slovenian-speaking environment, or of being taught Slovenian by someone else who speaks it. On the other hand the ability to acquire language as such *would* seem to be the product of genetic inheritance. With the possible exception of chimpanzees, who are genetically very close to human beings in any case, no other species is able to acquire language. And there are also specific genetically related conditions in humans which can impair language acquisition.

But when we come to discuss things such as personality traits, moral character, intelligence and abilities, then the argument becomes more difficult – and sometimes more heated.

The 'nature' viewpoint

The 'nature' viewpoint, as I'm calling it, is the view that what we are is mainly determined by our biological inheritance. The English philosopher Thomas Hobbes (1588–1679), for example, thought that human nature was wholly predetermined, that its characteristics were inherited and that it was based entirely on self-preservation. (It was he who famously described human life as 'solitary, poor, nasty, brutish and short'.) The French philosopher, Jean-Jacques Rousseau (1712–1778) by contrast believed that human beings were essentially good. Although his view of human nature is very different from that of Hobbes, they both have in common that they believe that there is *such a thing* as human nature: that human beings are born possessing a certain basic character.

Charles Darwin (1809–1882) showed how living things could change gradually over time as a result of 'natural selection', resulting eventually in new species. Animals or plants that thrived would pass on their characteristics to their offspring, so those characteristics would spread, but animals that coped less well would not be so successful in reproducing, so their characteristics would tend to die out. In essence, what 'natural selection' means is that nature accidentally achieves, over many thousands of years, the same kind of result that animal breeders achieve on purpose. In respect of physical characteristics, the evidence for Darwin's viewpoint is so overwhelming that there are few now who would dispute it.

Some would argue that the same principle can be applied to personality and behaviour. In *The Selfish Gene* the British zoologist Richard Dawkins (1976) starts with the conventional Darwinian premise that any gene that makes its bearer more likely to survive will multiply, while any gene that makes us less likely to survive will eventually die out. But he then extends this argument to genes which predispose us to different kinds of behaviour. If we assume that genes *do* shape behaviour, as well as physical characteristics, then it is hard to disagree with the idea that those genes which make us *behave* in ways that would enhance our chances of survival will be passed on, while other genes will eventually die out. Dawkins deduces from this that much of the behaviour that we think of as kindness or altruism must in fact serve the purposes of individual survival. A mother's care for her children, for example, is really about trying to ensure that they live to pass on her genes to yet another generation.

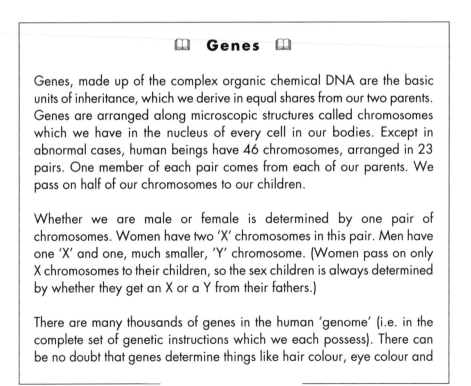

📖 Genes 📖

Genes, made up of the complex organic chemical DNA are the basic units of inheritance, which we derive in equal shares from our two parents. Genes are arranged along microscopic structures called chromosomes which we have in the nucleus of every cell in our bodies. Except in abnormal cases, human beings have 46 chromosomes, arranged in 23 pairs. One member of each pair comes from each of our parents. We pass on half of our chromosomes to our children.

Whether we are male or female is determined by one pair of chromosomes. Women have two 'X' chromosomes in this pair. Men have one 'X' and one, much smaller, 'Y' chromosome. (Women pass on only X chromosomes to their children, so the sex children is always determined by whether they get an X or a Y from their fathers.)

There are many thousands of genes in the human 'genome' (i.e. in the complete set of genetic instructions which we each possess). There can be no doubt that genes determine things like hair colour, eye colour and

continued

all kinds of other physical characteristics. (The fact that we are human and not another species is determined by our genes.) What is more controversial is the extent to which genes determine individual differences in personality, ability and so on.

The existence of genes had not yet been discovered in Darwin's day.

But, although few of us have any difficulty about the idea that genes determine our physical characteristics, to many it seems far-fetched – and perhaps also distasteful – to think of genes determining our behaviour as well. There are, however, countless examples in the animal kingdom of very complex and specific behaviours which are inherited rather than learnt. Spiders can build very intricate webs without being taught and birds navigate vast distances for their annual migrations without the benefit of maps or word of mouth.

Studies of twins are one way in which researchers have explored the influence of genetic inheritance on personality and other individual characteristics. There are two kinds of twins: so-called 'fraternal' twins are conceived at about the same time and grow together in their mother's womb, but they are no more closely related than any other pair of siblings (that is to say, that they share, on average, about 50 per cent of the same genes). Fraternal twins do not necessarily look alike and may not be of the same gender. 'Identical' twins, on the other hand, result when a single fertilised egg divides and the two resulting parts start growing into separate individuals. Such twins are not always *absolutely* identical because environmental factors – in the womb, at birth, or subsequently – may result in some differences. But they certainly look very alike – and they are *genetically* identical: they both have exactly the same set of genes.

Occasionally it happens that identical twins are separated at birth and this event allows scientists to look in reality at the kinds of questions that you considered hypothetically in Activity 1.2. Is it the genetic parents, or the environment and the adults who actually *raise* a child, who are the most powerful influence on the child's development? It is also possible to compare fraternal twins with identical twins.

Twin studies have shown that there are often surprising similarities between the lives, preferences, careers, and so on, of twins who have been separated. Twins Oskar and Jack were raised respectively as a Nazi in Czechoslovakia and a Jew in Trinidad, yet when they finally met as middle-aged men, both wore the same kind of shirt, and both had the habit of flushing the toilet before and after using it (Steen, 1996: 25). Recent research has tended to conclude that inheritance is the major factor in intelligence. The Minnesota Study of Twins Reared Apart concluded that variations in intelligence are 70 per cent related to inheritance, and only 30 per cent to all the environmental factors such as family circumstances, schooling, nutrition, and so on (Bouchard et al., 1990).

But there is a whole range of methodological difficulties with such studies, which should make us cautious of placing too much weight on such precise conclusions (see Steen, 1996: 26–32, for further discussion on this). Even extraordinary stories, such as that of Oskar and Jack just mentioned, should be treated with caution. Naturally people are amazed when they notice similarities like this and want to tell the tale, just as we all do when we encounter coincidences. We do not get to hear of instances where there are no such similarities, just as we do not tell the tale of the countless occasions in our lives when coincidences do not occur. Even in the case of Oskar and Jack we do not hear the things about them which they did *not* have in common.

There can be no doubt that genetics play an important role in making us who we are. But exactly how important a role this is continues to be a subject of debate. There have been claims in recent years, for example, that genetic causes have been identified for schizophrenia or autism, both of which have also been said to have been caused by childhood upbringing. It has even been suggested that a 'gay gene' making it more likely that a person will become homosexual, has been identified (see Steen 1996: 185ff.).

'Nature' ideas in everyday life

In common parlance the idea of the importance of inheritance is encapsulated in phrases such as 'blood will out', 'the leopard can't change its spots'.

The following exercise illustrates how 'nature' theories about human behaviour can crop up in a very direct way.

Activity 1.3

Matthew

You're a school teacher visiting a single-parent family, to discuss the problem of the son's poor attendance at school, and his poor work when he is there. The boy – Matthew, aged 13 – is getting in increasing trouble with the law as well as missing most of his schooling and he is staying out at nights. Matthew's father left the family home when Matthew was just 1, and now has no contact with him at all.

Matthew's mother says his father was violent towards her and constantly in trouble with the police. She says, 'Matthew takes after his father. There's nothing I can do about it.'

What is your reaction to this comment?

Comments on Activity 1.3

Matthew's behaviour may be similar to his father's in some respects, but, as you may have observed, this doesn't necessarily mean that this is some sort of unavoidable fate carried in the genes. There are all kinds of environmental reasons why Matthew might behave in the same sorts of ways as his father. For example, both Matthew and his father may have grown up in a community where there was a strong cultural expectation for boys to be 'hard'. There may be a long family history of fathers abandoning their families and for sons feeling hurt and angry as a result, so that they find it difficult in turn to stay in a stable family relationship when they grow up. You may well have thought of other reasons.

But one can see the attraction to Matthew's mother in taking a 'nature' view of this. By blaming his problems on his father's genes she completely absolves herself from responsibility for causing them – and also releases herself from the difficult job of trying to do something about them.

'Nature' ideas in the political arena

So: a 'nature' viewpoint can result in a rather fatalistic attitude – 'That's the way things are and there's nothing we can do about it!' – and it can have the attraction that it lets people off the hook.

I suggested earlier that we need to think carefully about why ideas become current and whose purposes they serve. You can see that 'nature' theories can be attractive not only to people like Matthew's mother in the above activity, but also to those in positions of privilege and power, because they can be used to argue that the status quo is inevitable. They seem to justify inequality and it is no accident that 'nature' ideas tend to be more popular with the political right. For example, the word 'aristocracy' comes from the Greek and means the 'rule of the good'. Like the expressions 'noble blood' or 'good breeding' the concept of an aristocracy was based on the idea that the upper class enjoyed more privileges and power because they were *innately superior* to other people. Racist theories are also 'nature' theories, as are ideas that women are innately inferior to men. And if those in positions of power can tell themselves that the poor are poor because they are 'by nature' incapable of earning a good living, or that criminals are criminals because they have criminal genes, then they can feel that they are absolved of responsibility.

But this is not to say that all 'nature' theories have no validity. It can hardly be disputed that many of our characteristics are inherited: and there is certainly scientific evidence that genetics plays an important role in intelligence, personality and perhaps even in things such as sexual orientation.

Nor is it right to say that 'nurture' theories are necessarily less oppressive, as we will see below.

The 'nurture' viewpoint

The word 'nurture' refers in particular to the care received by a child from her parents. Nurture in this sense is one important part of the environment in which human growth takes place and few would argue that nurture in this sense does not make a difference to the kind of person we become. But when we speak of 'nurture' in the context of the nature–nurture debate, we are talking more generally about *any* kind of environmental influence, which may include anything from events before, during and after birth, to factors as diverse as cultural expectations, nutrition, education, political circumstances and so on. In short, for the purposes of this discussion, the word 'nurture' will cover all the factors other than biological inheritance which might make a difference to who we are and what we become.

The English philosopher John Locke (1632–1704) considered that the mind of a new-born baby was a *tabula rasa*, a blank sheet, on which experience would subsequently write as she learnt to connect things together in her mind. Looking at the origin of moral principles, for example, he wrote:

> The ignorance wherein many men are of them, and the slowness of assent wherewith others receive them are manifest proofs that they are not innate. . . . Whether there be any such moral principles, wherein all men do agree, I appeal to any, who have been but moderately conversant in the history of mankind, and looked abroad beyond the smoke of their own chimnies. Where is that practical truth, that is universally received beyond doubt or question, as it must be, if innate? (Locke in Yolton (ed.), 1977)

In Chapter 5 we will look at the ideas of *Behaviourists* (or 'learning theorists'), starting with Pavlov (1849–1936) and his famous dogs. (Watson and Skinner are other well-known names.) As we will see, this strand within psychology has accumulated impressive evidence that the environment shapes behaviour according to certain predictable rules. Behaviours which are rewarded in some way tend to be repeated (they become 'conditioned'). Behaviours which are not rewarded, or which lead to a negative outcome, will become extinguished. As Darwin picked up on the long experience of animal breeders, behaviourists have explored an approach to learning that animal *trainers* have used for millennia.

Given that behaviourism sees all behaviour as being shaped by the environment, it could be regarded as one of the most extreme examples of a 'nurture theory'. One behaviourist, J.B. Watson, boasted that given a free hand he could train anyone to do anything, regardless of race, class, ability, background, or any other factor (see Watson (1931: 104)). But, of course, even if everything is learnt, this still presupposes some innate ability to learn.

Karl Marx (1818–1883) could also be described as a 'nurture' theorist. I don't mean by this that he wrote manuals on childcare (he didn't so far as I am aware). I mean that he regarded human thought and consciousness as being shaped by the society in which it took place. In particular he proposed that a society, including the roles that people play in it, their beliefs and their value systems, is the product of *economic* circumstances. The 'means of production' – the way that the economy is organised – was the determining factor, so that a certain set of values, ideas and behaviours would prevail in, say, feudal society, and another set in capitalist society:

> Consciousness is, therefore, from the very beginning a social product, and remains so as long as men exist at all. (Marx, in Elster (ed.), 1986:176)

You will find similar assertions in the writings of many who look at human life from a sociological perspective, whether they are inside or outside the Marxist tradition.

In the next chapter we will look at psychodynamic theories, and in particular at the ideas of Sigmund Freud (1856–1939). In some respects Freud's ideas also could be described as 'nurture' theories, both in the wide and the narrow sense of the word 'nurture'. They place a great deal of emphasis on early childhood experience, including very basic things like potty training, as a determining factor on how human beings grow and develop and as the source of most psychological problems in later life. But to describe Freud's ideas as purely 'nurture' theories is actually only to tell half of the story. Freud placed a huge emphasis also on instinctive drives (most famously, of course, the sexual instinct) which he saw as biological, inherited and present from birth: part of our *nature*, in other words.

'Nurture' theories in everyday life

Just as you find 'nature' theories not only in academic texts, but also in everyday life, so also do you find 'nurture' theories. The following activity gives one example:

Activity 1.4

Liz

You are a probation officer and you are meeting a new client, Liz, aged 19, to talk to her about a pre-sentence report which you've been asked to write (in which you will comment on the reasons for her offending and the likelihood of her offending again). Liz is charged with a series of violent assaults, using knives and other weapons, on other young women.

When you ask Liz about the reasons for her offending she shrugs:

> I can't help myself. I just see red and then my mind goes a blank. I was beaten myself as a child, you see. My dad used to beat me and then my stepdad. My mum pretended she didn't know it was going on. I was taken into care when I was 6 and my stepdad was sent to jail for assaulting me, but my mum got back together with him again when he came out. So I suppose that was it. It's just what was put into my head when I was a child and I can't help it.

What might your response be to Liz and what could you put in your report?

Comments on Activity 1.4

It may have struck you that if Liz doesn't take some more responsibility for her own actions, she is going to have difficulty persuading a court to be lenient with her. There can be little doubt that violent and unhappy relationships in childhood can predispose people to crime and other deviant behaviour in adult life (in Chapter 3 we will consider some reasons why this is), so Liz is not wrong in seeing her childhood abuse as a major contributing factor in her present problems. But in the long run it is not going to help her if she insists on seeing her problems in such a fatalistic way, even though in the short run it may seem easier to 'let herself off the hook' by blaming her unhappy childhood.

('Nurture' as well as 'nature' can be used to let ourselves off the hook, particularly for those, like Liz, who are genuinely the victims of mistreatment.)

But you could also argue that if it is possible to learn violent behaviour, then it must also be possible to learn another way of acting!

You could even argue that Liz's fatalism is in itself a learnt behaviour, which could likewise be unlearnt. (See the discussion on 'Learnt Helplessness' in Chapter 5.)

'Nurture' ideas in the political arena

Historically, 'nature' theories have been used as the rationale for oppression of various kinds, as we've noted above, and they tend to be associated with the political right. The idea that human beings are shaped by their environment, on the other hand, has always been attractive to the political left, which sees the poor as being at the bottom of the pile not because of their innate qualities, but because they have not been given access to the advantages enjoyed by the rich.

However, the idea that human beings are entirely the product of their environment has also been used in extremely oppressive ways by the political left. The Pol Pot regime in Cambodia, for example, justified the horrors of its notorious Year Zero with the idea that it was possible to change people by totally wiping out the influence of the past and retraining an entire population to start again. The Cultural Revolution in China, in which large numbers likewise lost their lives, was in some ways a similar kind of project.

Much closer to home, parents of schizophrenia sufferers, or of children with autism, might well complain about 'nurture' theories, fashionable in the 1960s and 1970s, that blamed them for the children's problems. It was suggested that a 'schizophrenogenic' family could drive its children mad with double messages and that 'cold' mothers turned their children into autists. Such theories must feel much more oppressive to parents than theories which propose a genetic origin for these problems.

Inherited and environmental factors

It is too simplistic to reduce the various factors that make people what they are to 'nature' and 'nurture'. In reality a whole range of different factors contributes to making us what we are, some of which could be described as nature, some as nurture, some of which could be assigned to either category. In many cases, a complex interplay between inherited and environmental factors is at work. Some of these factors are:

- genetic inheritance;
- other physical factors such as nutrition, health, physical injury, not only after birth, but from conception onwards – for example, a baby's growth may be inhibited if a mother drinks or smokes during pregnancy, and serious brain damage can be caused by complications during the birth itself;
- cultural factors – nationality, social class, geography (whether one grows up in the country or a town for example), ethnic background, time in history;
- sex/gender – which has both biological implications and social ones;
- upbringing, early relationships, position in the family (older children have a different experience from middle and youngest children for example), traumatic and/or positive experiences;
- random events (car accidents, lottery wins, chance meetings . . .).

One could think of many more. But the important thing to note here is how all these factors interact with one another. What sex we are, for example, *is* a matter of genetic inheritance and it has (of course) many purely physical implications: women can give birth and breast feed, men can't; boys are more likely to suffer from certain inherited conditions (haemophilia, colour-blindness); men and women have different hormones in their blood – and so on. But the way in which the sexes are viewed, the expectations of them, the roles and behaviour which are considered appropriate and inappropriate, will depend on cultural factors. (There is a further discussion on gender roles in Chapter 5.)

To give another example: physical appearance might seem a purely inherited feature at first glance, but in fact a whole range of environmental factors can affect physical appearance. A child's physical size can be drastically affected not only by malnutrition but by emotional deprivation. This is known as 'deprivation dwarfism' and is a recognised symptom of serious emotional abuse. And the *significance* attached to physical appearance will depend very much on culture, as can be seen from the fact that plumpness and white skin have been regarded as beautiful and desirable in some societies at some stages in history, thinness and sun-tanned skin at others.

In addition to the interacting influences of nature and nurture, our thoughts and beliefs must surely also be shaped by the fact that life poses certain unavoidable questions – 'existential' questions – which would faced by any thinking being, even, hypothetically, an alien from another planet or a sentient machine. For example, there is the fact of *death*. Our lives are finite. Even for an extraterrestrial alien or a robot, the possibility of non-existence would surely be an inevitable corollary of existence. And there is the fact of *individuality*. The fact that we exist as individuals means that there are other things in existence which are separate from us. So, as well as being limited in time, our lives are also necessarily located in space. (The way that we come to terms with the concept of 'self' and 'others' is something that is of particular interest to the object relations theorists whom I will discuss in the next chapter and in Chapter 3, and to theories of cognitive development, which are the subject of Chapter 4.)

Free Will versus Predetermination

Looking down my list of inherited and environmental factors above, you may have wondered why I missed out personal choice. We don't feel like automatons, after all, simply responding to our genes or our environment. It feels as if we are constantly making decisions, and often difficult and painful ones. As old, or older, than the nature–nurture question, and even more fundamental is the question of free will. Do we really in fact have choices, or is our feeling that we are free to choose only a kind of illusion? This is a debate you can find in Chaucer's *Canterbury Tales*, written in the fourteenth century:

> But I kan nat bulte it to the bren . . .
> Whether that Goddes worthy forwiting
> Streyneth me nedeley for to doon a thyng . . .
> Or elles, if free choys be graunted me
> To do that same thyng, or do it noght.
> (Crawley (ed.), 1992: 470)

> (Rough translation: 'But I can't sift the flour from the bran . . . [as to] whether God's worthy foreknowledge constrains me necessarily to do a thing . . . or whether free choice is granted me to do that same thing or not to do it.')

And indeed the same question is debated much earlier still in the writings of classical Greek philosophers, more than 2,000 years ago.

All the writers I have quoted so far in this chapter assume that there are causes for human behaviour, whether those causes are genetic or otherwise. Yet most of us also believe that there is such a thing as responsibility for our own actions, and there is certainly a long tradition that says free will is a reality. The entire edifice of traditional Christian theology – the Fall, the Day of Judgement, Heaven and Hell – is founded on this idea. How could it be just for souls to be condemned to eternal torment if their actions were simply the unavoidable consequences of nature or nurture? Or, if you would prefer a modern, secular example, look at the writings of the French existentialist Jean-Paul Sartre. 'I am condemned to be free', he wrote, '. . . we are not free to stop being free' (1943, cited by Howells, 1988: 21). When people like Liz (in Activity 1.4) blame their behaviour on external factors outside their control, Sartre would say that they were acting in 'bad faith'.

Here is one more activity, based on a real-life case, for you to consider where you stand on this issue:

✳ Activity 1.5 ✳

In England in 1993, Jon Venables and Robert Thompson, then both aged 10, were found guilty of the murder of a toddler, Jamie Bulger, whom they had picked up in a shopping mall, taken to a railway line and beaten to death by hitting him with bricks. Many have said that these boys committed this appalling act because they were 'evil', others have suggested that there must have been distressing events in their previous childhood that caused them to act in this way. What is your own view about why they might have done this and how they should be seen?

Comments on Activity 1.5

If you incline to the view that these boys were indeed evil (and few would dispute that evil is an appropriate word for what they did), you have to ask what you mean by that. Are you saying that they were born with a propensity to do bad things (a nature theory) and, if so, how can they be blamed for what they did any more than a person born blind can be blamed for not being able to see?

Or are you saying that we all make choices between good and evil, and these boys chose evil of their own free will? If so I'd have to ask you whether, at 10 years old, you were ever tempted to kidnap and murder a small child, and resisted that temptation? If not, clearly this was not just a matter of choice.

Or are you saying that these boys became evil as a result of something in their upbringing? If so, you are really agreeing with those who say the act must have been the result of environmental factors (a nurture theory). The obvious question then is why do other children, from similar or worse environments, not commit such crimes? One answer might be that no two environments are exactly alike and we can never know all the subtle influences that might tip a person one way or the other. Another might be that no two individuals are born exactly alike, so the environment never affects any two people in exactly the same way.

Clearly, whether we believe in free will or not can have quite major implications for how we act and how we view other people. In fact, as I noted earlier, we tend to make moral judgements in some cases and look for causes in others – and we don't necessarily do so in a very consistent way. But I am not here going to attempt any sort of resolution of this question that has troubled great thinkers for several millennia, beyond offering a pragmatic compromise.

I don't wish to dissuade anyone from believing that they make real choices in their lives. I also believe that the idea of personal responsibility is necessary for society to function. But if you look at the things that you think of as free choices, and consider why other people make different choices from yours, it is hard to escape the sense that there is a pattern. As we've discussed, a lot of evidence exists that people with the same genes are more likely to make the same choices. We also know that people can be trained to act differently by rewarding or punishing different behaviours – and that people with the same childhood experiences often have the same kinds of problems in later life.

We may not be automatons, but we are *shaped*, if not controlled, by our history and by the world around us. I suggest that this requires us to try not to judge other people in a moral sense, and to try and understand the reasons why people act as they do. And yet at the same time we cannot function without taking some responsibility for our own actions, and expecting others to take responsibility for theirs.

Chapter Summary

The Birth of A Human Being

- In this chapter we have considered the birth of a child and looked at some ideas about what will shape her as she grows and develops. But ideas themselves are not fixed, so I began by giving a warning about ideas and theories. They are not neutral. People use them for their own ends.

- In particular I have looked at the debate about the extent to which our identity is determined by our genes and by environmental factors (the 'nature and nurture' debate), and you should now have some flavour of the positions taken on this by behaviourists, Darwinians, Freudians and Marxists. I have also looked at the way this debate has very practical implications, both in daily life and in politics. I have proposed that we need to see human growth as being the product of a number of interacting factors, of which genetic inheritance is one.

- Finally, I considered another very ancient subject of debate – between free will and predetermination – and looked at the issues this raises.

In the next chapter we will look at the ideas of Freud, who saw human personality developing as the result of our having to try and strike a balance, from the moment of birth onwards, between instinctive drives, the external environment and previous learning.

Suggested Reading

INTRODUCTORY TEXTS ABOUT HUMAN GROWTH AND DEVELOPMENT:

- Durkin, K. (1995) *Developmental Social Psychology* (Oxford: Blackwell)
- Sugarman, L. (1986) *Life Span Development: Concepts, Theories and Interventions* (London: Methuen)

A CRITICAL LOOK FROM A RADICAL AND FEMINIST PERSPECTIVE AT MANY OF THE IDEAS IN THIS BOOK:

- Burman, E. (1994) *Deconstructing Developmental Psychology* (London: Routledge)

ON NATURE AND NURTURE:

- Steen, R.G. (1996) *DNA and Destiny: Nature and Nurture in Human Behavior*, (New York: Plenum Press)
- Wright, L. (1997) *Twins: Genes, Identity and the Mystery of Identity* (London: Weidenfeld & Nicholson)

2 The Balancing Act
Insights from Freud

In the last chapter I discussed various factors – some innate, some environmental – that might play a part in human development. I want to look now at a view of the human mind that sees human development as the product of a dynamic process incorporating both innate and environmental forces. From this psychodynamic viewpoint life is a struggle from the beginning to manage in a world where urgent innate needs are clamouring to be met, but where it is not always easy or possible to meet them. So as we grow up we develop psychological strategies, both conscious and unconscious, to deal with the situations in which we find ourselves. Strategies adopted in childhood are carried into adult life, where they may sometimes be maladaptive and cause problems for the individual concerned, unless she can get help in unravelling the patterns laid down in the past. Although this model has been developed, modified and expanded in many different directions, and although it had historical antecedents, its best-known exponent is certainly Sigmund Freud.

Freud, who was born in Austria in 1856 and died in London in 1939, remains a controversial figure, admired by some, rejected or condemned by others. Many criticisms can be levelled against him – and I will discuss some of them later on in this chapter – but it seems to me that he has left an important legacy which we now almost take for granted. Many of his ideas, have entered the language and we use them without thinking about their origin. In particular, I think the Freudian tradition has offered the possibility of new insights into the way that apparently irrational things – madness, dreams, obsessions, jokes, slips of the tongue – have a kind of deep logic of their own, rooted in the fears and longings of childhood and, even before that, in our biological origins.

Many people approach Freud's ideas with some fairly strong preconceptions, so you may find it useful to look at the following activity before going any further, in order to be aware of your own starting point:

✷ Activity 2.1 ✷

Some people are attracted by Freud's ideas, some find them repellent, others find them slightly ridiculous or comical? Where do you stand? What aspects of Freud's thinking make you feel as you do? What is attractive, or repellent, or funny about his ideas?

What would you say were the key features of Freud's ideas?

Comments on Activity 2.1

Many people say about Freud that 'he was obsessed with sex', 'he thought everything was to do with sex' – and you could argue that one of the legacies of Freud was to make sex something of an obsession in modern society. Whether that is a legacy of Freud, or whether Freud was simply a product of his time, is of course another question. What you will see, though, is that Freud's use of the term 'sexual' was fairly broad.

You may also have mentioned the therapeutic technique known as psychoanalysis which Freud developed, which has spawned a thousand cartoons featuring couches and Freud lookalikes with pencils and pads. Certainly a lot has been written about the efficacy or otherwise of psychoanalysis, its length, its costliness, its potential for abuse. I will not be covering this in any detail here, because this is a book about psychosocial development and not about therapeutic techniques. But it does rightly form a large part of most people's image of what Freud was 'all about' – and it is through material collected in psychoanalysis that much of Freud's thinking developed.

You may also have mentioned doubts about Freud's claim to be offering a genuinely scientific or objective theory, or concerns about Freud's attitudes and assumptions (particularly about women) or about whether his ideas can be generalised in the way that he did generalise them. These are important questions which will be discussed later in this chapter.

Many people also find some of the language in which Freud's ideas are expressed rather off-putting, or even at times a bit absurd, though many of them have passed into everyday speech ('penis envy', 'phallic symbol', 'anal personality'). It is important to try and look behind the language and the strange imagery and try and get some sense of the underlying ideas.

I'll now attempt to sketch out some of the main themes in Freudian thinking, with the warning that this is necessarily a very partial account of a rich and complicated set of ideas which Freud himself changed and developed repeatedly during his lifetime, and which has been developed further in many different ways since his death.

The Unconscious

Freud didn't begin his professional career in psychiatry but in the field of pathological medicine and neurology. At the age of 29, while working in Paris with a French physician called Charcot, he encountered the treatment of 'hysteria' using hypnosis. At that time 'hysteria' was a term used to refer to physical symptoms which had no apparent physical cause. Freud was impressed by the fact that observable physical symptoms could be caused not only by infection or by injury, but simply by distressing ideas in a patient's mind. And he was impressed by the fact that the symptoms could apparently be treated by hypnotising patients and talking to them to neutralise these powerful ideas.

When being treated by hypnosis, the patient listens while the doctor talks. Freud turned this on its head by developing a form of therapy in which the patient talks while the therapist listens. In other words, he moved on to 'talking therapy', now practised by many who would not regard themselves in any way as Freudians. He then developed this further into a technique which encouraged the patient to 'free associate' in order to allow exploration not only of the patient's conscious thoughts, but of connections of which the patient herself might not be consciously aware.

📖 **Free Association** 📖

In free association, the patient is asked to respond to a word or an idea with the first thing that comes into her head, without thinking about it and

---

continued

without holding anything back. It's a bit like the parlour game 'elbow tennis' except that the patient is not required to demonstrate a connection between one word and the next. On the contrary, the technique is based on the assumption that there will always *be* some link, though the patient may not be aware of it.

When I was giving a lecture on this subject one Christmas I tried hard to think of two completely unrelated words and came up with 'tangerine' and 'anger'. Later I realised that there *was* a Christmas-linked connection for me between these words. I do not like tangerines but my parents always put one in the very toe of my Christmas stocking. After the unwanted and unexciting *tangerine* there were no more presents.

Another more obvious connection has since been pointed out to me: that the word 'anger' is actually embedded in the word 'tangerine'.

Freud believed that, by exploring these links that our minds make without us being consciously aware of it, we obtain glimpses of the contents of the unconscious.

As a result of his explorations Freud became convinced that his patients' neurotic problems were rooted in traumatic events in infancy, and that these events were basically sexual. Again and again they seemed to be telling him that their fathers had sexually assaulted them. He came to the conclusion that most psychological problems in adulthood were caused by what we would now call sexual abuse in childhood. This theory is known – rather inappropriately – as the *seduction theory*. Freud did not subscribe to this idea for very long, however. The same stories came up so often that he decided that they could not be literally true. He concluded that these events had not actually happened, but were *phantasies* representing the wishes and desires of childhood.

What we now know about sexual abuse would suggest that Freud's original view was likely to have been much nearer to the truth. His difficulty in believing it was probably a fairly typical response of his time. Indeed he was ahead of his time in even countenancing the possibility that what he had been told was true. There is still, a century on, a widespread reluc-tance to accept that sexual abuse can and does often occur within families. But Freud's rejection of his own seduction theory led him to develop much more elaborate explanations for what his patients were telling him. And these explanations formed the basis for much of his subsequent thinking.

Why study a theory based on a mistake?

At this point, you might legitimately ask what is the point of looking any further at Freud's ideas, if they were indeed based on his denying the reality of his patients' experience? I would make the following suggestions:

- Whether we like it or not, Freud's ideas have been very influential – and it is important to know about them, even if we don't agree with them.
- It can be argued that, although Freud may have been wrong to abandon his original seduction theory, in fact in doing so he stumbled upon some insights into the nature of the unconscious which stand on their own as ideas, even if the way he came across them was wrong.
- Certainly I think it would be wrong to condemn Freud for not believing his patients. I think we must allow him to be a man of his own time and not expect him to know what we know now.

But on these matters, you will of course have to make up your own mind. You can read Masson (1984) for a much less sympathetic account than the one I have just given.

Suppressed desires

As a result of changing his mind over the seduction theory, Freud moved on from his original perspective that 'hysterics suffer mainly from reminiscences', to the idea that the primary problem was not so much memories – or suppressed memories – as suppressed *desires*. His view was that we have all kinds of desires, not all of which can actually be met, and some of which we cannot safely admit even to ourselves. Desires which we are aware of but which we don't allow ourselves to act upon we *suppress*. Other desires we *repress*, which means that we push them right out of our conscious mind altogether.

So (in Freud's view) we are not even aware of those desires that we repress, but they are still there. It is as if we were to put the lid on a pan of boiling water, so that we could no longer see its contents. But Freud believed that unconscious desires could not be completely contained. We might have put the lid on the boiling pan but we are nevertheless made aware, in various ways, of the heat and pressure inside. The contents of the unconscious, Freud thought, emerged in disguise in various ways: in jokes, in slips of the tongue (the famous 'Freudian slip') and in dreams. The technique of 'free association' is supposed to provide a means of tapping into them.

Freud's idea that we are not always aware of all the contents of our mind was certainly not new. If you reflect on it for a moment you will see that it is actually self-evident. You are not always thinking about everything that is in your memory. If I mention your last summer holiday, it is probable that, until I mentioned it, it was not in your thoughts at all. At times we may even be unable to retrieve something from our memory and into consciousness, even though we know quite well that it is there. 'It's on the tip of my tongue', as we say.

But things that are unconscious in this sense are like library books which are not currently being read, or which occasionally may be hard to find if we can't remember what subject they were filed under. In Freudian terminology these things are called *preconscious*, rather than unconscious. Freud's conception of the *unconscious* was much more dynamic than this. He saw the unconscious not as a kind of static library or storehouse but as a powerful, active player in the dynamic system that is the human mind. The unconscious is a source of energy, and it also contains things which are in some sense dangerous and therefore inadmissible to consciousness. Desires, unlike memories, have urgency about them.

The Structure of Personality

Freud moved on again from being primarily interested in the distinction between the conscious and the unconscious, to making a new distinction between what he called the *ego* and the *id*. In this new model the *id* – a Latin word meaning roughly 'it' – contains the instincts: the inherited part of ourselves, our basic biological drives. In other words it contains the *'nature'* part of us, to use the language of the previous chapter. And it operates on the *'pleasure principle'*. It is

> a cauldron full of seething excitations. . . . It is filled with energy . . . but . . . has no organisation . . . only a striving to bring about the satisfaction of instinctual needs subject to the observance of the pleasure principle. . . (Freud, 1933: 73)

The *ego* – from the Latin word for 'I' – is a part of ourselves that develops from the id as a result of experience, and is the part of ourselves where conscious thought takes place.

> The ego is that part of the id which has been modified by the direct influence of the external world. . . . The ego represents what may be called reason and common sense, in contrast to the id, which contains the passions . . . in its relation to the id it is like a man on horseback, who has to hold in check the superior strength of the horse . . . (Freud, 1923: 25)

According to Freud, the ego operates on the *'reality principle'*. It deals not only with the instinctual demands arising from the id (as powerful as a horse is in relation to a man), but also with the demands of the external world, and with what it has learnt through experience. One of the jobs that the ego does is the job of *repressing* desires which cannot safely be allowed into consciousness. The part of the ego that does this job is necessarily itself unconscious, which complicates the model somewhat by preventing a simple equation of ego with consciousness and id with the unconscious. In order to explain how this part of the ego decided what must be repressed Freud introduced the idea of the *superego*.

The *superego* is a kind of 'deposit' left behind in our minds from our childhood relationship with our parents and others who were in charge of us. The superego contains rules and restrictions which originally a child would have received from adults ('That's naughty', 'You mustn't do that', etc.), but which in due course become internalised. The superego is therefore the seat of conscience and self-criticism. A simple example of how this process of internalisation operates is that of a small child, who does not think to wash her hands after using the toilet. She has to be told to do so, and starts to do so in order to conform to adult wishes. By the time we are adults however, we wash our hands not to please others, but because it feels uncomfortable not to do so.

In the language of nature–nurture the superego in Freud's model is clearly the product of 'nurture', while the id is the product of 'nature'. The ego has the job of balancing the competing demands of id and superego, and the demands of external reality, as Figure 2.1 illustrates.

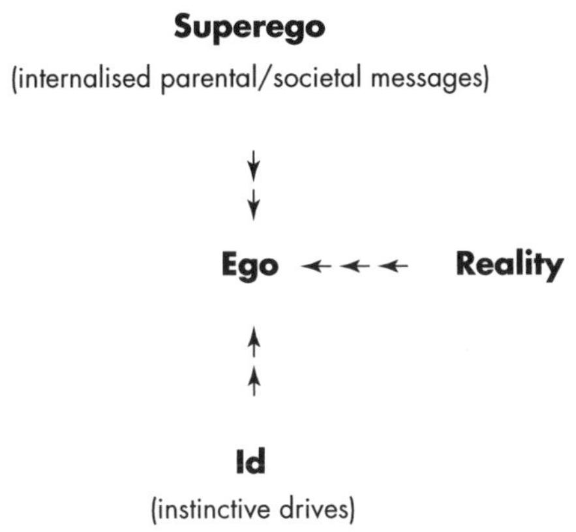

Superego

(internalised parental/societal messages)

Ego ← ← ← **Reality**

Id

(instinctive drives)

FIGURE 2.1   *Ego, superego and id*

The shaping of personality

We have seen that in Freud's model the individual starts with certain basic instinctual needs. The id constantly demands the satisfaction that comes from meeting those needs. The ego has the job of mediating between the demands of the id, the demands of the external world and the demands of powerful others (the parents), who end up being internalised (or *introjected*) as the superego.

A person grows as a distinct and separate personality as the result of her ego performing its own unique balancing act. Circumstances are never ideal, and everyone's circumstances are different. In an attempt to manage the unique circumstances in which it finds itself, each individual ego develops strategies for negotiating the competing pressures upon it and finds ways of resolving dilemmas, which in some cases will mean suppressing inconvenient things from consciousness.

If all goes well, the individual will progress to a stage where she can cope with adult life. But things can go wrong along the line, which may hamper growth. For example, traumatic events may be experienced beyond the capacity of the individual to cope with properly, or needs may go unmet. It is even possible that needs can be excessively *well* met in some circumstances, Freud thought, creating a 'warm bath' effect from which the individual feels reluctant to move on.

So blockages can result in an number of ways which, if not successfully resolved, will result in the individual being stuck to some degree, perhaps developing *fixations* for something from a previous stage. A person who is constantly eating might be fixated in the oral stage, for example. A person who is obsessed with neatness and order might be fixated in the anal stage (an idea which has now entered the language, as in 'I'm afraid I'm rather anal about my CD collection').

Freud saw the ego as employing a whole range of *defences* to protect itself against anxiety. One of the defences is *repression*, which works by shutting something out of consciousness altogether. (You will recall that *repression* is an automatic, unconscious process, resulting from anxiety, while *suppression* is voluntary, occurring when we choose not to act on an impulse or desire, even though that desire remains something we are consciously aware of.) But there are a number of other defences also. These defences are necessary at the time – the best that can be done under the circumstances – but they can subsequently become obstacles to development.

To consider this more closely, have a look at the following activity:

✄ Activity 2.2 ✄

Jenny

This small child aged 4 lives alone with a mother (Mandy) who is highly volatile and unpredictable. Occasionally Mandy treats her kindly, but at other times Mandy erupts into frightening rage and violence, hitting her, depriving her of food, threatening to abandon or kill her. Mandy also isolates her. Jenny doesn't know anyone else other than Mandy's friends. She does not know other children of her own age.

How would Jenny deal with this situation psychologically? How would she explain to herself what was going on? How would she comfort herself?

Please note: I am not asking you to guess what Freud might say about this. I am asking you to consider what you yourself think, based on your own experience and your own imagination.

Comments on Activity 2.2

The first thing that strikes me about this scenario is that a child cannot deal with it like an adult. An adult is aware of other possibilities, the possibility of escape, of sources of help (though, having said this, I should acknowledge that there are many adult women in the world who are living in abusive relationships because they feel there is no choice). Her mother may abuse her, but to Jenny Mandy is also the world, the source of her nourishment, the provider of her home.

A child also does not think like an adult in terms of logic, cause and effect and so on. (See Chapter 4 for a discussion of cognitive differences – differences in the structure of thought – between children and adults.)

The second thing that strikes me is just how intolerable it would be for a little child of this age to admit to herself that she was in real danger from the adult who cares for her, or that her mother was a bad person, or that her mother did not have her best interests at heart. The anxiety of this would be too much to bear and she needs to protect herself from it.

But Jenny is very little and the grown-ups are very big. There is no way in reality she can defend herself from what is going on. All she can resort to is psychological defences. She might tell herself: 'This isn't really happening to me', 'This isn't real', just as we do as adults, at least at first, when brought some terrible news such as news of a bereavement. This defence is known as 'denial' (another Freudian term that has entered everyday language).

Or she could tell herself that the Mandy who mistreats her is a different person from the Mandy who is kind to her. The kind Mandy is her real mum. This defence is known as splitting.

Or perhaps she could tell herself that she is bad, and that she deserves the treatment that Mandy gives her. This does not sound a very comfortable position to take, but it may well be less frightening to think of herself as bad, than to think of the large person who controls her life as being bad. This defence is known as turning against the self. In my experience, it is extremely common among children who have been seriously abused (as are denial and splitting).

Even very little children – who from an outsider's perspective are quite obviously powerless – often blame themselves for abuse perpetrated against them.

The point about these defences is that they are necessary, the best that Jenny can do in the circumstances to protect her sanity. They are less damaging in the short run than facing the full reality of the situation. But in the long run they may leave her with a seriously defective way of dealing with the world.

Jenny may grow up routinely blocking out painful feelings, or feeling of any kind. She may grow up with the habit of 'splitting' – holding in her mind contradictory stories at the same time. She may grow up with a view of herself as worthless and bad.

📖 **Psychological Defences** 📖

Defences are ways in which the ego tries to protect itself against anxiety – and anxiety may be caused by:

- increases in instinctual tension (tensions coming from the id: needs and desires demanding to be met);
- a bad conscience (i.e. pressures from the superego);
- reality. (One of the defences is *denial*. Probably most of us have observed, at first or second hand, the way that people go initially into denial to protect themselves against the impact of some catastrophic event – a sudden bereavement, for example – and will only gradually allow themselves to face the fact that this event has actually taken place.)

Other defences are, for example, *projection* (where the individual 'projects' their own feelings on to some other person or object), *reaction-formation*, *introjection*, *'undoing'* and *repression*, which were discussed earlier.

In *sublimation*, instinctual energies are discharged by non-instinctual behaviour (channelling sexual energies into creative work, for example). This is a kind of defence, but is seen in Freudian theory as a healthy and adaptive one, in that energies are not bottled up but are redirected to some constructive purpose.

Most children do not have a challenge as great as Jenny's to contend with, but all children have to deal with an imperfect world, using whatever psychological resources are available to them at their particular stage of development.

Psychosexual Stages

If Jenny – in Activity 2.2 – had been 13 when the mistreatment started, the emotional and intellectual resources available to her would have been different. They are different again for a baby subjected to abuse. Freud saw emotional development going through several stages (see Figure 2.2), each stage having its characteristic goals and its characteristic defensive strategies.

More controversially perhaps, Freud called these stages 'psychosexual' stages. And this is because he saw them as being based on the child's changing focus of *sexual gratification*. This can be a somewhat shocking concept to many people, even nowadays, because we are accustomed to thinking of childhood as time that is free, or relatively free, of a preoccupation with sex.

During the *oral* stage the principal source of gratification is food and the comfort obtained from sucking, the latter being as important as the nourishment itself.

> The baby's obstinate persistence in sucking gives evidence at an early stage of a need for satisfaction which, though it originates from and is instigated by the taking of nourishment, nevertheless strives to obtain pleasure independently of nourishment and for that reason may be termed sexual. (Freud, 1949: 24)

Stage	Age
Oral	First Year
Anal	Roughly ages 2–3
Phallic (Onset of Oedipus complex)	Roughly 4–6
Latency period	7 to adolescence
Genital	Adolescence onwards

FIGURE 2.2 *Psychosexual stages*

(Freud's definition of 'sexual' in the above quote is worth noting. Many people might agree with most of this sentence but might use the word 'sensual'. Or they might say that the gratification obtained from suckling was 'like sex' or 'analogous to sex', in the sense that sex is primarily about reproduction, but carries a whole range of other functions to do with pleasure, intimacy and so on. Freud's reputation is that he says everything is to do with sex. He certainly *does* give sex a very central role but, as this quote shows, his definition of 'sex' is quite broad.)

In Freud's model, people can get *fixated* at different stages for various reasons, which is to say they hang on to some aspects of behaviour characteristic of that stage – or *regress* (that is, go backwards) to such behaviour at a time of stress. The orally fixated person tends to have the mouth as their primary 'erotogenic zone', to be mother-fixated and 'to *identify* with others rather than to relate to them as others' (Rycroft, 1995: 122). This is because the oral stage is the most primitive stage, a time when a baby has not yet learnt that self and others are really separate things. (See Chapter 4 for further discussion on the growth of a child's sense of objects as separate to self.) The cartoon character who, when frightened, jumps into another adult's arms with a cry of 'Mummy!' is an example of regression to the oral stage.

During the *anal* stage, according to Freud, the anus and defecation are the major sources of sensual pleasure. And at this stage of ego development, control of the body and socialisation of impulses are the child's major preoccupations. A basic but very important example of body control usually acquired during this stage is that of potty training. When being potty-trained a child is learning to resist the immediate impulse to defecate and to control and defer it. The child is encouraged not to defecate whenever the urge takes her but is praised for producing faeces in the right place.

So compulsive orderliness and excessive pleasure taken in power and control are, in the Freudian scheme of things, examples of anal fixation. The pleasure we take in orderliness and control was seen by Freud as akin to the pleasure taken by a child looking into the toilet bowl after defecating and admiring some particularly fine stools. Like other of Freud's ideas, this one has entered everyday speech: the word 'anal' is sometimes used of someone who is very controlling and orderly. Interestingly the phrase 'tight-arsed' is used of someone who is mean, though I do not know whether the latter term followed or preceded Freud. Taking pleasure in cruelty (sadism) – again to do with power and control – is also supposed to be characteristic of the anal stage.

During the *phallic* stage the focus – for both boys *and* girls in conventional Freudian thinking – is the penis. (This is very controversial – and raises questions about how Freud viewed the sexes.) Fixation in the phallic phase might result in an adult who sees sexual activity as a test of potency, as opposed to an adult who has progressed to the *genital* stage, who would see it as the expression of a relationship.

It is during the phallic stage that the famous *Oedipus complex* is supposed to come into play. (In the case of girls, this is sometimes – though rarely – referred to as the *Electra complex*.) The idea of the Oedipus complex is that, at this stage, both boys and girls desire to have an exclusive sexual relationship towards their opposite-sex parent, and become murderously jealous of their same-sex parent. However, this is countered firstly by fear of the same-sex parent (in boys this is supposed to be a fear of actual castration by their father) and, secondly, by contradictory feelings of love for the same-sex parent. At this stage girls are supposed to become aware of their own lack of a penis ('penis envy').

Resolution of the Oedipus complex is supposed to be achieved initially by identification with the same-sex parent, and suppression of desire for the opposite-sex parent. So by identifying with his father a boy can, as it were, vicariously have a sexual relationship with his mother – and no longer feels the need to kill his father. Having accomplished this resolution, the child then enters the *latency* phase until adolescence. This is viewed as a relatively quiet period, in psychosexual terms, between the struggles of the Oedipal phase, and the struggles of adolescence.

The final phase of development (for Freud, that is: Erik Erikson, discussed below, suggested three further stages), and therefore not one in which a person can become fixated, is the *genital* phase, when the individual seeks an opposite-sex partner as a substitute for the opposite-sex parent, and as another and more permanent way of resolving the Oedipal conflict.

The following activity is to give you an opportunity to 'take stock' of what I have covered so far:

⚒ Activity 2.3 ⚒

Can you think of examples – among people you have met – of people with oral fixations, anal fixations, or fixations from the phallic stage, in Freud's sense? Do you find that these concepts shed any light on behaviour (whether other people's or indeed your own)?

Can you think of instances, from your own experience, of denial, splitting or projection?

At the beginning of this discussion, I asked you to consider your own preconceptions about what Freud was 'about'. Having considered this

continued

again, what do you think about Freud's ideas about sex – and its importance in human development?

What would you consider to be the major problems with Freud's theory, and what would you see (if any) as its strengths?

Comments on Activity 2.3

I can't comment on the people you know, of course, but it seems to me that certain characteristic patterns of behaviour are observable which could be described in Freudian terms as anal, oral and so on. I personally find it useful – and it makes some sense to me – to think of these as patterns which come from different stages of childhood.

Instances of denial, splitting or projection seem to me to be quite common in everyday life. An example of projection which I've encountered is projected anger as in: 'Of course I personally don't mind, but everyone else in the team is very angry with you.' In my experience the speaker may quite genuinely not be aware of being angry herself.

Although I've argued that Freud's definition of 'sexual' is broader than most people's, and in many instances the word 'sensual' could perhaps be substituted, Freud's preoccupation with the sexual drive over others is an issue for many people. It was one of the reasons that Carl Jung split with Freud.

Some other criticisms of Freud are discussed at the end of this chapter.

Developments of Freud's Ideas

Freud's ideas have proved to be very fertile ground for other thinkers and theorists. It would be impossible here to give an account of all the different strands that have emerged, split off from, or been influenced by Freudian thought, they are so numerous and diverse. Alfred Adler, for example, split off from Freud in 1911. Carl Jung did likewise, falling out with Freud on a number of points – including the central position Freud gave to sex – after initially being a close colleague and disciple. Influential thinkers in the Freudian tradition include Erich Fromm, Herbert Marcuse, Jacques Lacan (the latter still influential in the field of literary studies because of his ideas about language) and Freud's daughter Anna Freud.

Some of those who developed Freud's ideas would see themselves as remaining within his framework, others as moving on from it, branching off from it or making connections with other schools of thought. There have been feminist re-workings of Freud's and Lacan's ideas (for example by Dorothy Dinnerstein, Nancy Chodorow and Julia Kristeva).

Some ideas which have roots in Freudian thinking, have now developed a more or less independent life of their own. *Attachment theory*, which we'll discuss in the next chapter, is one example. Another might be Transactional Analysis (Berne, 1961).

For the remainder of this chapter I will briefly look at some development of Freudian thinking that is known as 'object relations theory'. I will look at the ideas of two members of the British 'Object Relations' school, Donald Winnicott and Melanie Klein, and at the related ideas of the American Erik Erikson about ego development. (Erikson is not always categorised as an object relations theorist – and was certainly not a member of the *British* object relations school – but for the purposes of this discussion I think it is appropriate to describe him as such.) Another member of the British object relations school, John Bowlby, will be discussed in more detail in the next chapter.

Object Relations and Ego Development

In classical Freudian theory, people are seeking to gratify primitive instinctual needs. An individual's relationship to others is seen in terms of 'drive reduction', the extent to which that relationship can be used to meet basic instinctual needs (such as for food and – of course – for sexual/sensual gratification). However, in the various developments of Freud's ideas described as 'object relations' theories, the development of the *relationship* between an individual (the 'subject') and others (the 'object') takes centre stage. (The use of the word 'object' is a little confusing. It is used here not in the sense of a 'thing' but in the sense in which we refer to the subject and object of a sentence.)

The mirror

In object relations theory human relationships are a prerequisite for a sense of selfhood. It is only through an intimate relationship with her primary carers that an individual can arrive at a sense of difference between self and others. Erikson wrote that our ability as adults to trust others stems in the first instance from learning as a child to trust that, when our mother goes away, she will come back (Erikson 1995, first published in 1951). Not all children have this experience, of course. If you know anyone who experienced neglectful or very inconsistent parenting early in life (or if this applies to you yourself) you will probably agree that people with these experiences do indeed often find it very hard to trust others in adult relationships.

This basic sense of trust, then, seems to be a precursor to satisfactory relationships later in life. Donald Winnicott (1896–1971) used the analogy of a mirror to talk about this. All small children express a variety of basic needs which they have to rely on others to meet. And Winnicott suggested that if these needs are reliably met when they are expressed then it is as if the carer is *mirroring* the child. A need seems to the child to bring a corresponding response, just as when we look into a mirror, our mirror-image produces actions that correspond to our own.

So, as a result of having her needs consistently met, the child would conclude (if not actually in words) that 'If I express my needs, they are met. If I express my feelings, they are acknowledged as valid.' This, Winnicott suggested, gives her a sense of possessing power (an *'illusion of omnipotence'*). As a result of this experience, the child is freed up to be creative, to make demands of life and to express needs and feelings spontaneously. Through having her needs mirrored the child develops what Winnicott called a *'true self'*. People learn who they are by having their needs and feelings reflected back, just as we can only come to know what our own face looks like by seeing it reflected in a mirror.

But children are not necessarily mirrored. Needs can be ignored, feelings can be ignored, demands can be rejected or even responded to with anger and punishment. And a child who does not have the experience of her needs being reliably met at this crucial early stage, or of her feelings being accepted as valid, will fail to develop a sense of trust and fail to properly develop a sense of herself as an autonomous being.

In fact, Winnicott thought, for a child who has not been 'mirrored', human interaction in general becomes terrifying, and the child attempts to defend herself by withdrawing into a state of *'false self'* in which she herself denies her own feelings and needs and compulsively anticipates the reactions of others. An extreme form of this would be the 'frozen watchfulness' of badly abused children, who do not play or explore but simply watch the adults around them, trying to guess what they are going to do next. But, of course, many of us have at least some difficulty in asserting our needs, and many of us feel more comfortable giving way to other people. Even in a very happy home environment, after all, a child's needs cannot always be mirrored. As Erikson said about early childhood:

> Even under the most favourable circumstances, this stage seems to introduce into psychic life . . . a sense of inner division and universal nostalgia for a paradise forfeited. It is against this powerful combination of a sense of having been deprived . . . and of having been abandoned that basic trust must maintain itself throughout life. (Erikson, 1995: 224)

Good breast and bad breast

Melanie Klein (1882–1960) put less emphasis than the other object relations theorists on the external world and more on the child's internal phantasies. And she presents what many find a rather bleak and disturbing picture of what is going on in the mind of a small human being. Klein suggested that babies from an early stage simultaneously feel intense love and murderous, sadistical hatred towards the same object – the mother, and in particular the mother's breast. (If you feel inclined to dismiss the possibility that babies can have such violent feelings, look closely next time you see a baby in a rage.)

The love felt by the baby for his mother relates to the comfort offered by the mother, while the hatred relates to the absolute power that the mother has, to give or withhold this comfort. (As we've just noted, no mother can hope to respond to *every* need.) To begin with, Klein thought, babies deal with these contradictory feelings by the classically Freudian mechanisms of *splitting* and *projection*. Instead of seeing the mother as one person, the baby splits her in his mind into two different people, or two different things, the 'good breast' and the 'bad breast' in Kleinian terminology. However, it is necessary for the child to move on from this stage (the *schizoid* stage); failure to do so could, in Klein's view, lead to schizoid/paranoid disorders in later life, including schizophrenia.

If this initial stage *is* resolved, the child moves from the schizoid phase to the *depressive* phase, which starts to appear at about three months. At this stage the child comes to see the mother as a whole person, so that

> disappointment with the mother no longer turns her into something wholly bad and dangerous: damage is no longer feared as total destruction. A good experience does not mean heaven forever; its loss is no longer the end of the world but is . . . mitigated by the hope of good experiences in the future (Segal, 1992: 38)

But guilt also appears at this stage, when the child realises that his own feelings are ambivalent, and feels badly about the violent and negative feelings he has towards his mother. Inability to manage this guilt could lead to depressive illness. According to Klein we repeatedly revert to a schizoid position at times of difficulty and stress. For example in a quarrel with a loved partner we may temporarily see them as wholly bad and malicious, and ourselves as wholly blameless and good. But she thought that real caring relationships require us to negotiate the difficulties of the depressive position, in which ambivalence has to be faced.

Incidentally, Melanie Klein saw the primary object of envy as being not the penis (as in conventional Freudian thinking), but the *breast*. This is because the breast is experienced from an early stage as providing something which is wanted and needed – and which is possessed and controlled by someone else. While it may seem more plausible that babies would be primarily interested in breasts, rather than penises, we should note that many children are not breast fed at all, and there is no evidence that they are psychologically traumatised as a result. But perhaps it is not so much the breast as such that the child envies, as the ability of mother, or indeed father or other carer, to provide sustenance and comfort in whatever form?

Erikson's stages

Erik Erikson (1902–1994) saw the ego developing through a series of stages at each of which it faces a 'crisis', which must be resolved for the individual to move on to the next stage (see Erikson, 1995: 222 ff.). This is a classically Freudian model both in its conception of stages, and in its suggestion that there are characteristic issues that have to be resolved at each stage before a person is fully capable of moving on. Indeed the first five stages in Erikson's model do correspond to Freud's oral, anal, phallic, latency and genital stages. But a major difference is that Erikson's model spans the whole life-cycle and not just childhood. In addition, while Freud referred to stages of *psychosexual* development, Erikson paid more attention to the social context of development and referred to *psychosocial* stages. Although there are many criticisms that can be levelled at his framework, it does provide a useful starting point for discussion of change across the human life-span – and I will be returning to it in later chapters. His stages are summarised in Table 2.1.

As you can see, each stage has a favourable outcome and an unfavourable outcome. The actual outcome for any individual would depend on how well the particular 'crisis', or challenge, of that stage had been successfully met. You will also notice that an unfavourable outcome in one stage makes it more difficult to meet fully the challenge of the next stage. Thus, as we've already discussed, Erikson saw the task of the first stage (equivalent to Freud's oral stage) as being the establishment of a sense of trust. Clearly if one had not established a sense of trust in the environment, it would be more difficult to achieve the sense of autonomy which is the next stage (the anal stage, in Freudian terms), and then in turn it would be harder to develop the capacity for initiative which is the optimum outcome of the next (phallic) stage – and so on.

Nevertheless, Erikson's model does not say that you have to have completed one stage before you go on to the next. In fact everyone is likely to have some unresolved issues from earlier stages (exactly as in the original Freudian model, everyone will have some fixations from earlier stages). But too much baggage from earlier stages will impede progress.

A new stage of life, according to Erikson, does however offer not only opportunities to tackle the new challenges that it presents, but also a chance to go back and deal with unresolved issues from earlier stages. Sometimes, for example, a person entering a 'midlife crisis', at the beginning of Erikson's sixth stage, may revisit unresolved issues from early adulthood and adolescence. (Indeed the 'second adolescence' at midlife has become almost a cliché. I'll discuss this further in Chapter 7.)

TABLE 2.1 *Stages of psychosocial development*

Life Crisis	Favourable Outcome	Unfavourable Outcome
First Year *Trust v. Mistrust* The child needs consistent and stable care in order to develop feelings of security	Trust in the environment and hope for the future	Suspicion, insecurity, fear of the future
Second and Third years *Autonomy v. Shame and Doubt* The child seeks a sense of independence from parents	A sense of autonomy and self-esteem	Feelings of shame and doubt about one's own capacity for self-control
Fourth and Fifth Years *Initiative v. Guilt* The child explores her environment and plans new activities	The ability to initiate activities and enjoy following them through	Fear of punishment and guilt about one's own personal feelings
Six to Eleven *Industry v. Inferiority* The child acquires important knowledge and skills relating to her culture	A sense of competence and achievement. Confidence in one's own ability to make and do things	Unfavourable reactions from others may cause feelings of inadequacy and inferiority
Adolescence *Identity v. Role Confusion* Young person searches for a coherent personal and vocational identity	Ability to see oneself as a consistent and integrated person	Confusion over who and what one is
Young Adulthood *Intimacy v. Isolation* The adult seeks deep and lasting relationships	The ability to experience love and commitment to others	Isolation: superficial relationships with others
Middle Adulthood *Generativity v. Stagnation* The individual seeks to be productive and creative and to make a contribution to society	The ability to be concerned and caring about others in the wider sense	Lack of growth; boredom and over-concern with oneself
Late Adulthood *Integrity v. Despair* The individual reviews and evaluates what has been accomplished in life	A sense of satisfaction with one's life and its accomplishments; acceptance of death	Regret over omissions and missed opportunities; fear of death

As good a way as any of looking at Erikson's model is to test it against your own life:

✂ Activity 2.4 ✂

What stage are you at in your life? Look through the stages you have already been through and see whether you agree with Erikson about the issues that were important at each stage?

Which stages do you think you negotiated most successfully? Which ones do you think you negotiated less successfully? (Everyone carries some 'baggage' from unresolved issues in earlier life – 'unfavourable outcomes' in Erikson's terminology.)

What do you see as the main drawbacks of Erikson's model?

Comments on Activity 2.4

One criticism of Erikson's model is that it is too linear and prescriptive. It may sketch out the issues we deal with, or try to deal with as we grow older, but it does not allow sufficiently for the many different routes that we may take.

You may also have felt that this model fits better with middle-class life in North America and Europe than it would in other cultures where decisions are made much more collectively and individuals have less choice (or no choice at all) about issues like marriage and career.

Criticisms of Freud and his Successors

I asked you earlier (in Activity 2.3) to consider what you saw as the main problems with Freud's model. I will conclude this chapter by listing some of the criticisms that are commonly levelled at Freud and psychodynamic theory. These criticisms apply to a greater or lesser extent, I would suggest, to most psychodynamic models, as well as to Freud's original ideas.

1 Freud constructed what purports to be a scientific theory as to the structure of the personality, the nature of psychiatric problems and the way that human beings develop and grow. However, his *methods* were certainly not scientific in a conventional sense. He did not test his hypotheses by controlled experiment, but developed them through his clinical observations. In particular, his methods are not of a kind that

could hope to eliminate his own subjective feelings and prejudices, and these are apparent in a number of his conclusions, most famously in his decision not to believe what his female patients told him about childhood abuse.

2 Freud's ideas therefore reflect the man himself, the time in which he worked and the particular culture in which he grew up: middle-class, Austrian Jewish in the time of the Austro-Hungarian Empire. This is particularly apparent perhaps in his attitude to women, as evidenced by his concept of penis envy (it has been said that Freud seemed to view women as essentially men without penises), and his ideas about the phallic stage and the Oedipus complex. In particular, Freud's change of heart over the 'seduction theory' seems to reflect a reluctance to face up to the extent that children and women are abused by men. Masson (1984) goes further and accuses Freud not just of abandoning the 'seduction theory' but of a more deliberate act of suppressing the evidence.

3 Freud's ideas also reflect his own personal life experience. His father was a somewhat distant figure, considerably older than his mother who was quite young when Freud was born – and to whom Freud was consciously sexually attracted. These circumstances, which of course do not apply to all of us, probably played a part in the shaping of the idea of the Oedipus complex. The considerable differences between Jung's ideas and Freud's, for example, may in part simply reflect their different childhood experiences.

4 We have been looking here at Freud's theories about human development and the structure of the personality, and have not discussed psychoanalysis. However there are a number of criticisms of psychoanalysis as a therapeutic technique, which would include questions about whether or not it is effective, and issues to do with the power relationship that exists between the analyst and the person analysed.

5 The claims that are made for Freud's ideas as original have also been challenged. Perhaps, for practical purposes, it makes little difference precisely who contributed to the development of these ideas, but, for example, if you look at the writings of the Greek philosopher Plato (who lived nearly 2,500 years before Freud), you find a dynamic model of the human mind in which it is likened to a chariot in which the rider is the soul while the two horses pulling it are reason and desire:

> First of all we must make it plain that the ruling power in us men drives a pair of horses, and next that one of these is fine and of noble stock, and the other the opposite in every way. So in our case the task of the charioteer is necessarily a difficult and unpleasant business. (Plato, translated by Hamilton, 1973: 51)

Webster (1995), in particular, argues that Freud's ideas are actually much less original than is usually thought.

6 Freud's thinking very much follows what we now call the 'medical model'. He and most of his successors use the language of illness ('pathology', 'symptom', 'therapy'). They label various types of behaviour with disease-like names ('neurosis', 'the psychoses', 'hysteria'). And they put the psychoanalyst in the doctor-like position of expert (offering inter-pretations of symptoms and dreams, for example). In this context, as in others, the medical model can have the effect of taking power and control away from the ordinary person. You could compare this to the application of the medical model to the field of disability or to the management of terminal illness, questions to which I will return in Chapters 9 and 11 respectively.

Clearly you must make your own mind up about the strengths and weaknesses of Freud's ideas, and those of his successors. However I would suggest that for all their shortcomings these ideas remain of value. Freud and other psychodynamic theorists such as Winnicott, Klein and Erikson have shed light on dimensions of human development which are not illuminated in the same way by any other body of theory.

I will conclude with a personal observation about Freud's abandonment of the 'seduction theory'. It seems to me that Freud was perhaps not wrong in concluding that his sexually abused patients were suffering as a result of desires repressed in childhood, rather than simply painful memories, but was mistaken about the kinds of desires that were repressed. Perhaps the desires that they really had to repress were the desires for love, security, freedom from fear, and the wish not to be abused? That the need for love and security is at least as fundamental a need as sex – and a need in its own right – is really the position of attachment theory, which I discuss in the next chapter.

Chapter Summary

The Balancing Act

- In the chapter I have looked at the development of Freud's ideas about the unconscious.

- Noting the controversy about his abandonment of the so-called 'seduction theory', I have looked at Freud's conception of the structure of the personality (ego, id, superego) and his idea of psychological defences (such as denial, repression, projection and splitting).

continued

- I then looked at his theory of psychosexual development (from oral, though anal and phallic stages, into the struggles of the Oedipus complex and the latency period and finally into the genital stage).

- I have discussed the range of different developments of Freud's ideas that there have been.

- Finally I looked at the developments which (loosely) can be categorised as object relations theories and at some of the ideas of Winnicott (the mirror, the true and false selves), Klein (good breast and bad breast, the schizoid and depressive positions) and Erikson (the concept of psychosocial development).

- I concluded by looking at the shortcomings of developmental models of this kind.

In the next chapter we will look at *attachment theory*, **a body of theory that developed out of object relations theory – but which would claim perhaps to have been put on a somewhat more 'objective' or 'scientific' footing. (One must remember however that even 'scientific objectivity' is a culturally bound concept, valued more in some societies than others.)**

Suggested Reading

ON FREUD AND HIS IDEAS:

- Storr, A. (1989) *Freud* (Oxford: OUP)
- Freud, S. (1949) *An Outline of Psychoanalysis* (London: W.W. Norton & Co.)

  (This latter is a short and perfectly readable summary of his ideas by Freud himself, not quite completed because of his death. Unlike some of his successors, Freud writes in a clear and lucid style.)

- Rycroft, C. (1995) *A Critical Dictionary of Psychoanalysis* (2nd edition), (Harmondsworth: Penguin)

  (Contains explanations of all the many terms and concepts.)

ON DEVELOPMENTS OF FREUDIAN THEORY:

- Elliot, A. (1989) *Psychoanalytic Theory, an Introduction* (Oxford: OUP)

  (An overview including Klein, Winnicott, Erikson, Lacan and others.)

- Erikson, E. (1995) *Childhood and Society* (first published 1951) (London: Vintage)
- Segal, J. (1992) *Melanie Klein* (London: Sage)

CRITICISM OF FREUD:

- Masson, J. (1984) *The Assault on Truth: Freud's Suppression of the Seduction Theory* (Harmondsworth: Penguin)
- Webster, R. (1995) *Why Freud Was Wrong: Sin, Science and Psychoanalysis* (London: HarperCollins)

3   A Secure Base

The importance
of attachment

At the end of the previous chapter I looked the development of Freud's ideas by object relations theorists. Attachment theory, the subject of this chapter, is an object relations theory *par excellence*. It is based on the proposition that the way we relate to others throughout our lives (subject–object relations, in other words) is shaped by our first relationship with our primary carer, who traditionally and still usually is the mother.

John Bowlby, who might be described as the 'father' of attachment theory, was a psychoanalyst and a member of the British group of object relations theorists which also included Winnicott and Klein. His emphasis was very different from Klein's, however, and he was less interested in speculating about phantasies that go on in children's minds and more interested in developing a scientific approach that drew on verifiable, objective research on human and animal behaviour. In modern attachment theory, which has moved on from Bowlby's original ideas, you can still find ideas that owe a debt to Freud, but you will not find much mention of Oedipus complexes, phallic stages, penis envy and the other more explicitly sexual – and to many, bizarre – aspects of Freudian thinking.

Although it has its critics, attachment theory has been very influential, particularly in fields where assessing parenting is a central issue. In Britain, for example, social workers working with children and families are often involved in addressing questions such as the following. All of them are related to attachment:

- Are a child's needs being adequately met within this relationship?
- Can the relationship change?
- Would the damage done by disrupting this relationship be outweighed or not by the benefits of providing other more consistent carers?
- Could the child settle with new carers?
- If so, what therapeutic work would be needed to make that possible?
- Is the respite and support offered to a family by a shared care arrangement, likely to be beneficial to relationships in that family?
- Does a child's rejection of their foster-carers reflect a real problem with those particular carers, or is it the result of the child's difficulties with attachment that would be a problem in any relationship?

In any of the caring professions – or indeed in life generally – you are certain to encounter many people who have problems with attachment. Attachment theorists argue that many other problems actually have their roots in difficulties in early attachment relationships and that early attachment has strong links with mental health in adult life, the ability to form relationships, the ability to parent and the ability to deal with loss.

The following activity may help you to gather your own thoughts on the subject:

Activity 3.1

(a) Think of a child you know who seems to have some problems in relating with his/her parent(s) or carer(s)? What is it that makes you think there is a problem? How does it affect the child?

(b) Now think of an adult you know who seems to have difficulty with intimate relationships. What makes you think that there is a difficulty? What are your theories about what may have caused the difficulty in the first place?

Comments on Activity 3.1

(a) You may have mentioned that this child is reluctant to go to his/her carers, or seems anxious in their presence. Alternatively you may have said that the child seems excessively clingy to his/her carers, and seems very anxious if separated from them at all. Or you may have said that the child appears to cling indiscriminately to any adult. Among the effects on the child, you may have noticed: poor concentration, difficulty in making friends, difficulty in judging social situations.

(b) You may have mentioned an adult who seems to have difficulty with commitment, and who is always ending relationships because he or she feels trapped. Or an adult who is unable to talk about feelings with his or her partner – or seems to talk about them compulsively. Or perhaps someone who always seems to be abused and dominated in relationships, and can't seem to end them, no matter how unhappy he or she feels . . . If you know anything about this adult's childhood, you will probably notice that their relationship with parents/carers was problematic in some way. There may have been neglect or abuse, or abandonment of some sort. Or the parents may have been excessively controlling or excessively protective.

John Bowlby (1907–1990) and 'Maternal Deprivation'

Although a trained psychoanalyst, and a member of the British psycho-analytic community, John Bowlby was critical of psychoanalysis in general for focusing so much on phantasies and imaginary fears, such as a small boy's supposed fear of castration by his father, as if there were not enough real dangers in the world. He thought Klein and the Kleinians in particular were excessively interested in children's phantasies about their parents, and suggested that it would be much more fruitful to look at their parents' real characters. Bowlby was interested in the *external* factors that influence a child's development.

Bowlby was also interested in reconciling the insights of psycho-analytic theory with ethology (the study of animal behaviour) and with verifiable, empirical research in general. However he was part of the psychoanalytic community, and though his ideas are expressed in much more 'common-sense' terms than those of some other writers in the psychoanalytic tradition, they recognisably follow the same pattern. As in classical Freudian theory, Bowlby's ideas included the concept of various unconscious strategies that come into play when needs can't be met at different stages, including strategies such as splitting or excluding things from consciousness. Like Freud, he saw these strategies being carried into later life.

Bowlby's particular interest was on the effects of separation of children from their parents. *Attachment, Separation* and *Loss* were the titles of the three volumes of his most famous work (Bowlby, 1997, 1998a, b). And, in 1950, he was asked by the World Health Organisation to carry out a study of children separated from their parents. (This was of course in the post-war context, when bereavement, evacuation, deportation and so on had disrupted millions of families in Europe.) He looked at children separated from parents in various ways and interviewed disturbed adolescents and adults. He found a strong link between what he called 'maternal deprivation' and problems in adult life such as delinquency, mental illness and difficulties in parenting.

Bowlby's definition of maternal deprivation, in his original thinking, included loss of the mother or separation from the mother, as well as neglectful or abusive mothering. Both the word 'maternal' and the word 'deprivation' are targets of criticism, the former because of its exclusive emphasis on the mother, as opposed to the father and other carers, the latter because it conflates several very different things. As attachment theory has developed, it has taken on board some of the criticisms in both these areas.

In addition to these studies on the long-term effects of maternal deprivation, Bowlby also looked at the short-term effects on children of separation from their mothers (see Robertson and Bowlby, 1952). What he observed was that children went through several stages:

- a stage of *protest*, including crying, screaming, trying to find the mother and so on;
- a stage of *despair*, when the child becomes listless and apathetic;
- a stage of *detachment*, when the child seems to lose interest in the missing parent and starts to become involved again in other activities, though this involvement may be quite superficial and unengaged.

This last stage seemed to Bowlby to be the result of defensive mechanisms coming into play which meant that the child *repressed* (to use the Freudian term: Bowlby also used the phrase *'defensively excluded'*) feelings of grief and anger and distress. If they were never resolved in any way, could these painful, angry, distressing feelings lead to the long-term problems which his other research seemed to indicate were associated with so-called maternal deprivation?

As you will see, attachment theory tries to bring these different observations together into a coherent whole.

Bowlby and social reform

Bowlby's interest in this topic was not, however, primarily academic. He was passionate about the need of children for love and security and he was influential in bringing about many changes in this area that we now take almost for granted. For example, parents in the 1950s and 1960s were routinely told not to visit their children in hospital, because 'it only upsets them'. Bowlby decided that this was nonsense. Children did not get more upset when their parents visited, but just felt safe enough to *show* how upset they already were. Bowlby was a key figure in bringing about a change towards the modern approach of encouraging parental contact.

Some of the other causes he championed were:

- Consulting children and letting children express their own views and feelings.
- Not judging parenting, or removing children from parents, just on the grounds of poor physical conditions.
- Being aware of the negative effect of institutional care on young children.
- Not placing children in temporary care situations without long-term plans in place.
- Abandoning what he called 'the astonishing practice' of separating mothers and babies immediately after birth. Arguing that this was hardly the way to promote a close mother–child relationship, Bowlby described this practice, common in the 1950s, as a 'madness of Western society' which he hoped would never be copied by 'the so-called less developed countries' (Bowlby 1990: 180).

The Biological Origins of Attachment

A much-quoted comment by Bowlby was that 'mother love in infancy and childhood is as important for mental health as are vitamins and proteins for physical health' (Bowlby, 1951). He saw the need for a close relationship – an attachment – between child and carer (and particularly *mother*) as being a basic biological need. And he differed from Freud in that he didn't see this relationship as being important only in so far as it met basic primary needs – sexual needs and the need for food. He saw it as a need in its own right. After all, we can easily observe, not only in humans, but also in other mammals, how strong the bond is between a mother and a child. Both mother and baby animals of many species become distressed and agitated if they are separated, and mother animals will often fight ferociously to prevent a baby being taken from them. Bowlby quoted this vivid description from a piece of research in which baby monkeys were separated from their mothers for five-minute periods:

> Separation of mother and infant monkeys is an extremely stressful experience for both mother and infant as well as for the attendants and for all other monkeys within sight or earshot of the experience. The mother becomes ferocious . . . the infant's screams can be heard over almost the entire building. The mother

struggles and attacks the separators. The baby clings tightly to the mother and to any object which it can grasp to avoid being held or removed by the attendant. With the baby gone the mother paces the cage continually . . . bites at it and makes continual attempts to escape. The infant emits high-pitched screams intermittently and almost continuously for the whole period of the separation. (Jensen and Tolman, 1962, cited by Bowlby, 1998a: 85)

So both mother and baby monkey called to each other and signalled their distress, and the mother made frantic efforts to get back to the baby. These are examples of what Bowlby termed '*attachment behaviour*'. Attachment behaviour includes crying and distress calls but also behaviour by the child that has the effect of attracting the mother's interest in a positive way. Indeed any behaviour that appears to have the function of bringing mother and child together is attachment behaviour. And it is by observing the amount of attachment behaviour that we gain some sense of how strong an attachment exists. For instance, from the account just quoted of a baby monkey being separated from the mother, we conclude that a strong attachment exists between the two.

📖 Attachment and Animal Experiments 📖

Bowlby was interested in learning from animal experiments. But such experiments are controversial for two reasons. Firstly, there is a question about *ethics*. Secondly, there is the question as to whether they are *valid*. Can information from animals tell us anything about human beings? The sociologist, Erica Burman, emphatically rejects this (Burman, 1994: 87–9).

The best-known animal experiments in the field of attachment were carried out by Harry Harlow and his collaborators. In one experiment baby rhesus monkeys were separated from their mothers within twelve hours of birth and placed in cages with two types of surrogate mothers: one made of soft cloth and one made of wire. They found that the babies preferred the cloth mother, spending their time cuddled up to it, even if the experimenters arranged things so that it was the wire mother that actually provided milk. Babies raised with these surrogate mothers, or with no mothers at all, grew up incapable of normal sexual or social behaviour, and were neglectful and abusive mothers to their own babies.

There must be serious ethical questions about such experiments, but there do seem to be striking parallels here with human experience. (Indeed the striking parallels with humans seems to me to be one compelling reason why these experiments should be regarded as unethical.)

Bowlby believed that attachment behaviour is innate, part of our 'nature', and he theorised that this behaviour had evolved for a specific reason. A baby (human or animal) needs to explore to learn about the world. It cannot permanently be physically in contact with its mother. But it also needs to retain some proximity to the mother, on whom it depends for food and protection. The effect of attachment behaviour is to act as a kind of invisible elastic, maintaining a link between mother and child. Too much separation, whether in terms of distance (too far away), or in terms of time (too long), increases the anxiety levels of mother and child and increases the amount of attachment behaviour. When closeness is restored, attachment behaviour can go into abeyance and other behaviours can be resumed. Attachment behaviour is not about 'drive reduction' in the sense that, say, the appetite for food or sex is. It is about *homeostasis*, which means maintaining a balance.

The effects of this can be observed quite readily. If you are a parent you will probably be familiar with the scenario in which you are sitting in a room with your children playing round you and you then decide move to another room. After a period of time you find that your children have followed you. They may not necessarily want anything in particular from you, and they may well quietly resume their games when homeostasis has been re-established. Or, for a more extreme example of attachment in action, you only need to consider the reactions of both parent and child when they accidentally lose one another in a busy street.

Parents, mothers, carers

You may have noticed that I sometimes use the word 'mother' to describe a child's primary attachment figure, which was also Bowlby's practice. As I've already mentioned, this is one source of criticism of attachment theory.

In the case of some animals, there can be little doubt that the mother *is* the primary attachment figure (and indeed, in some species, the males take no part in child-rearing, and may not even have any way of knowing which are their own offspring). But children can and do have attachment figures other than the mother. And, even if the main attachment figure *is* the mother, they may well have other figures who are also important sources of protection and comfort. A further criticism of attachment theory, as originally expounded by Bowlby, is that it is too 'monotropic' – meaning that it makes the assumption that there has to be one single primary focus of attachment behaviour. In all cultures to some extent, and in some cultures to a great extent, childcare is of course a task that is *shared*, not only by mothers and fathers but also by grandparents, uncles, aunts and friends.

I will use the words mother, parent and carer in this chapter to describe adult attachment figures. They can in most instances be used interchangeably. At its core, attachment theory is about the way that childhood needs are met – and the long-term effects of needs being met or otherwise. Bowlby may have made the assumption that the primary carer is the mother, but it is not in my view essential to the theory itself. What *is* central to the theory, though, is that attachment is not indiscriminate. It is in the nature of attachment that, if not focused on just one individual, it is at least focused on particular individuals.

The Secure Base and Attachment Behavioural Systems

In Bowlby's model, attachment behaviour is seen as instinctive, and as serving a basic biological purpose. But this is only the starting point. One way of looking at attachment is that the attachment figure is a kind of emotional anchor, a source of security, or, in Bowlby's phrase, a *'secure base.'* In the absence of the attachment figure, there is insecurity. Attachment behaviour is designed to restore the sense of security that comes from knowing that the secure base is there in case it is needed. But for all children, on occasion the secure base will not be there. There will be unavoidable separations of one kind or another and there will also be occasions when the mother or primary carer is physically there, but is not really available as a source of comfort, perhaps because she is preoccupied, or because she is angry with the child, or for some other reason, such as ill-health for example. This will be the case more for some children than others.

Children will adopt different behavioural strategies, depending on their circumstances, to obtain as much support as they can. Attachment behaviour is modified in the light of experience, in other words. Each individual adopts a different repertoire of characteristic attachment behaviours. This repertoire Bowlby called an *attachment behavioural system.*

There are some children who grow up with no real sense of a secure base at all. Such children are, in Bowlby's term, in a state of *dissuagement*, a state of permanently having an unmet need. This is an extremely difficult situation to be in – and the child will resort to various defensive manoeuvres in order to minimise the pain of separation anxiety or to try and obtain support. Here of course – in the idea of defences – is a concept derived directly from the Freudian model.

Children use these defences and strategies to obtain as much support as they can and to minimise anxiety. But Bowlby did not see them as merely temporary behaviours. He saw them being internalised by degrees into what he saw as a distinctive working model of the world, which an individual carried with him into later life. Again this is a classically Freudian approach. You will remember from the last chapter how the superego develops as a result of the internalisation of adult messages.

I hope you can see how these ideas lead outwards from what begins as a relatively straightforward idea about the biological origins of attachment, into a theory about how human personality develops, and how relationships in early childhood shape and influence behaviour and relationships throughout life.

The following three propositions, extracted from Bowlby's book *Separation* (1998a: 235), may help to clarify what we have just been discussing:

> . . . when an individual is confident that an attachment figure will be available to him whenever he desires, that person will be much less prone to either intense or chronic fear than will an individual who has no such confidence.
>
> . . . confidence in the availability of an attachment figure, or lack of it, is built up slowly during the years of immaturity – infancy, childhood and adolescence – and . . . whatever expectations are developed during those years tend to persist relatively unchanged throughout the rest of life.
>
> . . . the varied expectations of the accessibility and responsiveness of attachment figures that different individuals develop during the years of immaturity are tolerably accurate reflections of the experiences those individuals have actually had.

(This last proposition, as Bowlby went on to say, was controversial in analytical circles because many psychoanalysts, such as Klein, put so much more stock on phantasy than on actual objective experience.) I will return to these ideas later, in the discussion about *working models* and about *secure* and *insecure* attachment.

The following activity is to give you an opportunity to think about how different patterns of relating to others can become established in childhood:

⚒ Activity 3.2 ⚒

Think of three or four children, preferably of similar ages, from different families, and think about how they relate – or related – to their parents (or to their primary carers if these are not their parents).

Assuming that all children are seeking the reassurance that their carers are available to them for support, but that this is not equally available to all children all the time, what do you notice about the different ways in which these children gain their parents' attention? Can you see ways in which these children have adapted their attachment behaviour to meet the particular circumstances in which they find themselves?

Comments on Activity 3.2

The possibilities here are, of course, endless. The following are a few patterns which I have noticed:

- Some children learn that presenting symptoms of illness is a good way of attracting parental interest and attention. This is particularly so, of course, when parents are anxious about health. I have encountered children who have developed what seem like quite intractable health problems, which have consumed a good deal of their parents' time, yet which seem to disappear when the children are with other carers.
- Sometimes children of parents who are emotionally fragile can seem unusually 'grown-up', 'independent' and 'well-behaved'. Perhaps these are children who have learnt from experience not to make excessive demands on their parents?
- Some children, on the other hand, seem to subject their carers to an incessant barrage of demands.
- Youngest children often continue to use 'cuteness' to attract positive attention at a much later stage than their older siblings did. ('Acting cute' is a form of attachment behaviour.) The older children in the family, faced with younger and 'cuter' rivals, have needed to develop other ways of getting parental attention.

We will return later to look in more detail at patterns established in childhood. But I want to look now at stages in the development of attachment.

The Growth of Attachment

Attachment develops in early childhood, going through several stages. If you look at the attachment literature, you will find some variation in the terms used and in the indicative ages given for each stage. One would expect, in any case, that there would be some differences between individuals in respect of the speed at which they develop. But, taking the ages as rough guidelines only, the following are the stages through which attachment is thought to develop. (The indicative ages which I have used here are from Howe et al., 1999: 19–21.)

Pre-attachment (0–2 months)
This stage is characterized by *undiscriminating social responsiveness*. At this stage babies enjoy social interaction. They are interested in human voices and human faces. But they can be left with different caregivers without seeming to be distressed. Experiments on monkeys carried out by

Harlow (1963) and others in the 1960s and 1970s showed that very small babies could be separated from their mothers without causing any long-term difficulty, but that older babies separated from their mothers for the same period, showed long-term behavioural problems: this suggests that for monkeys too there is a pre-attachment stage. Also of relevance here are the findings of cognitive psychology, which will be discussed in the next chapter. Piaget's model would suggest that at this very early age the baby would have no concept of the mother, or carer, as a separate individual with her own existence. At this stage the baby does not even know that objects exist when she is not looking at them. (According to Piaget, the concept of 'object permanence' does not develop until about 6 months.)

Attachment-in-the-making (3–6 months)

We now see *discriminating* social responsiveness developing. Babies start to show different responses to different people. They respond more to familiar people than to strangers and they become increasingly focused on their main carer.

Clear-cut attachment (7 months to 3 years)

During this stage a child will *actively seek proximity and contact* with her main carer whenever the distance between them becomes too great. And the child will display full-blown separation anxiety when the carer leaves the room. As well as becoming more active in seeking out the carer, the child will also become more active in maintaining contact. For example, the child will read the situation and alter her behaviour accordingly in order to optimise the response from the carer. (So we see *different* attachment behavioural systems developing, depending on circumstances, as discussed above in Activity 3.2.)

Reciprocal relationship (from 3 years)

As the child becomes more mobile and spends more time away from the carer, the pair enter a reciprocal state in which they share responsibility for maintaining equilibrium. Increasingly a feeling of security can be main-tained even during temporary separations – assisted by cognitive devel-opments which allow the child to think in more sophisticated terms about things like time and space, the reasons for a carer's absence and so on. (The child can feel that the carer is 'there for her', even when the carer is not physically present.) Cognitive developments also allow the child to begin to be able to see things from the carer's point of view and to adjust behaviour accordingly, understanding that their carer also has goals and plans. The relationship becomes more of a partnership.

The description of the reciprocal relationship stage which I have just given does suppose that, by and large, the relationship between carer and child has gone well. Rather different patterns would otherwise emerge. Whatever pattern is established by this stage, though, will become an *internalised working model*, that the child will use as a standard to guide interactions with other people – and will carry on into the rest of her life.

Internalised Working Models

What differences in behaviour are noticeable between children who have a secure relationship with their carers and those who don't? Have a look at the following activity:

⚒ Activity 3.3 ⚒

What characteristic behaviours might lead you to think that there was a secure relationship between a child and her carer? What behaviours would lead you to feel that the relationship was problematic?

The fact that children behave differently suggests that they have different ideas in their minds. What ideas might those be?

Comments on Activity 3.3

You may have described a secure relationship as being one in which a child goes easily to her carer, but seems confident enough of her carer's support to leave the carer's side and explore. A securely attached child has learnt the basic lesson of trust which you may remember Erikson saw as the first developmental task (see p. 42). The child has the belief that the carer can be depended upon. You may also have mentioned eye contact, mutually rewarding physical contact and mutually rewarding verbal communication.

In the case of an insecure attachment you may have thought either of clinginess or the opposite: the child avoiding or ignoring the carer (or perhaps you may have thought of children who exhibit a strange combination of both of these). Some children seem to have the idea in their minds that there is no point in going to their carers for support – or that to do so might actually do more harm than good. Other children seem to see it as their job to look after their carers rather than the other way round, or to feel guilty about the burden they are to their carers. Such children may seem preoccupied with the carer, constantly watching the carer for approval, or constantly checking that the carer is okay.

You may have mentioned a lack of specificity about the relationship: the child treats other adults in just the same way as she treats the carer. You may have mentioned a lack of mutuality: eye contact, touch or verbal communication do not seem to be pleasurable or rewarding to either party.

Insecure children exhibit a number of different characteristic ways of behaving (different attachment behavioural systems). We will discuss different patterns of insecure attachment later on. For the purpose of the present discussion, though, what I would like you to note is that children in different kinds of relationships (secure and insecure) appear to have different ideas in their minds about what they can expect from their carer, what is expected of them, and what is an appropriate way to behave.

We are thinking beings and our actions are based on ideas about the world that we carry in our minds. We avoid fire and hot things, for example, because we have in our minds the idea that they can cause injury and pain. The same, Bowlby suggested, applied to attachment behaviour:

> each individual builds working models of the world, and of himself in it, with the aid of which he perceives events, forecasts the future, and constructs his plans. In the working model of the world that anyone builds, a key feature is his notions of who his attachment figures are, where they may be found, and how they may be expected to respond. Similarly, in the working model of the self that anyone builds a key feature is his notion of how acceptable or unacceptable he himself is in the eyes of his attachment figures. (Bowlby 1998a: 236)

The working model that a child uses, then, includes three elements:

- an idea about other people and what can be expected from them
- an idea about self
- an idea about how self and others relate

A securely attached child (a child who has been 'mirrored', to use Winnicott's term) will have a working model of the world in which she herself is worthy of love and attention, others are expected to be responsive and reliable (at least in the absence of evidence to the contrary) and relationships with others are seen as rewarding and fun.

But what about a child whose caregiver is unpredictable or rejecting? In such circumstances, according to attachment theory, children develop a working model that is based, not on reality or on an accurate representation of self and others, but on *coping*. To achieve this working model, the child will use *defensive exclusion* (or 'denial' as Freud would have called it) to shut out aspects of reality which do not fit the model. The resulting model is 'faulty'. It sacrifices the child's own needs, including the child's need for an accurate representation of reality, in order to accommodate the caregiver in some way. Children with grossly neglectful parents, for example, will think of all kinds of excuses for the neglect in order to protect themselves from concluding that their parents do not care about them. They may tell themselves that they deserve the neglect, or that they prefer things the way they are.

This concept of the *faulty working model* is very much in the psycho-dynamic tradition. Freud saw defences coming into play to protect an individual against the anxiety that comes with needs not being met. Winnicott's concept of a 'false self' (see p. 40) also seems to me to mean pretty much the same thing as a faulty working model. And, like Freudian theory, attachment theory maintains that, once established, defensive mechanisms become part of our make-up, so that as we move into adult life, and try to form new attachments, these will be informed by these faulty working models. In other words, adults who have internalised faulty working models as children try and form relationships *on the basis of incorrect information*. Thus, although faulty working models may be a necessary survival mechanism at the time they are established, a way of maintaining relationships which are the best currently available, there is a cost to pay in the long term.

These costs can be summed up as follows:

- Faulty models contain inaccurate information on which to base relation-ships, and therefore cause difficulties in forming new relationships successfully.
- 'Defensive exclusion' means that models can't be updated in the light of new experience. (Defensive exclusion is *why* faulty models tend to become 'set in stone'.)
- These systems tend to include *splitting* – the co-existence of incompatible ideas (for example, 'My mum loves and cares for me very, very much' co-exists in the same mind as 'Unless I am very, very careful, my mother punishes me and tells me she never wanted me.') (See Chapter 2 for more on splitting.) The habit of splitting prevents the development of a coherent sense of self. People prone to splitting never know what they *really* think or who they *really* are.
- Defensive exclusion removes the opportunity to process painful feelings (such as grief or anger), and this leads to the perpetuation of primitive unresolved feelings of hate, abandonment and so on. This in turn restricts growth and development. (If you can't admit to yourself you are angry, then you can never deal with it.)

Mary Ainsworth's Attachment Classification System

We've already noted that both clinginess and aloofness, though apparently opposite, can both be the consequences of poor attachment. When a child's attachment needs are not fully met, and the child develops a faulty working model, this may take one of several forms.

Mary Ainsworth, a collaborator of Bowlby, proposed a classification, based on her own studies of mother and baby interactions, which included three categories of attachment: *secure, anxious–avoidant* and *anxious–ambivalent* (Ainsworth et al. 1978). A fourth category, *disorganised* attachment, has since been recognised and there are also some individuals who have not experienced any type of attachment at all who can be termed *non-attached*. So we now have five categories, as follows:

Secure

The child shows a clear preference for the mother (or other primary carer) over others. The carer is sensitive to, and responds to, the child's attempts to communicate. The child is confident that the carer is available to give support and takes pleasure in the presence of the carer. The child shows distress on separation from the carer. On reunion she seeks some reassurance, but then settles again.

Anxious–avoidant

This is also known as 'insecure–avoidant' (the word 'anxious' and the word 'insecure' are used interchangeably in this context) and one might describe it as the 'aloof' strategy. The child doesn't show much distress on separation from the carer and when she returns the child ignores or avoids her. The child does not seek out physical contact and is watchful and wary around the carer. Her play is inhibited and she shows little discrimination between her carer and others, including strangers. This pattern emerges when the parent is insensitive to, or rejecting of, the child's needs. The child has therefore learnt to minimise needs for attachment (through defensive exclusion) in order to avoid rebuff. It is as if the child is saying: 'Who cares? I didn't want it anyway.'

Anxious–ambivalent

Also called 'insecure–ambivalent' or 'resistant', this might be described as the 'clingy' strategy. Here the child is distressed on separation but does not settle down on reunion. The return of the carer is longed for, but when it comes it is not reassuring: the separation anxiety continues. The anxious–ambivalent child is frightened to go off and explore the world, because she is uncertain about whether the carer will be there when needed. This pattern is the result of a parenting style that is not consistently hostile or rejecting, but is inconsistent, and where parents are lacking in empathy for the child's needs. Not surprisingly, separations from parents, and threats of abandonment, are also associated with this strategy. The child may adopt all kinds of strategies to keep the attention of the carer. Role reversal may take place, for example, where the child cares for the caregiver, paying more attention to the caregiver's needs than her own. But at the same time the child is angry about the unreliability of the carer. This anger may be defensively excluded, so that the child is not consciously aware of it.

Disorganised

This occurs when the carer is viewed by the child as frightening (as in abusive situations) or as frightened. Either way the carer is not available as a source of comfort or reassurance, though the child has nowhere else to go. In the case of abusive situations, the carer may simultaneously be the main *source* of danger or fear, while at the same time the only place to go for comfort. In a situation like this there is no 'right' response. Children exhibiting disorganised attachment may show a confused mixture of both ambivalent and avoidant responses (for example, seeking to be held, but then looking away and avoiding eye-contact). Or they may simply 'freeze', showing neither positive nor negative reactions to separation and reunion.

Non-attached

This applies to children who have had no opportunity to form attachments of any kind. For example, it applies to children raised from an early age in institutions, where, even if they are adequately fed and clothed and so on, they may have had no opportunities to form personal relationships with carers. It may also apply in some cases to families where the carer is totally unavailable emotionally, as the result perhaps of mental illness. Non-attached children show serious problems in social relationships. They may show little preference for, or interest in, one person rather than another. They have difficulty in controlling their impulses. Their cognitive development may be impaired.

Michael Rutter, whose criticisms and modifications of Bowlby's ideas I will discuss next, is currently involved in research on the effects of institutional care on Romanian 'orphans' (see Rutter et al., 1998: I put the word orphan in inverted commas, because many so-called orphans have living parents, but have been given up by their parents for economic or other reasons). But before looking at Rutter's ideas, the following activity may give an opportunity to reflect on what I have been discussing.

Activity 3.4

(a) Thinking about adults that you know (perhaps the ones you thought of in Activity 3.1), can you think of some whose way of relating to others could be described as anxious–avoidant and of some whose way of relating to others could be described as anxious–ambivalent?

(b) If you would like to consider how your own childhood relationships affect your relationships now, one way to look at it would be to write down a list of messages that you characteristically received from your parents – positive ('You are special'), negative ('I'm too busy to attend to you') or neutral. You can then consider how these messages have affected your characteristic stance in relation to other people. Please note, though, that this can be surprisingly distressing.

Comments on Activity 3.4

(a) Probably most of us know people who are avoidant or ambivalent in relationships, sometimes to surprising extremes. If you are familiar with the childhood history of these people, you may well see, I suspect, that the parents were either rejecting or unresponsive (in the avoidant case) or inconsistent (in the ambivalent case)

(b) If you decided to do the second part of the exercise in full, you will probably have noticed how powerful some of those parental messages are in terms of the emotional response they produce – and it may have struck you that these messages from your childhood do indeed affect the way you deal with the world now. One could argue that this is a demonstration of internalised working models in action. (Parent message cards, incidentally, on which a large number of such messages are written out, one per card, can be used as a therapeutic tool: the idea being to sort them into two piles, those that apply and those that don't – or those that you would wish to pass on to your children, and those you would not.)

Rutter's Modifications to Bowlby

Michael Rutter is a British psychiatrist active in research on the effects of childhood experience on later life. If Bowlby started with psychoanalytic theory and moved from it towards a more empirical approach (drawing on systematic research on human behaviour, rather than just clinical observations, as well as animal experiments), Rutter could be said to have taken attachment theory still further down the same path.

Research by Rutter and others confirms Bowlby's original insistence on the importance of early life experiences on children's long-term psychological development. In a study published in 1998, for example, Rutter and his collaborators in the English and Romanian Adoptees Study Team, found that gross early privation was a major cause of cognitive deficits in Romanian orphans adopted in the UK, 'with psychological privation probably more important than nutritional deprivation'. But Rutter has pointed out that Bowlby's concept of 'maternal deprivation', as originally formulated, was a confusing one because it lumps together many different factors, and because the words 'maternal' and 'deprivation' are both somewhat misleading.

He argues that things such as cognitive delay and language delay in children from deprived backgrounds, may be due to lack of *stimulation* in those environments. This is a different thing from the lack of emotional warmth, which research by Rutter and others confirms is linked to deviant and anti-social behaviour in later life. Emotional warmth and cognitive stimulation are different factors, and the lack of each of them has different effects, though in certain environments both may be lacking.

Importantly Rutter also argues that *privation* (that is to say, a chronic *lack*) rather than deprivation (that is, a specific *loss*) is what causes long-term psychological problems.

> Loss of an attachment figure, although a major factor in the causation of short-term effects, seems of only minor importance with respect to long-term consequences. . . . Indeed the evidence strongly suggests that most of the long-term consequences are due to privation or lack of some kind, rather than to any kind of loss. (Rutter, 1981: 121)

Rutter questions the 'maternal' part of 'maternal deprivation' because it gives a unique importance to the mother. Rutter does not think this is substantiated by research evidence and writes:

> most children develop bonds with several people and it appears likely that these bonds are basically similar . . . the chief bond need not be with a biological parent, it need not be the chief caretaker and it need not be with a female. (Rutter, 1981: 127)

Criticisms of Attachment Theory

Certainly some of the earlier formulations of attachment theory, with their emphasis on mothers and their claim that children were essentially 'monotropic' (forming a primary attachment to just one person), can be criticised from both a feminist and from a multicultural point of view.

Bowlby's old-fashioned view of the roles of mothers and fathers is illustrated by the following quote from a book first published in 1953:

In the young child's eyes father plays second fiddle. . . . Nevertheless, as the illegitimate child knows, fathers have their uses even in infancy. Not only do they provide for their wives to enable them to devote themselves unrestrictedly to the care of the infant and toddler, but, by providing love and companionship, they support the mother emotionally and help her maintain that harmonious contented mood in the atmosphere of which her infant thrives. (1990: 15)

I would suggest that not only mothers but also many fathers would object to the restricted roles to which Bowlby seems to be consigning them, respectively, here.

A number of feminist writers (for example Burman, 1994) have criticised Bowlby for 'tying women to the home', by implying that if the mother leaves her child at all, this will result in long-term harm. In fact it has been argued that one reason that Bowlby's ideas became popular when they did is that they provided a rationale for taking women out of paid work following the war years when so many women had joined the industrial workforce, and expecting them to stay at home. Attachment theory could be used as a pretext for not providing good daycare facilities, for example.

From a multicultural point of view, one could argue that this insistence on the monotropic mother–child bond has the effect of setting up the European / North American 'nuclear family' as the model for child-rearing, ignoring the more communal approaches that are the norm in other parts of the world. In other words: attachment theory, in its original formulation, is distinctly 'Eurocentric'. Even within the terms of Western culture, over-emphasis on the monotropic mother–child bond seems to undervalue other relationships, such as those with the father and grandparents.

It can even be argued that if a child relies too exclusively on care from one person, her mother, this may in the long run itself be damaging, placing undue pressure on the mother which will itself harm the relationship if she is worn out, or bored, or becomes resentful of the child.

The idea of a 'critical period' in early childhood during which patterns are laid down for the rest of life, is also one which has seen some challenges. It can be demonstrated to be the case that some aspects of development are 'set in stone' at particular stages, but not all. Ann and Alan Clarke, for example, have been arguing for many years that there is nothing unique about early childhood and that

the widespread belief in the disproportionate effects of early experiences is likely to lead to underestimation of what can be done for deprived children, and hence, on the one hand, less than adequate interventions, or, on the other, total inaction. (Clarke and Clarke, 2000: 105)

They are not saying, then, that early experience is unimportant, but rather that later experience is equally important, and can change the effects of early experience.

However, although there are many criticisms that can be made about attachment theory as originally formulated by Bowlby, attachment theory has proved to be something that can grow and develop in the light of new evidence. It would be a mistake, I think, to discard Bowlby's ideas about the importance of attachment and a secure base in childhood, or his ideas about the influence of childhood experience on adult life, merely because his conception of what this might consist of was limited by the particular perspective of his own times.

Bowlby's ideas were related to the ideas of other object relations theorists such as Winnicott, and also to the ideas of Freud himself. One lasting legacy of Freud seems to be an increased recognition of the deep emotional needs of young children and of the profound damage that can be done if these needs are ignored. Bowlby translated this insight into a practical concern which has been a major influence on public policy, and on the way we think about children and their needs.

Chapter Summary

A Secure Base

- In this chapter I have looked at John Bowlby's ideas about the importance of early attachment for long-term psychological health.
- I have considered his ideas about the biological origins of attachment and attachment behaviour.
- I have looked at stages in the development of attachment.
- I have considered the idea of internalised 'working models' – of self and others – learnt in early relationships and carried into later life.
- I have looked Mary Ainsworth's classification system for secure and insecure attachment (the latter being divided into anxious–avoidant and anxious–ambivalent – disorganised attachment and non-attachment are two additional categories).
- I have considered Rutter's modifications to Bowlby.
- I have looked at criticisms of attachment theory from feminist and multicultural points of view, among others.

In this chapter and the last I have looked primarily at emotional development. In the next chapter I will move on to look at cognitive development: the development of thinking.

Suggested Reading

ON AND BY BOWLBY:

- Bowlby, J. (1990) *Childcare and the Growth of Love* (first published 1953) (Harmondsworth: Penguin)
- Bowlby, J. (1997) *Attachment* (London: Pimlico)
- Bowlby, J. (1998a) *Separation* (London: Pimlico)
- Bowlby, J. (1998b) *Loss* (London: Pimlico)
- Holmes, J. (1993) *John Bowlby and Attachment Theory* (London: Routledge)

OTHER PERSPECTIVES:

- Burman, E. (1994) *Deconstructing Developmental Psychology* (London: Routledge)
- Rutter, M. (1981) *Maternal Deprivation Reassessed* (2nd edition) (Harmondsworth: Penguin)

GENERAL INTRODUCTIONS TO ATTACHMENT THEORY AND ITS APPLICATION (LIKELY TO BE OF INTEREST TO OTHERS AS WELL AS SOCIAL WORKERS):

- Howe, D. (1995) *Attachment Theory for Social Work Practice* (London: Macmillan)
- Howe, D., Brandon, M., Hinings, D. and Schofield, G. (1999) *Attachment Theory, Child Maltreatment and Family Support* (London: Macmillan)

4 The Emergence of Reason

Piaget and cognitive development

Suppose you are a teacher in a nursery school. In your class is a 4-year-old child whose mother has to go to hospital for an operation. She is a single parent with no relatives in the area, and it is going to be necessary for the little boy to go to a foster home for seven nights. How do you help a 4-year-old make sense of the fact that he must go and live with strangers for a week? It's not just a matter of making him feel cared for, or of helping him cope emotionally, and giving him an opportunity to express his feelings (as Bowlby advocated), vitally important though that this. It is also a matter of making the facts intelligible to him. What is a hospital? What is an operation? What is a foster home? What, for that matter, is a *week*? All these concepts need explaining.

This chapter represents something of a change of gear from the two previous chapters. We have been considering how childhood experience influences emotional development. We are now going to look at how a child learns to make sense of the world. We are moving into what is known as cognitive psychology – or, more specifically, into developmental cognitive psychology.

In particular, I am going to focus on the work of Jean Piaget. If Bowlby is the father of attachment theory, Piaget could perhaps be described as the father of developmental cognitive psychology. Just as with Bowlby, many of Piaget's ideas have been challenged by subsequent research, and I am not offering them here as the 'last word'. Nevertheless, because of Piaget's importance in the development of thinking in this field, the easiest way to introduce this topic is to begin with Piaget and then to discuss some of the problems with his ideas that subsequent research has identified.

I began this discussion by making a distinction between cognitive development and emotional development. But in reality the two are closely interlinked. If you look back after reading this chapter at the stages of development proposed by Freud or Bowlby, or those of Klein or Erikson, you will see that each stage presupposes a level of cognitive development also. Children cannot reach an understanding about their relationship with others, for example, until they are able to grasp that others do actually have a separate existence.

As discussed in the previous chapter, a secure emotional base allows exploration and learning to take place. The insecure baby monkey puts all its energies into attempting to find comfort, and does not explore as much as does a monkey that is confident that its mother is available when needed – and any teacher will confirm how difficult it is to get troubled children to settle and concentrate in class. So a solid emotional base gives the security that supports learning. But the reverse is also true. Learning about the world helps us to make sense of troubling events. Moves and losses, for example, are particularly difficult for children at an age when they are old enough to know what is happening but not old enough to make sense of it. It is easier for a child to spend a week away from home, when that child is capable of grasping the concept of 'a week'.

For those who work with children, it is important to have some understanding of cognitive development as well as emotional development because the two go hand in hand.

Cognitive Psychology and Cognitive Development

To us as adults, most of the time, it seems as if the outside world – the world of people, objects and events – is just self-evidently *there*. But in fact all that we can ever know about that outside world comes to us in the form of millions of electrical impulses that reach our brains from our various sense organs: light-sensitive cells in our eyes, cells in our ears that are sensitive to vibrations in the air, pressure sensors in our skins. The 'world' that we feel ourselves to inhabit is not 'just there' at all, but is something which we have somehow reconstructed from these countless signals. Once in a while we may get a sense of this. You have probably had the experience of seeing someone out of the corner of your eye and noticing all kinds of details: a beard, glasses, a slight stoop. But then you look round and see it was only a coat hanging on the back of a door. All those details were just intelligent guesses made by your brain on the basis of the limited information available.

Cognitive psychology is the branch of psychology that deals with the interpretation of sensory events. How they *register* (perception), how we store them in memory and retrieve them. How we learn from experience and make use of images, symbols, concepts and rules in thinking, reasoning and problem solving. In short it is about how we process and interpret *information* (in contrast to psychodynamic theory which is more about how we process *feelings*).

And this business of processing and interpreting information is a skill. Some skills are innate and present at birth (horses are born with the ability to walk) but some skills have to be learnt. The study of human development suggests that most of these cognitive skills are not present at birth, not even very basic ones such as the ability to understand that the patterns of colours in front of our eyes represent objects out there in the world. The skills have to be learnt, though the process of learning follows pathways that may in themselves be innate (as with the growth of the body).

The study of this developmental process is developmental cognitive psychology.

Before we move on to discuss the work of Piaget, the following activity may help you to start to think about the different ways in which children function cognitively at different ages.

Activity 4.1

Think of a child of 4 or 5 that you know or have worked with. What is different about the way this child thinks and understands the world, from the way adults think about the world? What kinds of ideas does this child – and others of this child's age – characteristically find difficult to grasp?

Comments on Activity 4.1

Some things you may have thought of:

- Geography. Small children have little grasp of geography, not only in the sense of not knowing so many facts, but in being unable to grasp ideas such as distance (if you go on a journey with a small child, she may repeatedly ask 'Are we nearly there?'), or the idea that, say, a different town may still be in the same country.

- Time. You may have thought of examples where small children have similar difficulties with adult ideas of time as they do with space. 'Next month' does not mean much to a 5-year-old.

- Money. Small children have difficulty with the concept of money. When you go to a shop and receive change, they have difficulty understanding what change is, however carefully it is explained to them. Small children may think that change is simply a gift.

Jean Piaget (1896–1980)

When dealing with children, adults (and that includes adults who work with children) are prone to make one of two incorrect assumptions:

- That children think and understand just like we do. For example, if you are a parent, you might possibly have had an experience like the following. A family is setting off in the car on the annual holiday which has been discussed for months. Twenty miles down the road and the youngest child suddenly asks: 'By the way, where are we going?' It may have been discussed for months, but never in terms which were comprehensible to the child.

- That children don't think at all about the world about them. Some parents discuss all kinds of adult matters in front of their small children, and, if the wisdom of this is queried, simply say: 'Oh don't worry about him, he's not listening to us and anyway he doesn't understand. . . .'

Piaget realised that *both* those assumptions about children are untrue: children do think, as adults do, but they don't think in the same way as adults. This insight came to him early in his career when he was working on intelligence tests and realised that children regularly made the *same kinds of mistakes*. There was a pattern to their mistakes, in other words, which suggested that they were thinking in a consistent way that had a logic of its own, even though this was not consistent with adult logic. This interested him philosophically from the point of view of the nature of human knowledge.

Jean Piaget was born in 1896 in Neuchâtel in Switzerland. Although one of the most famous names in developmental psychology, he in fact did not see himself as primarily a psychologist at all, but as a biologist (when he was still at school, apparently, he was for a time the curator of molluscs at Neuchâtel Natural History Museum) and as a philosopher. He described himself as a 'genetic epistemologist'. Epistemology is the philosophy of knowledge, so what he meant by this was that he studied the origins of knowledge.

Piaget believed that a child is actively involved in the development of her own thinking and he saw the active search for knowledge as being something that children do, and want to do, for its own sake, and not just as a means to other ends. In other words, he disagreed with the Freudian view that we are driven primarily by a desire for sensual gratification: the desire for knowledge was also a basic innate human drive. If you consider how energetically children seem to explore and experiment, you will probably agree that this is almost certainly the case.

In Piaget's view a child finds her way through successive stages of cognitive development rather like a scientist, experimenting and developing ever more sophisticated models to explain the world, until eventually a level is reached where she is able to reason abstractly, think about hypothetical situations and organise rules about the world in her mind.

Piaget saw cognitive development moving – in all children – through several stages, each one of which is characterised by a different way of thinking about and understanding the world. And he identified four factors that might be involved in this developmental process:

- physical maturation (that is: actual physical changes in the brain during childhood, resulting in the emergence of new abilities)
- experience
- social transmission (what we learn from other people)
- equilibration (a concept which I will explain and discuss a little later on)

Given that Piaget saw all children, regardless of culture, as going through the same basic stages, one might think that he would see physical maturation as being a major factor. But Piaget did not think that physical maturation could explain much of the change. His reasoning was that although children in different cultures go through the same stages of cognitive development, they reach different stages at different speeds, whereas if it was purely a matter of brain growth, one would expect the speed to be constant across cultures. (It is a fact, however, that the central nervous system is still growing in early childhood.)

Experience and social transmission are (of course) factors in a child's learning, but Piaget did not take the view that our knowledge and understanding are simply the sum of what we have experienced or been taught. His view was more that children would use the information presented to them by experience as experimental data with which to develop their thinking about the basic rules that operate in the world. So children with very diverse experiences would nevertheless come to the same basic conclusions and develop their thinking along essentially the same paths.

You could learn the concept of number, for example, in almost any environment, though some children may begin by counting marbles, others by counting stones, others again by counting sheep.

As far as social transmission is concerned, teaching could be used to speed up a child's progress, provided that it was pitched at an appropriate level. There are some things that a child simply cannot be taught below a certain age. Certain ideas cannot be grasped until other more basic ideas are in place, just as one cannot place a building block one metre up until there is a pile of building blocks beneath it to hold it in place. Outside factors make a difference, but the essential driving force of cognitive development is something from *within* the child.

Studies carried out by Jerome Kagan and others in the 1970s seem to give some support to this view. These studies compared urban US children aged 7–11 with rural Indian children in Guatemala (see Mussen et al., 1974: 283). The former had, of course, plenty of experience of books, TV and pictures of all kinds. The latter had apparently never even seen photographs or pencils and paper. If learning was simply a matter of accumulating experience, one would expect the US children to perform much better on tests to do with pictures, so, in the experiments, children were shown line drawings containing visual puzzles. In fact the US children only did a little better than the Indians overall, and in some cases – for example when asked to find hidden triangles embedded in pictures – the two groups performed identically.

Accommodation, Assimilation and Equilibration

The basic building block of learning, according to Piaget, is what he called a *scheme*. 'Schemes' are basic patterns of co-ordination between perceptions and actions. Grasping at a colourful object, for instance, could be described as a 'scheme'. When a child encounters a new object or situation, she will try and deal with it in the first place by applying ideas and habits learnt from dealing with other objects and other situations. For example, if she is familiar with eating Smarties she may try and eat a coloured bead. This process Piaget called *assimilation*, taking the word from the work of another psychologist, James Baldwin, who was a major influence on Piaget.

However, a new object often turns out not to fit into an old scheme. Schemes then have to be changed to fit the new object. If given a magnet, for example, the child may treat it initially like any other small hard object – a stone, perhaps – but when she discovers its property of attracting metal, she will change the way she plays with it. This process Piaget called *accommodation*.

Mental growth involves both assimilation and accommodation. The only way we can deal initially with a new situation is to try and apply ideas learnt from other situations (assimilation), but no one would progress with learning about the world if they did not modify their ideas in the light of experience (accommodation). The balancing act between assimilation and accommodation he called *equilibration*.

So, to sum up: according to Piaget, a child gradually arrives at an adult understanding of the world by assembling, to use the analogy again, a series of building blocks. More complex ideas develop from simpler ones through an alternating process of accommodation and assimilation. Moreover, Piaget argued that this process could only take place in a certain sequence. More complex blocks can only be put in place when simpler ones have already been laid. This is why Piaget saw experience and social transmission as being of secondary importance in learning. No amount of information or stimulation could impart a new idea to a child unless she was at a stage where she was able to grasp it.

I have now used the analogy of building blocks twice, because this seems to sum up the assumption behind Piaget's theory. Before going on to look at Piaget's stages of development, the following activity is an opportunity to consider this analogy:

Activity 4.2

Piling up building blocks is one metaphor for human development. Another might, for example, be going on a journey. Think of some other metaphors that could be used for human development.

Do different metaphors make us look at the process in a different way?

Comments on Activity 4.2

The metaphor of building bricks may seem to be a reasonable way of describing human learning – and it may be – but one should always be careful about the power of metaphors. For example, you might have described learning as being like colouring in a picture, or of accumulating useful objects in a sack. If so, you may have noticed that the implications of these analogies are different. With building blocks you have to start at the floor and work upwards. But with colouring books and filling sacks you don't have to start in any particular place, or perform tasks in any particular order.

In thinking critically about Piaget's ideas, one question you could ask is whether building blocks are the best metaphor? Does colouring fit better? Or are some aspects of learning like building and others like colouring?

The same discussion could take place in relation to the theories discussed in the last two chapters, all of which contain the idea of development following a certain necessary sequence.

Stages of Cognitive Development

Piaget identified four basic stages in the development of a child's thinking, illustrated in Table 4.1:

TABLE 4.1   *Piaget's stages of cognitive development*

Stage	Approximate Ages
Sensori-motor	0–18 months
Pre-operational	18 months to 7 years
Concrete operations	7–12
Formal operations	12 +

I'll now look at the stages one by one:

The sensori-motor phase (0–18 months)

Piaget characterised this stage as 'intelligence manifested in action'. His idea was that babies start with basic physical reflexes, learn to modify these and then extend them by a process of assimilation and accommodation until – at the end of this stage – they are able to hold representations of things in their minds and plan out what they do.

He sub-divided the sensori-motor phase into six parts, as shown in Table 4.2. Piaget's idea was that development in different areas – the understanding of space, say, or of number, or of cause and effect – proceeds in parallel. They all require the same basic underlying structures of reasoning. You can see below how in Piaget's thinking the stages of sensori-motor development correspond with the development of the idea of *object permanence*: the idea that objects still exist, even when you can't see them. Piaget would argue that you could add further columns to a chart like this – for example a column showing the parallel development of a child's understanding of cause and effect.

If you look through the table you will see how, under the object permanence column, the child starts out with little or no idea that objects really exist at all. Why, after all, should a baby be able to know that the colours and shapes that she sees are anything more than just colours and shapes? The child then progresses to a point where she doesn't just see objects but actively looks for them. Under the sensori-motor column, you will see the child similarly progressing from movements which exist for their own sake

TABLE 4.2 *Stages within the sensori-motor phase*

Stage		Approx. ages	Sensori-motor development	Object permanence
(i)	Modification of reflexes	0–1 month	Innate reflexes become more efficient (accommodation)	Fleeting images
(ii)	Primary circular reactions	1–4 months	Simple actions are repeated for their own sake	Child follows objects with eyes but objects out of view are not followed
(iii)	Secondary circular reactions	4–6 months	Actions are repeated when they produce interesting results	Child will grab for objects she can see, but still acts as if objects she can't see don't exist
(iv)	Co-ordination of secondary reactions	7–10 months	Child begins to solve problems	Child will reach for an object hidden from view (and is surprised by disappearances) – believes in permanence of objects.
(v)	Tertiary circular reactions	11–18 months	Child varies responses and tries out new ones (experimenting – exploring potential of objects)	From 12 months: if object is hidden under one pillow but child then sees it hidden under another pillow, she will look there
(vi)	Interioration of schemes	From 18 months	'Invention of new means by internal mental combinations.' Child thinks through in advance what she is going to do	Child will search for objects which she didn't see being hidden

and have no other purpose, to movements which are not only purposeful but planned in advance.

Pre-operational stage (18 months to 7 years)

At the conclusion of the previous stage, the child was beginning to hold representations of things in her mind. This ability develops in the pre-operational stage when representations of many kinds are used with increasing sophistication. The child acquires language, learns to make and interpret pictures and uses one object to represent another in imaginative play (a box is a car, a doll is a baby). So the *meanings* of objects and events are now being manipulated as well as the actual objects which the child learnt to manipulate in the previous stage. This is a major advance in the ability to think. But, as you probably concluded in Activity 4.1, a child during this stage still thinks in a very different way from an adult.

The following are some of the ways in which, Piaget suggested, the thinking of a child is different during this stage:

- The child tends to be *egocentric*. This is not to say that the child is *selfish* (I am not sure that children of this age are any more or less selfish than anyone else), but that the child finds it difficult to see things from a point of view other than her own. For example, a child talking on the telephone may point to something in the room and refer to 'that thing over there', seemingly unaware that the person on the other end of the phone cannot possibly know what she means. Or a child playing hide-and-seek may hide her face, without thinking that the rest of her body is quite visible to others, though invisible to her.

- The child is prone to *centration*. She tends to fix her attention on one aspect of a situation and ignore other aspects. She has difficulty in recognising that a situation may have a number of dimensions. To give an instance: a child of 4 is talking with his mother about how all his friends go to the same school. This is an interesting idea which hasn't struck him before. 'But how come I know granny then?' he asks. 'She doesn't even *go* to my school!' Struck with the idea of school as the place where you get to know people, he has failed to hang on to the idea that there are other contexts in which you can meet people.

- There is a *lack of reversibility* in the child's thinking. This means that the child is unable to mentally reverse a series of events or steps of reasoning. To us as adults it follows that if we take three Smarties away from a pile of twenty, there will be twenty Smarties there again if we add another three. Or, if some water half fills a glass and we pour it into a mug, it will still half fill the glass when we pour it back again. There is a whole range of operations which we understand to be reversible. But these things are not self-evident to a pre-operational child. Piaget, in fact, used the word *operation* in a specialised sense to *mean* these reversible logical processes. The term *pre-operational* thus refers to the stage when the child has not learnt to use 'operations'. I mentioned earlier the inability of small children to grasp the concept of giving change in shops. Buying something, paying for it and receiving change is a good example of an operation in Piaget's sense. The price of the item bought and the change, we as adults understand, add up to the amount handed over to the shopkeeper. If we change our minds about the purchase and return the item, we will get back the price of the item which, with the change, adds up to precisely the same as the money we first handed over. But this is very difficult to explain to a 5-year-old.

So a child at this stage has a 'pre-logical' understanding of the world, based on subjective impressions and hunches, rather than on logical thinking, and based on a view of the world that has themselves at its centre. That is, after all, how it subjectively *appears* to all of us, but as we grow older we learn that this is not really the case. One aspect of this is that children at this age in particular are prone to 'magical thinking'. The following conversation is reported by Piaget with an 8-year-old child (child's words in italics).

> You have already seen the clouds moving along? What makes them move? – *When we move along, they move along too.* – Can *you* make them move? – *Everybody can, when they walk.* – When I walk and you are still, do they move? – *Yes.* – And at night, when everyone is asleep do they move? – *Yes.* – But you tell me that they only move when somebody walks. – *They always move. The cats, when they walk, and then the dogs, they make the clouds move.* (Piaget, 1930: 62)

Those who work with children have to watch out for the combination of magical thinking and egocentrism which can make pre-operational children in particular feel that they are responsible for events which in reality have nothing to do with them: a traffic accident in which a relative was injured, perhaps, or their parents' divorce.

The following activity is a further look at the practical implication of pre-operational thinking.

✖ Activity 4.3 ✖

Suppose you are a doctor, explaining to a child of 6 why he needs to have an operation – and what will be entailed.

Bearing in mind that a child of 6 thinks in a different way from adults, how should you go about this?

Comments on Activity 4.3

- Many people, when talking to children, are careful to adopt a kind and reassuring tone of voice, to talk about things familiar to the child and to use words which the child is likely to know – and all these things are of course important. But it is also important to ensure that the ideas presented to the child are comprehensible at his age.
- Because children at this age tend to centration, a complex discussion of the kind 'on the one hand, on the other hand' is likely to mean nothing to the child.

- The child's concerns may be focused on particular aspects of the situation which can be quite different from an adult's. To give an example: it may be that the thing that most worries the child is not the operation at all but having the bandages removed later, because he is terrified of pulling off sticky plasters.
- The child may come with powerful preconceptions which are quite irrational ('People who have surgery always have their legs removed', 'My illness is a punishment because I hit my little brother'). It might be a good idea to ask the child to describe his understanding of the situation – though of course the child may not want or feel able to tell you all his thoughts.

Being aware of children's very different ways of thinking is of course only part of successful communication with children. There are a lot of other issues too: awareness of a child's emotional needs and of his relationships, for example. And any adult trying to communicate with a child, such as a doctor in the above example, needs to be aware of the huge power difference between an adult and a child. But these are questions outside the scope of this book.

Concrete operations stage
(7–12)

In this stage the child is now able to grasp what Piaget called 'operations'. A child at this stage will have no difficulty grasping that when water is poured from a tall container to a broad one, it is the same amount of water and will come back to the original level when poured back into the first container. But, although the child becomes at home with external, *concrete* operations of this kind, she is still less at home with more abstract kinds of operations.

During the concrete operations stage, Piaget thought, there is a gradual waning of egocentric thinking (again, I must emphasise, this word is meant here in a cognitive sense and not a moral one). There is an increasing ability to *decentre*: to recognise and take into account the fact that many phenomena have several dimensions to them.

The child now grasps the idea of *reversibility* and growing logical insights lead to development of concrete operational structures such as *classification* (sorting things out into categories), *seriation* (placing things in a logical order: of size for example) and *conservation* of size and number (for example: water poured into a different shaped container is still the same amount of water; plasticine squeezed into a different shape has not increased or decreased in quantity; when a bag of marbles is strewn across the floor there is still the same number of marbles . . .).

The reason that a pre-operational child has difficulty with conservation of size and number is that she understands the concept 'more' in a *perceptual* way, as a description of the way things look, whereas the concrete operations child has got hold of the more abstract concept of *number*. Likewise, a child at the pre-operational stage can find the way from A to B if it is a familiar route but she does so on the basis of remembering things on the way, and could not make a map of the route, which a child at the concrete operations stage could do.

Another example of this shift is in the understanding of what are called *relational* terms (for example: 'This colour is *darker* than that one'). It can be shown that a concrete operations child understands that such terms describe a *relationship* between two things (between two colours in my example). But a pre-operational child sees words such as darker, bigger and so on, more as synonyms for 'very dark' or 'very big'. Once again, the concrete operations child is using logical concepts to organise experience, while the pre-operational child is relying on perception.

The contrast is apparent again in *classification*. Small children have difficulty with the idea of categories within other categories. I mentioned, for example, when discussing Activity 4.1 that small children have difficulty with the idea that a different town may still be in the same country. A statement such as 'We're driving from London to Bristol, but we'll still be in England', may be baffling to a pre-operational child. The concrete operations child is at home with such concepts.

But while able to use these sorts of rules and structures, a child at the concrete operations stage still finds it difficult to think in a self-conscious way about the rules she is using.

📖 Comparisons with Psychodynamic Stages 📖

If you compare Piaget's concrete operations stage with Freud's psycho-sexual stages, or Erikson's psychosocial ones, you'll find that it corresponds roughly to what Freud called the latency period (a period when the turmoils of the Oedipus complex were set aside while the child pursued more outward and practical concerns). Erikson saw this as a stage whose successful outcome was a sense of competence and achievement, and confidence in one's own ability to make and do things. These seem broadly consistent with Piaget's view of this stage as one in which concrete operations are mastered. While Piaget's model is not a psychodynamic theory, and does not even purport to address the same kinds of questions, Piaget *did* have a psychoanalytic training.

Stage of formal operations (12+)

According to Piaget the stage of formal operations is normally reached at the beginning of adolescence and it is the final stage. This does not mean, of course, that Piaget was suggesting that a 12- or 13-year-old functions in exactly the same way as an adult in every respect (the ways in which this stage is different will be the subject of Chapter 6). But he thought that, when it comes to using rules and solving problems, a young person at this stage does indeed operate in much the same way as an adult. Piaget's theory would suggest that 11-year-olds, though very proficient in all kinds of ways, are less flexible in the way they think about problems and new situations than 14-year-olds – who, on the other hand, operate with much the same degree of flexibility as adults.

At the formal operations stage we are able not only to master basic, concrete operations, but also to perform operations *with* operations. Faced with a problem, we are able:

- to be self-consciously deductive (consciously going into problem-solving mode, so to speak) and to consider all the possible ways a problem might be solved;
- to use abstract rules to solve a class of problems;
- to reflect on the rules we are using and to be aware of our thought process;
- to use 'higher order' or analogical reasoning, for example making connections between problems that at a surface level seem quite different, but which have some likeness in terms of their logical structure.

The following experiment (Piaget et al., 1977, described in Goswami, 1998: 275) may make this slightly clearer. Piaget and his colleagues gave children a set of jumbled pictures and asked them to sort them into pairs. So, for example, given pictures including: *dog, feather, vacuum cleaner, car, dog hair, ship, bird . . . etc.*, they might pair *bird and feather*, and *dog and dog hair*. Children at the concrete operations and formal operations stage do not find this difficult. Children at the pre-operational stage will tend to pair pictures in idiosyncratic ways of their own.

Children were then asked to *pair up the pairs*. Thus, for example the pairs *dog and dog hair*, and *bird and feather* might go together as they both describe a similar relationship (as might the pairs *pilot and aeroplane*, and *driver and car*, for instance). This is an example of 'higher order' analogical thinking, because the participants were being asked to make connections not on the basis of anything visible on the cards, but on the basis of types of relationships. They were being asked to consider the rules that they used to form the pairs in the first part of the experiment, and then to find a second level of rules which could be used to pair up the rules themselves. In other words, they were being asked to make rules about rules, or to categorise categories. This was possible for young people in the formal operations stage, but it was too abstract for concrete operations stage children.

Summary of stages

Before going on to look at challenges and criticisms of Piaget's ideas, here is a brief summary of the stages:

- **Sensori-motor (0–18 mths)** – The child's learning is based around movement and the senses.
- **Pre-operational (18 mths to 7 years)** – The child is able to use language and symbols as well as actual objects, but not able to grasp ideas like reversible operations, relational terms and so on. The child has an 'egocentric', non-logical worldview. Magical thinking is particularly prevalent at this stage.
- **Concrete operations (7–12)** – The child is able to understand and use operations, along with basic logical concepts such as classification, seriation and conservation of size and volume, but does not solve problems in a self-conscious way. The child does not think about thinking.
- **Formal operations (12 +)** – We are able to solve abstract problems in a consciously deductive way. We are able to think about how to think.

Challenges to Piaget's Model

Criticisms of Piaget's theory come from many different quarters. I will discuss here criticisms of his assumptions, criticisms of his methodology and experimental challenges to his findings.

Piaget's assumptions

Erica Burman (1994) points out that Piaget depicts the developing child as 'a budding scientist systematically encountering problems in the material world, developing hypotheses and learning by discovery and activity'. She continues: 'Logic . . . is cast as the pinnacle of human development. This produces a model of thinking which treats the individual as prior and separate, and celebrates activity and discovery', things which, in most cultures, are seen as stereotypically masculine. In Piaget's model, Burman argues, the 'quintessential developing child is a boy' (Burman, 1994: 157).

It could be argued that, if our culture sees 'activity and discovery' as essentially masculine, then that is a problem with our culture, rather than with Piaget. (Activity and discovery do in fact seem to be very characteristic of all small children, both boys and girls. But there are gender differences. Whether these are the result of 'nature' or 'nurture' is discussed in the next chapter.) Nevertheless, Burman is surely right in saying that Piaget focuses very much on one particular aspect of the development of thinking, the development of deductive reasoning. What about creativity? What about intuition? What about aesthetic judgement?

By the same token, Piaget's priorities could be described as stereo-typically Western, since by giving pride of place to deductive reasoning he is making a value judgement which is characteristic of modern, Western, scientific society – and with which other cultures would not necessarily agree.

The role of language

One aspect of Piaget's thinking is the surprisingly secondary importance he assigns to language. The Russian psychologist Lev Vygotsy (1896–1934), for example, put much more emphasis on language and saw the capacity to learn through instruction as a basic feature of human intelligence.

The fact that small children chatter to themselves was seen by Piaget as an example of egocentrism, because the child chatters away and it doesn't occur to her that what she is saying means nothing to anyone else, and because private speech disappears as the child grows older. But Vygotksy saw language as basic to thought and suggested that a child using private speech was giving instructions to herself as a strategy to keep her focused on a task. He suggested that the role of language and instruction is so crucial in guiding action that, when it is not provided externally, we learn to provide it for ourselves. Private speech, in Vygotsky's view, did not disappear as a child grew older, but simply became internalised as the interior monologue which goes on in our heads even as adults (Vygotsky, 1962).

Piaget's whole approach was to look at the kinds of underlying conceptual structures which children use when solving problems. And his exploration of those underlying structures may have been flawed by the fact that he did not address issues to do with language. Thus it is possible that children may actually *possess* concepts such as object permanence but may not demonstrate this if questions are put to them in an inappropriate way. To complicate this, the opposite can also be true. Children may be taught to repeat a rule, but without understanding the underlying concept. In a small experiment of my own, I poured water from a tall glass into a wide one and asked a 7-year-old whether the amount was the same or not. 'The same', she said, but then added: 'I know because my teacher told me.'

Experimental challenges to Piaget

One of the advantages to any field in having a 'grand theory' like Piaget's is that this provides a framework for research. An enormous amount of experimental work – and many highly ingenious experiments – have taken place to test aspects of his theories.

Some research seems to confirm Piaget's ideas about different kinds of thinking at different stages. But a lot of experimental evidence now suggests that development of cognition occurs much earlier than Piaget envisaged. There is experimental evidence, for example, that the concept of object permanence is present at least as early as 3 months. Renée Baillargeon (1987) devised an elaborate apparatus whereby a toy car rolled down a track. A screen could be placed in front of part of the track and a box could be placed behind that screen either *next* to the track or *on* it, so that it looked as if the car could not get past it. In both cases the car could in fact pass the box. She compared babies responses to the apparently 'possible' event of the car reappearing from behind the screen when the box had been seen to not be in its way and the apparently 'impossible' event of the car seeming to have passed through the box. She found that babies stared for much longer at the apparatus in the 'impossible' case. If they had no concept of object permanence, Baillargeon argued, why would the 'impossible case' be any more interesting than the other case?

Other researchers have challenged what Piaget said about 'egocentricity' and demonstrated that small children *are* able to view many types of problem from points of view other than their own (see Cox, 1991; Donaldson, 1978). It can also be demonstrated that children as young as 2 can make deductions by analogy. This is done by showing children how to do one task with one set of materials, and then giving them another analogous but different task with a different set of materials. They do better at the new task than children not previously shown the analogy. Chen et al. (1997) even claim to have demonstrated analogical reasoning in children less than a year old.

One challenge to Piaget's theory comes from the simple observation that babies at only three days old will imitate an adult sticking out her tongue. How can a baby know that the tongue of another person is in some way equivalent to her own, if she has not yet learnt to interpret the signals in her optic nerves as objects at all?

Conversely, forms of thinking characteristic of children do not simply disappear in adulthood. Adults can be prone to magical thinking of various kinds. So what seems to be emerging is that Piaget's 'building block' model, in which each block can only be put in place when the previous block is already there, is too rigid. Or, at least, it does not apply to every aspect of cognitive development. Perhaps a more complicated analogy needs to be found which allows for the fact that some aspects of the structure are already in place at the outset, and that others can emerge at different speeds?

Nevertheless, Piaget's insight that children do think in *systematically* different ways from adults does, I think, remain interesting and useful, even if the details are still being worked out. As I said earlier on, many people make the mistake of assuming, on the one hand, that children don't think at all or, on the other, that they think in exactly the same way as adults. Even though many aspects of Piaget's model may in the long run be superseded, its existence helps us to recognise that children's minds are just as full of thoughts as the minds of adults, but those thoughts may work in very different ways at different ages.

Chapter Summary

The Emergence of Reason

- In this chapter I have looked at the concept of cognitive psychology and at cognitive development, including its relationship to emotional development as discussed in the previous chapters.

- I then looked at the work of Jean Piaget and his ideas about the nature of human cognitive development. His key insight was that children's thinking differs from adult thinking in consistent, systematic ways.

- I introduced some of Piaget's basic concepts including *accommodation*, *assimilation* and *equilibration*, as well as specific uses of the terms *scheme* and *operation*.

- I then described Piaget's stages of cognitive development: the *sensori-motor* stage, the *pre-operational* stage, the *concrete operations* stage and the *formal operations* stage, looking at the characteristic thinking that Piaget suggested occurred at each stage.

- Finally I looked at challenges to Piaget's assumptions, his methodology and his findings and I concluded that while Piaget's original insights remained useful, experimental evidence shows the picture to be much more complex than he believed.

We have now looked at Piaget's theory of cognitive development and at psychodynamic theories. Though they may seem worlds apart, they do have in common (a) that they are 'stage' theories, and (b) that they are attempts to map out what goes on in people's heads. This is in stark contrast to the behaviourists, whom we will consider in the next chapter.

Suggested reading

- Boden, M. (1994) *Piaget* (London: Fontana)
- Goswami, U. (1998) *Cognition in Children* (Hove: Psychology Press)
- Wood, D. (1998) *How Children Think and Learn* (Oxford: Blackwell)

5 Making Connections

Ideas from learning theory

Piaget was interested in the logical structures within the mind that underlie thinking and understanding – and he gave a secondary importance to the influence of the outside world on learning. But there is a completely different way of looking at learning, which says that what is really important about learning is not what goes on in our heads, but the making of *connections* between external events: connections between a word and an object, or between one event and another, or between an action and its consequences.

This was the view taken by the seventeenth-century English philosopher, John Locke (1632–1704), whom I mentioned in Chapter 1. Locke believed that learning was essentially a matter of forming connections or associations between things that came together in time. If you have a cat you will know how it learns to recognise the sound of a tin of cat food being opened, or perhaps the engine sound of your car.

A whole branch of experimental psychology is based on this idea of learning by association. Once called *connectionism*, then *behaviourism*, this body of ideas is also often referred to as *'learning theory'*. I will refer to it in this chapter either as behaviourism or learning theory. The characteristic style of this school of psychology is an experimental method, based on the physical sciences, in which guesswork and intuitive hunches are avoided, and connections are only asserted to exist when this can be proved statistically in a controlled experiment. So learning theorists typically try and avoid speculating about what is going on inside the heads of their subjects, and even try to avoid using words like 'feelings' and 'thought'. Many of them assert that such things are not proper subjects for scientific study, because science should concern itself only with things that can be objectively observed.

This experimental, objective approach – excluding talk of internal states and excluding any assertion that can't be demonstrated experimentally – is in very stark contrast to the approach of Freud and his successors. One may well feel that psychodynamic theory is sometimes very over-elaborate and not sufficiently solidly grounded on the evidence available. Behaviourism is very much at the opposite extreme: its preoccupation with precision and with experiments as rigorous as those in the physical sciences can make some of its findings seem simplistic.

Unlike all the other theories we have discussed in the last three chapters, learning theory does not offer a model of development. It is not a stage theory. It is simply a series of generalisations about how new behaviour is learnt. Learning theory could be described as a 'nurture' theory (see Chapter 1) of the most extreme form, because it sees learning as originating in the external environment. On the other hand, most of its data comes from animal experiments (some of them cruel, I am afraid). And, as learning theory contains an assumption that certain basic patterns of learning are common to humans and animals alike, it does in fact assume that there is some underlying 'nature' on which nurture can act.

You may ask why, if it is not a developmental theory and if its findings are largely derived from animal experiments (rats and pigeons in the main), I have included learning theory in this book at all, given that the subject of the book is human development. My reasons for including it, however, are:

- It provides an important contrast to the stage theories discussed so far, a reminder that development doesn't have to be looked at as a stage process.
- It describes a mechanism for learning which can be used to consider many aspects of social development – for example the learning of gender roles, which I'll discuss at the end of this chapter.
- Learning theory looks at patterns of behaviour and asks a very simple question 'What is it that keeps that behaviour going?' This has been a fruitful source of ideas for schools of therapy that avoid the

psychoanalytic emphasis on delving into the past, and look instead at the here and now. So learning theory has had important practical applications – and been an important influence – in the caring professions. And, although some learning theorists have made some rather sinister proposals for the use of conditioning for social engineering, some of these other applications seem to me to be humane and useful.

Before going any further, though, you might like to use the following activity to review your own experiences of learning by association:

⚒ Activity 5.1 ⚒

Can you think of examples in your own experience where a particular sensation (sight, sound, taste, smell) regularly evokes a particular response? Can you think of an instance where a particular set of circumstances seems to bring about an automatic response in you?

Comments on Activity 5.1

Probably most people can think of particular smells, or pieces of music that set off associations. Certain pop songs, for example, immediately call to mind for me a whole string of memories of the time when that particular song was commonly being played, and of my feelings associated with that time. The smells of certain kinds of disinfectant immediately call to mind for me childhood fears about hospitals and operations. These are instances of connections which are learnt when things come together at the same time.

An example of a certain situation seeming to bring about an automatic response is this: if you are a driver, you will probably have had the experience of getting in your car and being on the way to work before you realise that in fact it is the weekend, and you were not intending to go to work but to drive in the opposite direction. Being in the car set you off on a chain of actions so familiar that you didn't even think about it. Smokers trying to give up, often report that certain situations – the end of a meal, for example – trigger an intensely strong desire to light a cigarette.

Ivan Pavlov (1849–1936) and Classical Conditioning

Pavlov was a physiologist, not a psychologist, and his primary interest was in the digestive system: he received a Nobel Prize for his work in this area.

As part of this work, however, he became interested in finding out what psychological stimuli set the digestive juices flowing. He demonstrated that dogs start to salivate at the sight or smell of food. And this appeared to be an innate, involuntary *reflex*, like the automatic knee-jerk reaction when one is struck above the knee. Pavlov then tried sounding a buzzer every time food was given to the dogs. He found that after a while the dogs started to salivate as soon as they heard the buzzer. Now, dogs would not normally salivate on hearing a buzzer, so this response is not innate. It is what Pavlov termed a 'conditioned reflex'. An innate reflex had been 'conditioned' so that it occurred in response to a new stimulus.

Pavlov then went on to explore exactly how this kind of connection worked, by experimenting with different possibilities. Some of his key concepts can be summarised as follows:

- **Extinction** – Pavlov found that if a dog had been conditioned to salivate in response to a buzzer that preceded food, it would then continue to salivate in response to the buzzer alone. However, this effect did not last forever. If the buzzer ceased to be followed by food, then after a while the conditioned reflex would wear off and the sound of the buzzer would no longer result in salivation. In Pavlovian terms the conditioned reflex had become 'extinct'. To give a human example: a quitting smoker may for a long time feel a strong craving for a cigarette after a meal. But after some time that craving fades, until a point is reached where the end of a meal does not trigger a desire to smoke. The connection between 'end of meal' and 'smoking' has become extinct.

- **Spontaneous recovery** – But Pavlov also found that, if a conditioned reflex has been allowed to become extinct, it can very quickly be re-established. So a dog may have been conditioned to salivate at the sound of a buzzer, and this conditioned reflex may then have been allowed to become completely extinct, so that the dog does not salivate at all in response to food. But if the buzzer now starts to be sounded at feeding time again, the original conditioned link will reappear rapidly at full strength, much more quickly than it would appear in a dog which had never previously been conditioned. In other words, even though the link has been extinguished in terms of behaviour, some record of it clearly remains in the dog's brain. Again, we can use the comparison of a quitting smoker. After a sufficient time has elapsed this person may no longer feel a craving for a cigarette at the end of a meal. But if that person takes up smoking again, all those links seem to reappear very rapidly at full strength.

- **Generalisation** – If a dog has learnt to salivate to a buzzer, this response will tend to generalise to other sounds also. For example the dog will salivate not only if it hears a buzzer but also if it hears an electric bell. (This concept has some similarities, I think, with Piaget's assimilation, discussed in the previous chapter.)

- **Discrimination** – However, while generalisation occurs by default, dogs can be trained to finely discriminate between different stimuli. Amazingly Pavlov found that a dog can apparently be trained to salivate on hearing a pure tone of middle C, but not to salivate to a pure tone that is one-eighth of a tone below middle C, if one is consistently followed by food and one consistently isn't. (The interval between a white note on a piano and the adjacent black note is half a tone.) Owners of cats or dogs will know how animals can learn to distinguish the particular engine sound of the family car, and respond to this one sound, while ignoring all others.

These basic concepts are central to learning theory. What you may notice about them is that, unlike either psychodynamic theories or Piaget's theory of cognitive development, these concepts of conditioning, extinction, spontaneous recovery, generalisation and discrimination are not descriptions of anything that might go on in the dogs' minds. They are purely and simply descriptions of relationships between different types of stimulus and observed and measurable responses.

The insistence of behaviourists that only observable behaviour – and not thoughts or feelings – should be studied, can seem perverse. But of course we cannot know directly what goes on in the mind of another person, let alone an animal. It is possible to train a pigeon to discriminate, say, between red and other colours, just as a dog can be trained to discriminate between middle C and other notes, but it is impossible to know what red looks like to a pigeon. Indeed we cannot know whether the colour red looks the same to me as it does to you, even though we could both agree that tomatoes and fire engines are red.

Therapeutic approaches derived from behaviourism do not try and get inside the patient's mind in the way that psychoanalysis does. Instead they are aimed at finding practical ways of unlearning behaviour that is causing problems, or learning new behaviour.

J.B. Watson (1878–1958) and Behaviourism

A very influential figure in psychology in the middle of the twentieth century, Watson coined the term 'behaviourism' because he wanted to throw out entirely all psychology based on introspection, or anything other than observable behaviour. He was an enthusiastic advocate of the use of conditioning techniques to make people conform to the needs of society, and was extremely confident in their ability to actually do so, as the following quote illustrates:

> Give me a dozen healthy infants . . . and my own specified world to bring them up in and I'll guarantee to take any one at random and train him to become any kind of specialist I might select . . . regardless of his talents, penchants, tendencies, abilities, vocations, and race of his ancestors. . . . (Watson, 1931: 104)

He was also a pioneer of the use of sexual imagery as an advertising tool, believing that if people could be taught to make a connection (even if an unconscious one) between a brand of cigarettes, for example, and sex, it would make them buy more. His views were parodied in Aldous Huxley's famous futuristic novel *Brave New World*:

> Patiently the D.H.C. [Director of Hatcheries and Conditioning] explained. If the children were made to scream at the sight of a rose, that was on grounds of high economic policy. . . .
> 'A love of nature keeps no factories busy. It was decided to abolish the love of nature, at any rate among the lower classes. . . . Hence those electric shocks.' (1955: 29)

In Huxley's novel children were shown flowers and given an electric shock. An electric shock causes an involuntary response of pulling back. A flower does not normally provoke this response, but could be made to do so by associating flowers with shocks. This is an example of classical conditioning, which is about connecting a new stimulus to an existing basic reflex. In Pavlov's experiments a new stimulus is connected to something that provokes an automatic response – and, incidentally, also gives pleasure or pain, though Pavlov did not concern himself with these subjective experiences.

But Watson argued that rewards or punishments were not necessary to make a connection between two things. Simply the fact that two things occurred together was enough. The connection would be stronger if the two things occurred together *frequently* or if they had occurred together *recently*. Thus an animal placed in a maze might wander around until it found its way out. If placed back into the maze it would find its way out more quickly, not necessarily because it had been rewarded for finding its way out, but simply because finding its way out was the last thing it did in the maze. A human parallel here might be my example of getting in a car and driving without thinking along a familiar route. It is not as if this is particularly rewarding: it is just that this is what I did last time I got into the car.

B.F. Skinner (1903–1990) and Operant Conditioning

Animal trainers have known for centuries that animals can be taught to behave in certain ways when this behaviour is followed by a reward – and discouraged from behaving in other ways with punishments. Parents, of course, have also applied this principle to children. This kind of learning is slightly different from that studied by Pavlov because it is not just about conditioning innate reflexes to new stimuli. It has become known as *operant* conditioning, for reasons which I will explain, as opposed to Pavlov's *classical conditioning* which is also known as *respondent conditioning*.

Concepts such as extinction, generalisation, and spontaneous recovery apply to operant conditioning also. And researchers into operant learning, no less than Pavlov, avoided speculating about insight or thought on the part of animals. Animals are simply seen as trying various behaviours more or less randomly at first. Those that are rewarded become part of the animal's repertoire, while those that are not rewarded do not. It is a process analogous to Darwin's theory of natural selection, but applied to behaviours rather than to genetic variations: those that prove successful survive, those that don't, die out.

> In both operant conditioning and the evolutionary selection of behavioural characteristics, consequences alter future probability. Reflexes and other innate patterns of behaviour evolve because they increase the chances of survival of the species. Operants grow strong because they are followed by important consequences in the life of the individual. (Skinner, 1953: 90)

B.F. Skinner was the actual inventor of the term 'operant conditioning' (although he was not the first to explore this kind of learning) and he was a dominant figure in post-war behaviourist research. His classic experimental tool was the so-called Skinner Box, consisting of a cage in which there was a food dispenser with a lever above it. In the most basic version of this experiment, a rat presses the lever and the food dispenser drops a pellet of food into the tray beneath it. Not surprisingly, when this happens on a regular basis, the rat goes on pressing the lever in order to get the food.

In Skinner's terminology, the rat's original pressing of the lever is termed *operant behaviour*, meaning a behaviour that occurs with no obvious stimulus, as opposed to *respondent behaviour*, an example of which would be pulling your hand away from a hot stove, or Pavlov's dogs involuntarily salivating at the smell of food. (Hence 'operant conditioning', as opposed to 'respondent conditioning'.) The reward of a pellet of food has the effect of increasing the frequency of the particular operant behaviour of pressing the lever, so in Skinner's terminology it is called *positive reinforcement*.

Negative reinforcement could also be used, such as an electric shock which the rat can only stop by pushing a lever.

If a particular stimulus occurs regularly with a reinforcer, that stimulus itself can act as a positive reinforcer. This is the principle behind 'click-training' of dogs. The dog is taught to make an association between the clicking sound and the reward of food. The click can then be used on its own as a reinforcer, with the advantage that it can be given *at the same moment* that the behaviour you want to reinforce is happening. Of course, if you don't ever follow a click with food, though, the connection between click and food will in due course become extinct, and the click will no longer be effective as a reinforcer.

📖 Skinner and the Mind 📖

As we've noted, behaviourists study observable behaviour rather than processes within the mind. But Skinner was at pains to say that he was not denying that there were such things as thoughts and feelings, or that these were important. What he did argue was that we are accustomed to think of such things in the wrong way.

He wrote, for example, that 'what is felt or introspectively observed is not some nonphysical world of consciousness, mind or mental life, but the oberserver's own body'. What went on in that 'world within the skin' was, he argued, the product of the external environment which 'made its first great contribution during the evolution of the species, but [which] exerts a different kind of effect during the lifetime of the individual, and the combination of the two effects is the behaviour we observe at any given time'.

His point is that, when we explain things in terms of what is going on inside our minds, we are not really explaining anything. For example: if I say 'I did X because I was angry', this begs the question as to what it was, in the present or in my past, that made me angry at that particular time.

'When what a person does is attributed to what is going on inside him, investigation is at an end', wrote Skinner (1974: 17, 18).

Schedules of reinforcement

Skinner's experimental work consisted essentially of altering the patterns of reinforcement and seeing the effect this had on behaviour. A certain behaviour can be rewarded *every* time it happens, or it can be rewarded only intermittently. To give an example: rat 'A' is rewarded with a pellet every time it pushes the lever. Rat 'B' only gets a pellet every twenty times it pushes the lever. Not surprisingly, rat 'A' learns lever-pushing behaviour more quickly than rat 'B'. But now suppose that both rats stop being given food pellets at all for lever-pushing. For which rat would lever-pressing behaviour become extinct more quickly? People tend to guess that rat 'A', which had always been rewarded for lever-pushing, would be slower to give up pushing the lever. In fact, though, experimental evidence shows that it is the opposite that is the case. The rats that are only rewarded occasionally for lever pushing go on trying to push the lever for longer. They learn the behaviour more slowly – and they also unlearn it more slowly.

Shaping

As I've said, Skinner's techniques resemble those of circus animal trainers – and some of his students did in fact go on to become animal trainers. He and his co-workers set themselves such tasks, for example, as to train pigeons to play skittles in a miniature bowling alley or to knock a ping-pong ball to and fro (Skinner, 1960). You clearly can't get an animal to learn a behaviour as complex as this in the same way as you get it to learn something simple like lever-pushing. If you adopted the method of just waiting for the bird to start playing skittles by chance, and then reinforcing this behaviour, you would wait forever. What Skinner did was this:

- Ensured the pigeon was hungry.
- Established a strong conditioned connection between food and a certain sound (a clicking sound, say).
- Every time the pigeon did anything even vaguely approximating to the required task, he made the clicking sound and then gave it the food. (This was important because a click can be done at precisely the moment that the behaviour he wanted to reinforce occurred.) For example, he might start by making the clicking sound every time the pigeon pecked at the ball.
- Once ball-pecking had become established, he would then move on to another stage and, let's say, only click when the ball was pushed in the general direction of the skittles.
- Once *that* was established, he would then take it a stage further and, say, only click when the ball was knocked more than a certain distance in that direction.
- And so on . . .

This process is called *shaping* and is a powerful training technique with many applications. Its particular strength is that it avoids 'setting the trainee up to fail'. At every stage, the trainee is encouraged to continue to produce operant behaviour: in other words, to keep trying. By contrast, if the pigeon was only to be rewarded for completing the full task, none of its intermediate behaviour would be reinforced, and so it would have no reason to even change its behaviour in the right direction. Or if the pigeon were trained by punishing it for doing the wrong thing, then this would have the effect – as a result of generalisation – of reducing active behaviour of any kind.

Discrimination

Using techniques like this, it has been possible not only to teach animals to do complicated tricks, but also to teach them extraordinary feats of discrimination. For example, pigeons (not known for their large brains) can be taught to distinguish a photograph of one person from 100 other people, even if they were all taken against the same range of backgrounds and even if that one person was shown in 100 different poses (Herrnstein et al., 1976).

Strength of different reinforcers

Learned behaviours normally extinguish over time, if they are not reinforced – positively or negatively – any longer. As we've seen, the rates of learning and 'unlearning' a given behaviour depend in part on the schedules of reinforcement used. But the kind of reinforcer used also makes a difference. Interestingly, an exceptionally powerful *positive* reinforcer has been found to be the drug morphine. When rats received an injection of morphine for pushing a lever, lever-pushing never completely became extinguished, even if morphine stopped being given and even if the experiment was carried on past the time when there could possibly still be an actual physical dependency on morphine.

The only other kinds of reinforcer comparable in power to this were strong negative reinforcers such as a powerful electric shock. (I believe that there are strong ethical arguments against giving animals powerful electric shocks, but I am reporting the findings of experiments where such things have been used.) Given such a shock for pushing a lever, an animal might never push that lever again, regardless of the length of time that had passed. Given the tendency of responses to generalise, this means that negative reinforcement can have a general disinhibiting effect on learning.

Stress and Learnt Helplessness

While we are on the subject of cruel experiments on animals, I want briefly to describe the experiments carried out by Martin Seligman (1975) and various others on 'learnt helplessness'. In these experiments, one group of animals (call them group X) is subjected to electric shocks in an environment where they are strapped in and cannot do anything to get away. A second group, Y, is not subjected to this experience. Both group X and group Y are then given a shock-avoidance task (that is, a task where they are given shocks which can be stopped by, for example, pressing a lever). What was found was that the group X animals performed less well on the shock-avoidance task than the group Y animals. There are different ways of interpreting this, but a simple behaviourist explanation would be that the group X animals had (of necessity) been doing nothing when the shocks stopped in the first part of the experiment. The behaviour of 'doing nothing' had therefore been negatively reinforced, so that this was the behaviour that they adopted when placed in the second situation. This phenomenon was called 'learnt helplessness'. It has been applied in various ways to thinking about human development. For example, it has been suggested that depression could be a form of 'learnt helplessness'.

Pavlov also did some experiments on stress. As noted, he trained his dogs to carry out quite extraordinary feats of discrimination, and one of the things he trained them to do was to distinguish a circle from an ellipse (oval). However, when he carried this task to the point when the distinction between the oval and the circle was extremely small, the dogs barked and struggled. In one particularly cruel experiment he tried using an electric shock instead of a buzzer as the signal for food. The dogs involved in this didn't perform reliably in normal learning tests for months afterwards, even if they were given no more shocks.

I am now going to move on to look at some developments of learning theory which move outside the original prohibition against thinking about internal phenomena such as thoughts and feelings. But before doing so, I would like to pause to look at the relevance (or otherwise) of what we have been discussing to human development, bearing in mind that all the findings discussed so far are based on experiments with dogs, rats and pigeons. The following activity is intended to give you an opportunity to consider this:

⚒ Activity 5.2 ⚒

1 Skinner found that the rats unlearned behaviour more slowly when that behaviour had only intermittently been reinforced. Can you think of any parallels here with attachment theory?

2 Can you think of situations where human beings are placed in a similar situation to the helpless rats in Seligman's experiments? Can you think of instances of 'learnt helplessness' in human life?

3 Can you think of any human parallels with the experiment of Pavlov's cruel experiments on stress just described?

4 Can you think of practical applications of the idea of 'shaping' – or of similar ideas – in a therapeutic context or elsewhere?

Comments on Activity 5.2

1 The parallel that may have struck you is this: children who have been anxiously attached – whose attachment behaviour has only intermittently been reinforced – find it harder to cope with moves, let go of old attachments and make new attachments, than children who have been securely attached.

2 Many children in abusive situations are in much the same position, since the abuse is something outside of their control. Certainly depression in adult life is a common result of childhood abuse, as is a feeling of not being in control. People in institutional care – old people, for example, or people with mental illness – often experience a huge reduction in their control over their own lives, and often exhibit a kind of learnt passivity (there will be more discussion on this in Chapter 10).

3 You probably were struck by the fact that these poor dogs were in a no-win situation. Children in seriously abusive situations can be in the same position: the most dangerous thing in their lives is also their only source of physical care. You'll remember that attachment theorists suggest that the most dysfunctional form of anxious attachment – disorganised attachment – arises in these kinds of circumstances.

4 You may have remembered that some phobias have been successfully treated by a kind of shaping procedure called desensitisation, in which, for example, a sufferer from cat phobia is first shown a cat in a cage and helped to feel relaxed with that, then a cat out of a cage but across the room . . . and so on. So-called 'brief therapy' or 'solution-focused therapy' has a similar underlying idea. In this technique, a client is encouraged to think and talk as much as possible about positive things she has achieved, however small, and is rewarded by the therapist's attention for discussing these. The idea is to reinforce 'solution-focused' thinking to the point where the client is able herself to address whatever problem it is that has brought her to therapy. Exponents of this kind of therapy argue that traditional talking therapy tends

to reinforce 'problem-focused' thinking, by encouraging people to talk about their difficulties and reinforcing this with attention and sympathy (see De Shazer, 1985).

The behaviourist tradition has produced a number of therapeutic ideas which are in some ways the antithesis of Freud's, in that behaviourists are not interested in looking at the original causes of problem behaviours, or of the behaviour's meaning for the individual, but at the contingencies of reinforcement that are maintaining the behaviour in the here and now. Such approaches are often criticised for being superficial and for failing to get to the root of the problem, but they do have the advantage that they offer practical solutions, and avoid making us seem like the prisoners of our distant past.

Cognitive Factors, Observational Learning and Social Learning Theory

Although Skinner, Watson and others tried to avoid any sort of speculation about what was going on in the minds of humans and animals, and to focus purely on the observable and measurable phenomena of behaviour and stimuli, the experimental evidence alone does make such an approach hard to sustain. There are phenomena which cannot really be explained without postulating internal working models that animals and humans carry in their minds. An increasing recognition of this has led to cross-fertilisation between the cognitive and behaviourist branches of psychology that existed in the mid-twentieth century, to the extent that they no longer really exist as distinct branches (we speak now, for example, of 'cognitive-behavioural' therapy.)

Edward Tolman (1951) provided a number of simple demonstrations of the way that cognitive concepts could not really be left out of the picture. In one experiment, for example, he showed that if rats learn to run through a maze, they will still be able to find their way through it if it is flooded and they have to swim. This may seem unsurprising, but it does demonstrate that when rats learn how to get through a maze they are not just learning a sequence of muscle movements, because the muscle movements involved in swimming are quite different from those involved in running. They must therefore be learning some sort of 'mental map' of the maze.

Another cognitive factor that can be demonstrated to be a part of learning in animals – and which we all know to be a part of learning in human beings – is *observation*. Animals consistently learn tasks more quickly if they have previously observed other animals completing them, than if they are only taught by the traditional operant conditioning procedures. In fact, learning from observation seems to be very deep-rooted. (In the last chapter

I mentioned the fact that one-day-old babies, for example, can be shown to be able to copy simple movements such as sticking out the tongue.) A psychologist called Albert Bandura (1977) explored observational learning in human children. In his basic experiment, a child is shown a live or filmed model doing something, and is later observed to see how much of the model's behaviour she copies. Bandura identified several variables that influenced the amount of copying that occurred:

- Children were more likely to copy models identified as high prestige in some way. (Advertising agencies have presumably discovered the same thing, since they routinely use celebrities to endorse products.)
- They were more likely to copy models similar to themselves in some way.
- They were also more likely (not surprisingly) to copy models that they had seen rewarded for their actions.
- He also found that there was a distinction between acquiring the *capability* of performing a task and actually copying it. So, for example, children who didn't mimic a certain action after seeing it, could do so if asked (again, perhaps, not a very surprising finding).

Bandura's work formed part of the basis for an area of psychology known as social learning theory, which uses ideas from learning theory to look at how we acquire complex social behaviour. This can be applied to any aspect of social behaviour – for example: how do we learn the behaviour that is characteristic of our culture or our social class? But I want for the rest of this chapter to concentrate on just one area, which is obviously a crucial one in the study of human development: the acquisition of gender roles.

But before going any further, you may find it useful to look at the following activity. This will give you an opportunity to consider what you have read so far about learning theory by trying to apply it to the question of gender roles:

✹ Activity 5.3 ✹

Looking back at the ideas from learning theory which we've discussed (operant conditioning, classical conditioning, observational learning, generalisation, discrimination, etc.), consider how these might apply to the way that children learn different 'masculine' or 'feminine' gender roles.

Comments on Activity 5.3

Ideas you may have mentioned are:

- Different behaviours are positively or negatively reinforced, by parents or other adults (that is, aggression is encouraged more in boys, playing with dolls is discouraged, etc.).
- Observational learning means that boys will tend to copy male role models (at home, on TV and elsewhere), and girls female ones. Boys will also tend to copy males who are seen as successful and having high status, girls will tend to copy famous, high-profile girls or women.
- From an early age different stimuli are offered, even in connection with meeting basic needs for food and warmth. (Girls are given pink cups, boys blue, for example.)
- You may also have considered ways in which connections learnt in one context tend to generalise to others – or children may learn to discriminate very subtly different clues as to what is appropriate for boys and what for girls.

Learning and the Acquisition of Gender Roles

Men and women – and boys and girls – behave in different ways in all kinds of respects. Until recent times, most people would have assumed that this was mainly the result of 'nature' – boys and girls are simply born different – but there has been a growing awareness that many, and some would argue most, of these 'masculine' and 'feminine' characteristics are the result not of nature but of nurture. From a sociological point of view, one would say that gender roles are 'socially constructed' – that is created by the particular circumstances of a particular society in order usually to serve the interests of powerful groups within that society. From a psychological perspective (the main perspective of this book) one would say that they are *learnt* – and learning theory provides some ideas about the mechanisms through which this might come about.

For the remainder of this chapter I will give a brief tour of some of the research in this area, concluding with some evidence that at least part of the difference between boys and girls *is* to do with 'nature' (see Golombok and Fivush (1994) for a fuller account of this topic).

📖 **Different Attitudes to Masculinity in Ancient Greece** 📖

The fact that gender stereotypes are different in different societies is illustrated by the fact that in ancient Greece there was once a crack army regiment consisting entirely of gay men. The Sacred Band of Thebes, as it was known, apparently played a crucial part in many battles. In our own time, gay men still tend to be stereotyped as 'unmanly', and at the time of writing homosexuality is still   not permitted in the American armed forces, but in the ancient world men whose preference was for other men were seen, at least by some, as being *more* manly than men whose preference was for women. (See Boswell, 1996: 62–4)

Operant and classical conditioning and gender roles

Many researchers have suggested that behaviours such as aggression or dependency are differentially rewarded depending on whether they are produced by boys or girls. Baby boys have been found to be given more physical stimulation than girls, whereas girls are touched and talked to more (see Golombok and Fivush, 1994: 77–88).

Boy and girl children are also exposed to different learning environments. Different toys are given to them, or different things are drawn to their attention: 'Look at that fire-engine, John!' 'Look at that pretty dress, Jane!' There is clear evidence that children *are* differentially reinforced for taking part in what are seen as 'gender-appropriate' and 'gender-inappropriate' activities. So, even if it were not the case that things like aggression and dependency *per se* are reinforced differentially, play *is* selectively reinforced that will develop different patterns of behaviour – a form of 'shaping'.

As we noted above, appropriate activities are even colour-coded in our culture to assist children to choose the 'right' activities, and to allow them to generalise their social learning about gender. To give an example from my own experience: a 9-year-old boy is going through a Lego catalogue, pointing out the space models, cowboy models, aircraft models and so on. Coming to a page depicting models made with pink bricks, he dismisses it as 'girlie stuff', turning to the next page without a second glance.

Children are actively discouraged from what are seen as 'gender-inappropriate' activities. Interestingly, researchers have found that boys are more likely to be discouraged from 'girl-appropriate' activities than vice versa, and that fathers more than mothers do the job of discouraging them.

Girls are not discouraged from 'boy' activities to the same extent, but are equally discouraged by both parents (Langlois and Downs, 1980).

Observational learning and gender roles

Bandura showed that children are sensitive to the characteristics of the model they use, and are more likely to copy those that seem 'like them'. It therefore seems likely that children will tend to model themselves on the same-sex parent. The picture is complicated by the fact that, in a traditional family or in a single-mother family, or indeed a modern primary school, where women teachers heavily outnumber men, role models are of course much more to hand for girls than for boys.

However Bandura and others (such as Perry and Bussey, 1979) have found that this relationship is subtler than you might think. Children do copy role models of both genders, but will notice the behaviour of a large number of models and work out which behaviour is more *typical* of their own sex. Experiments have been carried out in which children were shown a number of models, male and female, choosing between pairs of items. If all the members of one gender were seen to have made the same choice, then, if the children were presented with the same options, they would tend to make the same choice as the models of their own gender. When one member of one gender was noticed by the children to consistently make choices different from the majority of their gender, then the children would tend to discount this person as a role model. The implication of this seems to be that, even if a boy sees his father changing the baby's nappy, for example, or a girl sees her mother mending the car, they are much less likely to copy this behaviour if their wider experience suggests to them that this is not typical behaviour for the respective genders.

Interestingly, some experiments have also found that girls will imitate male role models more readily than boys will imitate female role models, the exception being when boys perceive a female role model to have power. You will remember that Bandura found that children would be more likely to copy models they saw as prestigious or powerful. In a society where more power is still held by men, this appears to mean that both boys and girls will be more prone to try to copy men in the main, but that both boys and girls will imitate women when they perceive them as having power.

Other factors in gender differentiation

Social learning theory suggests a number of mechanisms whereby children learn gender roles, although it does not have anything to say about how those different roles arose in the first place – a very interesting sociological and political question, but one which is outside the scope of this book.

We should also note that the fact that roles can be clearly shown to be shaped by learning in very many ways, does not rule out the fact that there may be some actual biological differences (nature as well as nurture). In fact there is evidence that the hormonal differences that exist between boys and girls prenatally do actually have some influence on behaviour. (See Golombok and Fivush, 1994: 43–50, for details of the experimental evidence here.) For example, there is a condition called *congenital adrenal hyperplasia* which results in abnormally high levels of androgen (a male sex hormone) in the bloodstream. Babies with this condition who are genetically female will have internal female organs but external organs which resemble male organs. Some of these children have been raised as boys, and seem to socialise normally as boys. Other children with the same condition, however, have been treated by surgery and by hormone treatment so that the children appear and grow up as girls. Comparisons have been made between these girls and other children. Even though they are treated as girls from an early age, it seems that they are more interested in 'masculine' toys than other girls and spend more time playing with boys, suggesting that the early high doses of androgen, even if subsequently corrected, have predisposed them in some way towards more stereotypically 'boyish' behaviour (Berenbaum and Hines, 1992). There is also evidence that these girls are more likely than other girls to grow up defining themselves as bisexual or lesbian, thus suggesting that the prenatal exposure to the male sex hormone predisposes them to be sexually attracted to women (Golombok and Fivush, 1994: 51).

This is not to say that learning is not a major factor, but it does seem clear that some actual biological differences – nature as well as nurture – may underlie the social stereotypes of masculinity and femininity.

Concluding Comments on Learning Theory

As already noted, gender roles are only one of many areas to which learning theory and social learning theory can be applied. Social learning theory could also be used, for example, to look at the ways in which different patterns of behaviour are learnt by people from different social classes or ethnic backgrounds, differences which, again, in the past have often been seen as innate rather than learnt.

Learning theory has its limitations: there are biological factors and cognitive factors in development which cannot usefully be explained in terms merely of learnt connections. It can also be misused (as Aldous Huxley's satire colourfully illustrates.) But it can be useful as a way of understanding the influence of the external environment in shaping our behaviour.

The following activity is an opportunity to consider the value of this point of view in a practical context:

⚒ Activity 5.4 ⚒

Suppose you are a member of staff in a team that provides support to adults with learning disabilities living in supported group homes in the community, the aim of the team being to promote independence. One of the group home residents, Angie, arrives in your office having got in a muddle with her benefits, with the result that she currently has no money and is in a very distressed state.

You give her some sympathy, calm her down, make her a cup of tea and then go off and sort the whole thing out on the phone with the benefits office.

Angie is very grateful.

But what could be the drawbacks of this response from a behavioural point of view – and what might have been a better response?

Comments on Activity 5.4

While Angie saw your response as helpful and has no complaints whatsoever, you may not have really have done her a good turn if your aim is to promote independence. What you have done is to reinforce the behaviour of bringing her problems to you to sort out (positive reinforcement being provided by the tea and sympathy, and negative reinforcement being provided by the anxiety of having no money, which has now been taken away). You might have done better, for example, to have talked Angie through what she needed to do, given her a phone and then given her the tea and the encouragement after she had sorted it out for herself. That way you would have been reinforcing her own problem-solving behaviour.

Incidentally, the learning is not all one-way in such situations. Just as you were reinforcing Angie's 'helpless' behaviour, she was no doubt reinforcing your helpful behaviour by being happy and grateful when you had sorted it out for her.

This seems to me a common pattern in the work of the helping professions: dependency can be rewarding for both the professional and her client, so it keeps getting reinforced.

Chapter Summary

Making Connections

- In this chapter we've considered the tradition in psychology known as connectionism, behaviourism or learning theory, which explores the ways in which we connect events and actions. I began by looking at the work of Pavlov and the basic concepts of 'classical conditioning'.

- I looked briefly at J.B. Watson (who coined the word 'behaviourism') and considered the idea of learnt connections based purely and simply on proximity.

- I looked at operant conditioning (conditioning that links behaviour with particular stimuli) and the work of B.F. Skinner in this area.

- I described the concept of 'learnt helplessness' and looked at stress.

- I then looked at cognitive aspects of learning which cannot easily be explained in pure behavioural terms, and then at observational learning and at social learning theory.

- I discussed the application of learning theory to the question of how children acquire distinct gender roles.

Up to now we have looked at general theories of human growth and development, most of which have focused mainly on childhood. In the next section, however, we will look not at a particular theory, but at a particularly crucial stage of life: adolescence, the time of transition from childhood to adulthood.

Suggested Reading

ON LEARNING THEORY IN GENERAL (INCLUDING SOME OF ITS APPLICATIONS):

- Walker, S. (1984) *Learning Theory and Behaviour Modification* (London: Routledge)

ON SOCIAL LEARNING THEORY:

- Bandura, A. (1977) *Social Learning Theory* (Englewood Cliffs, NJ: Prentice-Hall Inc.)

- Durkin, K. (1995) *Developmental Social Psychology* (London: Routledge)

  (Gives an overview of social learning theory, in addition to covering many other topics in social psychological development.)

ON GENDER ROLE DEVELOPMENT:

- Golombok, S. and Fivush, R. (1994) *Gender Development* (Cambridge: Cambridge University Press)

6 Who Am I Going to Be?

Changes in adolescence

Unlike, say, the transition from Freud's oral to anal stage, or from Piaget's pre-operational stage to his stage of concrete operations – both of which are theoretical constructs, open to debate and challenge – the transition from childhood to adulthood is in part indisputably a biological change, a part of our nature. It is the transition to sexual maturity, the stage at which for the first time we become capable of reproduction. But the majority of girls in Western countries have now passed menarche (that is, begun having periods) by the age of 13 and of course we do not see 13-year-olds, or even 16-year-olds, as adults. So the stage of life between childhood and adulthood which we call adolescence is really only partly defined by biology. It is also a psychological transition, which is seen differently in different societies, just as childhood and adulthood themselves are seen differently.

I will begin this chapter, therefore, by looking at two questions which are of relevance to other changes in life as well as adolescence. Firstly I will consider the interaction between social and biological factors in development. Then I will look at the psychology of transitions in general. I will then go on to look at some ideas about adolescence itself.

One note of caution. In this chapter and the next, I will present an assortment of ideas from research. In a book of this kind it is not possible to go into detail on the methodology of the various research studies. Those I am going to describe in this chapter are based in the main on surveys of samples of young people in various circumstances (in the next chapter the studies quoted are based on surveys of adults). Inevitably bias creeps in, both in the way that questions are framed and the way that answers are interpreted. For example: when people answer researchers' questions, are they saying what they really feel, or are they saying what they think they ought to say? I describe the findings of these studies, therefore, because they are interesting and will, I hope, provide some new insights. They cannot however be regarded as final statements on the subject. The picture is further complicated by the fact that society is constantly changing, so that the experience of adolescence thirty years ago is different in some respects from the experience of adolescence now.

Before going further you may find it useful to use the following activity to take stock of your own ideas and experiences of adolescence:

Activity 6.1

Looking back on your own adolescent years, what would be the themes that you would notice? What was different about being a teenager from being a child, or from being an adult? What was easy or difficult about being a teenager? If you had to pick three words to describe your adolescent years, which words would you choose? What was helpful and unhelpful about the way that adults responded to you? Did your adolescent years correspond to the stereotype of this time of life? What would you say was the stereotype at that time?

If you ask yourself the same sorts of question about adolescents that you know now, do you come up with the same kinds of answers?

Comments on Activity 6.1

I can't comment, of course, on what you may have thought about these questions. What I suggest however is that you bear in mind what your thoughts were and test them against the ideas which I will discuss for the rest of this chapter. I hope that these ideas will give you some new perspectives on adolescence. But it is also possible that some of the ideas do not seem to you to fit with your own experience at all – or do not seem helpful in explaining your own experience.

Culture and Biology

The period of transition from childhood to adulthood has very different meanings in different cultures, and indeed adulthood and childhood themselves (as well as old age) are viewed in very different ways.

Segregation between adults and children is really only common in industrialised societies, where children go to school while adults go to work, or work at home. In pre-industrial societies (that is to say: in Western Europe and America in the past, and still in many developing countries around the world), both adults and children are involved in the same daily activities and routines: for example in caring for domestic animals or harvesting crops. There is, of course, still a biological transition, but the change in role between childhood and adulthood is very much less pronounced.

The significance of adolescence is therefore different in non-industrial cultures, and – not surprisingly since less change is involved – the period of transition tends to be briefer. Marriages will tend to take place much earlier, particularly for girls. There are still many cultures where girls can be married at 12. In many countries boys are already serving as soldiers in civil wars at the same age.

However, all cultures do recognise some kind of transition, often marked by a ceremony of some sort. The bar mitzvah, for example, marks this transition for boys in Jewish culture. Secular Western culture does not set a precise date, but it does include a relatively long period in which young people are biologically adult but legally children (for example, they are required by law to go to school). In Britain, where the full rights and responsibilities of adulthood are not legally acquired until the age of 18, this period may last for five years or longer.

Adolescence is in some ways a modern, Western invention (the word 'Western' is used loosely to refer to the industrialised world). In one study, a Samoan-born teenager commented that she had never heard of adolescence until she came to New Zealand:

> I don't think it was part of my life because it is a western concept, and from a non-western society all those development stages didn't relate to me. All I know is that my . . . [family] and my culture are important. They determine the way I behave and think and feel. . . . Sometimes I think that we [Samoans] are children for much of our lives. . . . It doesn't matter how old you are, if you are not considered worthy or responsible enough by our elders then you will not be treated as an adult. You really have to earn your place in the Samoan culture. (Tupuola, 1993, cited by Kroger, 1996: 5)

Nevertheless there *is* clearly a major biological change which is common to all cultures – the onset of fertility, and also a period of rapid growth and physical and biochemical change. These biological changes do not take place at the same time, or in the same order, for boys as for girls (the growth spurt starts earlier in girls), and there are also substantial differences in the timing of these changes from one individual to another. So biology is undoubtedly a major factor, not only in adolescence generally, but in shaping different responses to this stage of life from boys and girls and from one individual to another. But the impact of the biological changes cannot be assessed without looking at the meanings attached to them by a culture.

To add a further complication, the relationship between biology and social factors is in fact a *two*-way one. Culture and society do not just respond to biological events – they also influence those events themselves. The onset of menstruation (menarche) is known to occur earlier in affluent societies, and to be getting earlier in our society, probably due to changes in diet. Other factors are known to alter the timing of menarche. It may be delayed in the case of girls who are exceptionally physically active. A New Zealand study found that family conflict and absence of a parent could lead to an earlier onset of menarche (Moffit et al., 1992).

📖 **Menarche and Spermarche** 📖

The male equivalent of menarche (that is to say: the point at which boys become capable of reproduction), is the first ejaculation of semen, and this is known as spermarche. Both menarche and spermarche are still clouded in secrecy in our society. Research shows that while most girls do discuss their first period with their mothers, a significant minority do not – and boys do not usually discuss spermarche with their fathers, or indeed with anyone (Gaddis and Brooks-Gunn, 1985). It does seem that, even now, boys and girls often find their way into this new sexual territory on their own.

Once again, then, we see how biological inheritance and environment – nature and nurture – interact, to the extent that what we think of as adolescence in industrialised societies is really not universal at all, but simply one way adopted by one kind of society for dealing with the biological transition to sexual maturity.

In this chapter we will be looking primarily at adolescence as it occurs in Western industrialised societies. But it is important to remember that, even in this context, there are many going through this transition with very different cultural expectations. As a social worker, teacher or doctor in Britain or the USA, for example, you may well encounter women from the

Indian subcontinent who were married at the age of 12. Or indeed you yourself may have a background in such a culture.

Transitions

I have used the word transition a number of times now, and it is a subject we will return to later in this book when we look at other stages of life: the mid-life transition, the transition to parenthood, the transition to old age. But clearly the transition from childhood to adulthood is one of the biggest transitions we have to make, so this seems an appropriate point to look at transitions in general and what is involved in them.

The psychology of transitions

Transition is defined by the *Concise Oxford Dictionary* as 'passage or change from one place or state or act or set of circumstances to another'. Any such change in human life clearly involves a psychological readjustment. Many different studies have looked at the way that people deal with transitions of various kinds and it seems that there is a common pattern which applies both to positive and negative changes. The duration and intensity of the experience may vary but people characteristically go through the same kind of cycle when faced with a new situation – which may be anything from bereavement (which is a process of adjusting to the new situation created by a loss: a subject we'll come back to in Chapter 11) to a change of job or a new house, or indeed a lottery win. All these situations involve both an ending and a coming to terms with something new.

In Figure 6.1, the horizontal axis indicates time. (The diagram and the following discussion are based on Sugarman, 1986, who adapts Hopson,

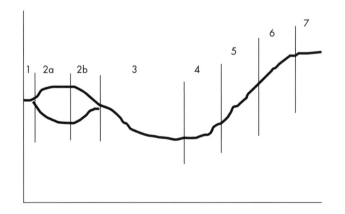

FIGURE 6.1 *Transitions (adapted from Sugarman, 1986)*

1981.) The vertical axis indicates changes in mood. Of course the size and timescale of changes will vary according to the event. Even a cancelled evening out involves an adjustment, but it is likely to be modest in scale and duration. It also is not necessarily the case that people emerge from this process at a higher level, although even from painful negative events people can of course emerge having gained something. The following is a summary of the stages involved in dealing with transitions:

1 *Immobilisation*: This is the initial response of being stunned, frozen, dazed. (Typical comments which we make in the aftermath of both positive and negative events are: 'I can't believe this is happening.' 'It feels like a dream.' 'It hasn't sunk in.')
2 *Reaction*: (a) Elation or despair: after a period of time our initial stunned response gives way to a sharp mood swing (either up or down depending on the nature of the event). (b) Minimisation: our initial post-shock reaction will be followed by some kind of minimisation. (Think of a lottery winner saying 'This isn't going to change my life' or a bereaved person at the early stage when they still haven't faced the permanence of their loss.)
3 *Self-doubt – (and sometimes depression)*: This phase is characterised by fluctuations in energy level, often between anger and apathy, self-doubt ('I was really pleased to get this new job', we might say, 'but now I'm wondering whether I'm really up to it.') and self-blame ('If only I'd not let her go out that night, she'd still be here today.')
4 *Letting go*: Until now we have been maintaining an attachment to the old order of things as they existed prior to the new event. There has been an element of denial and we have been clinging on in defiance of the new circumstances. At some point these old attachments have to be broken if we are to move on. These may include ties of affection to other people, or to old habits, or old beliefs. We may feel grief and anger at this, but if we are not completely stuck there will be a gradual recognition of the need to put the past behind us.
5 *Testing*: As we let go of the past, we become free to explore the new circumstances in which we find ourselves. We can try out new identities and start to form new attachments.
6 *Search for meaning*: 'Putting the past behind us' does not mean denying that it ever happened. During this phase, we look back at the past from our new viewpoint, reappraise it and try to make sense of it.
7 *Integration*: The transition process is complete when we feel 'at home' in the new reality. New behaviours, new ideas about ourselves have become part of our sense of our own identity.

People do not necessarily successfully negotiate this process and can get stuck within it. Successful negotiation of a transition puts a person in good shape to deal with other transitions in the future. But a transition which has not been successfully negotiated makes it difficult for people to cope successfully with adapting to new life changes. To give a simple example: it is difficult to make a commitment to a new sexual partner, if one is still attached to and grieving for a previous partner.

Transitions and adolescence

The transition from childhood to adulthood is not quite as sudden an event as, say, a bereavement or a lottery win, but it is nevertheless an event to which we have to adjust. We have to adjust to becoming a sexual being and to forming new kinds of relationships, to having new responsibilities and new freedoms, to having to earn a living. Some of these adjustments are necessary for biological reasons, some for cultural ones, but they are all adjustments that have to be made. And in fact, if you look back at Figure 6.1 and the stages in it, I think you will agree that it fits quite well with the changes that are involved in adolescence, if you allow for the fact that like all stage models it is a simplification and that in reality we tend to pursue a rather more winding path. As with other transitions, adolescence does involve a letting go of childhood, forming new attachments and (as we will discuss shortly) trying out new identities. As with other transitions, we can get stuck (become fixated in Freudian terminology) and never quite finish moving on.

You may like to use the following activity to reflect on different kinds of psychological transitions:

✵ Activity 6.2 ✵

1 You have been planning an exciting holiday with a partner or friend for some time and are much looking forward to it. Not long before the day of your departure, your friend is involved in an accident resulting in a broken leg, which means that the holiday will have to be cancelled. Suppose you have just received the phone call. What would your initial reaction be – and what stages would you then go through?

2 Looking back at your own teenage years and early adulthood, can you chart the stages you went through between the time you thought of yourself as a child and the time you thought of yourself as an adult?

Comments on Activity 6.2

1 I suspect that you will have found yourself going through stages of disappointment, anger at your friend, guilt for feeling angry and so on, but eventually reaching a point where you were able to give up on the old plan and either make some new plan, or rearrange the plan for a later date, so that instead of grieving over what did not happen you are once again looking forward to something. You might even have found some advantages in having postponed your original plan.

2 People take many different paths through adolescence, but you will probably have noticed yourself experiencing grief at the loss of childhood (when Christmas presents stop being exciting, for example) and ambivalence and fear about becoming an adult, but then gradually coming to terms with the change.

Although these two questions relate to a major life change and a comparatively temporary problem, I am suggesting that there will have been a somewhat similar pattern of response in each case.

Features of the adolescent transition

What is specific about adolescence as against other kinds of transition?

For Piaget, adolescence when children reach the stage of 'formal operations', and are able to deal with the same complex abstract ideas as adults. For Freud, adolescence is the time of the genital stage, the final stage of psychosexual development, when an individual's sexual interest, originally directed towards an opposite-sex parent, is redirected towards finding a partner of the opposite sex. For Bowlby, it is the stage at which attachments to parent-figures are loosened, in order to form new adult attachments.

Erik Erikson offered a stage model that divided the whole lifespan into eight stages of which adolescence was the fifth (see p. 43). And he described the characteristic crisis of adolescence as *identity versus role confusion*. His is one of several models of adolescence which see identity as the central theme of this stage in life (see Kroger, 1996, for an account of the models of Blos, Kohlberg, Loevinger and Kegan, for example). And while all transitions involve establishing a new identity, most commentators seem to agree that this is particularly central in adolescence. The shift from the status of a child to that of an adult, which adolescence represents, is probably the largest such shift that we have to make in our conception of ourselves.

I am going to use Erikson's model to provide a framework for the rest of this chapter, because of the emphasis he places on identity and because his ideas about the adolescent transition have been the basis of a good deal of research. But, as before when I have highlighted the work of one particular authority, I must emphasise that there *are* other models and that I am not offering Erikson as the only possible way of looking at this question.

Identity versus Role Confusion

As was discussed in Chapter 2, Erikson spoke of *psychosocial* stages, rather than Freud's psychosexual ones and, though he was a psychoanalyst, he felt that traditional psychoanalysis did not take sufficiently into account the external, social environment. Each of his eight psychosocial stages was marked by a distinctive life 'crisis' or task, a reasonably successful resolution of which would provide the individual with qualities which would assist with other tasks ahead (see Table 2.1, on page 43).

During adolescence, as with other stages, unresolved crises from earlier years may need to be fought again, and may provide obstacles to success-fully negotiating the current crisis. A new identity needs to be built on a foundation made from the gains from earlier stages. The gains that could be achieved from successful outcomes of the four previous stages could be summed up, according to Erikson as *hope*, *will*, *purpose* and *competence*. A successful negotiation of the adolescent transition could in turn equip an individual for the challenges of young adulthood by providing her with a sense of identity: one needs a secure sense of oneself in order to be able to negotiate adult intimate relationships with others.

Erikson thought that during the adolescent stage, a combination of rapid growth, hormonal changes and a growing awareness of adult tasks ahead, leads to a questioning of the 'sameness and continuity' relied on earlier. Old certainties simply do not work any more, and new ones are needed. He thought that, at least in Western culture, sexual and occupational identity was paramount, and he saw these as being the areas in which a new secure identity would chiefly need to be negotiated. He didn't dispute that this could be different in different cultures – and he also thought the issues would be different for boys and girls – we'll come back to this.

Of course children have a sense of identity before adolescence, but Erikson saw this identity as being based on introjection of others' qualities, or identification with others. During adolescence a process of *identity formation* takes place in which the individual makes her own decisions about what constitutes 'the real me'. Successful resolution of this stage will lead to a secure sense of ego identity: the individual has developed a defined personality within a social reality which he or she understands; she has a secure sense of herself as a consistent person.

Someone who has difficulty with this stage, though, may remain stuck with some confusion about who or what she really is. We can probably all think of adults who seem rather immature or who we might describe as rather 'adolescent' (if we do not feel so ourselves, at times). Difficulties in resolving the adolescent stage, Erikson argued, can lead to over-identification with peer groups, or with things like cults, or deviant sub-cultures (the drug sub-culture, the criminal sub-culture) on the basis that any identity is better than none.

Identity status

As I've mentioned, a good deal of research has focused on Erikson's ideas about adolescence and the idea of 'identity formation' in adolescence. One writer, James Marcia (1993 and elsewhere), defined four different kinds of 'identity status' found among adolescents. These are:

1 **Identity diffusion**: an identity status characterised by the avoidance of commitment and indecision about major life issues. The stereotypically difficult teenager who lies in bed, watches TV and refuses to think about or discuss the future, might be said to be in a state of identity diffusion.

2 **Identity foreclosure**: a status of preliminary commitment and value orientation but characterised by the acceptance of others' values (those of parents, for example, or teachers), rather than self-determined goals. The teenager who does not seem to question or rebel against adult expectations at all might be said to be in a state of identity foreclosure. Such a young person might seem to the adults in their life to be less of a 'problem' than the identity-diffuse teenager, but in fact in Eriksonian terms is likewise failing to tackle the challenges of this stage because she is relying on introjection and identification rather than seeking her own identity.

3 **Moratorium**: a status of intense identity crisis characterised by active attention to major decisions and exploration of possibilities for the future, but not yet resolved in firm commitments. So, like the identity-diffuse young person, a young person at the moratorium stage is avoiding making a commitment, but is doing so constructively, because it is constructive to consider actively all the options before making a serious decision. Moratorium is an *uncomfortable* position, which individuals may be tempted to avoid by opting for foreclosure.

4 **Identity achievement**: individuals with this status have resolved their crises and made firm commitments to ideals and plans, based on their own thinking and not simply on ideas imposed by or uncritically accepted from others. In Erikson's terms they have successfully negotiated the challenge of this stage of life.

Two of these statuses are characterised by lack of commitment to particular goals or values: moratorium and diffusion. But in another sense moratorium is closer to identity achievement because it is about actively seeking one's own identity, rather than avoiding the issue.

One could thus group Marcia's four kinds of identity status as in Figure 6.2.

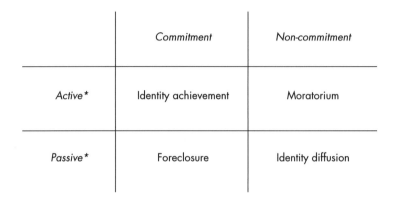

	Commitment	Non-commitment
Active*	Identity achievement	Moratorium
Passive*	Foreclosure	Identity diffusion

*My choice of words, not Marcia's

FIGURE 6.2 *Types of identity status*

These kinds of identity status are not necessarily stages in identity formation, in that young people do not necessarily move through them in linear order. (In fact, as discussed previously in relation to Piaget, stage models in general are probably a considerable simplification of the uneven process of development.) But, as one would expect, studies have shown that young people tend to move from diffusion and foreclosure status to moratorium and achievement status. Referring back to the 'transitions' curve (p. 114), one could say that both foreclosure and identity diffusion correspond to the early three stages. Moratorium might be said to correspond to what were referred to there as 'letting go', 'testing' and 'searching for meaning', and identity achievement with 'integration'. But of course many people remain in a state of foreclosure or diffusion into adult life.

(One of the features of Erikson's model is that at later times of transitions, we may revisit unresolved issues from earlier stages. As we'll discuss in the next chapter, the mid-life transition is sometimes marked by revisiting issues that were prematurely foreclosed in adolescence or at the beginning of adult life. Permanent relationships or careers or parenthood entered into too early, for example, may when revisited later be seen as examples of foreclosure: commitments entered into prematurely in order to avoid the anxiety of leaving matters unresolved.)

One group of researchers (Adams et al., 1994), who used Marcia's four basic categories of identity status, suggested that patterns of identity diffusion would tend to be characteristic of young people from rejecting, detached families. Identity foreclosure would tend to be a pattern with child-centred, conformist families. Young people from warm, supportive families that encouraged independence would be better at reaching the stage of moratorium and subsequent identity achieving.

The following activity may help you to measure these ideas against your own experience:

✷ Activity 6.3 ✷

Looking back at your own adolescent years are you able to identify times when you were in a stage of identity diffusion, foreclosure, moratorium or identity achievement? Do these ideas make some sense in terms of your own experience? Were you more prone to diffusion or foreclosure? How would you describe your family at the time? Does this fit in with Adams' suggestions about the kinds of families that produce different identity statuses?

Try and list four or five teenagers whom you know – as diverse as possible. Write their names down in a column. In a second column write what you see as their 'identity status', in Marcia's terms, and in a third column describe their families. How do your results fit in with Adams' theory?

Comments on Activity 6.3

Obviously I can't tell what conclusions you may have reached. Later in this chapter we will look a bit more at ways in which adults can help or hinder the process of identity formation in adolescents. You may like to reflect on your own thoughts and beliefs about this.

The adolescent ego

I have been discussing Erikson's idea that a secure sense of ego identity would be the successful outcome of the adolescent phase, a phase during which earlier conceptions of one's identity no longer work and have to be replaced. So how does the adolescent ego function during the intermediate period?

Many people would say that adolescents are particularly *egocentric*, preoccupied with their own needs, inconsiderate of the needs of others, and with an exaggerated sense of their own importance in the world. Is this in fact so? And if it is, how does this fit with Piaget's idea of egocentrism being characteristic of earlier stages of development (the sensori-motor and pre-operational stages – see pp. 77–81)? After all, if Piaget's model is correct, egocentrism ought to be on the decline, not on the increase, with the onset of the stage of formal operations?

Elkind (1967), however, suggested that the adolescent *recognises* the thoughts of others and therefore is not egocentric in the same strictly cognitive sense that little children are, but she tends to give *undue weight* to her own. Perhaps, if adolescence does indeed coincide with a qualitative change in thinking as Piaget suggests (an adolescent finds herself much more capable of using abstract ideas and much more aware of the underlying principles behind different ideas), it is precisely this change that makes adolescents feel that they are in possession of remarkable new insights? Piaget's own view was that adolescence was characterised by a 'belief in the omnipotence of reflection' (1968: 64). You may recall from your own adolescence being excited by new thoughts and insights, and feeling that you and your friends must be the first to have had them.

Elkind noticed that young people are prone to feeling they have an *imaginary audience*, to exaggerated self-consciousness, intense awareness of other's watching. Elkind also proposed that it is typical of adolescents to construct a *'personal fable'*: 'I am different', 'It won't happen to me', etc. Empirical evidence supports Elkind's view that these patterns peak in adolescence.

Other research (see Simmons et al., 1987) shows that *self-esteem* tends to drop at the beginning of adolescence and then climb up again, which is precisely the pattern one would expect from what we know of transitions in general.

Relating to Others

Having talked about what is going on 'inside' young people during adolescence, we'll now consider what adolescence means in terms of relationships with other people. This is of course a two-way question. How do adolescents relate to others – and how does the behaviour of others affect adolescents?

Rebellion

The stereotype of adolescence in this culture is that it is a stormy time characterised by unreasonable behaviour and rebellion. While few who deal with adolescents would dispute that there is some basis in reality for this stereotype, it is interesting that many researchers who have looked into this have come to the view that it tends to be exaggerated. Only a minority of adolescents seem to go through a period of exceptional emotional turbulence. A 1989 study compared the emotional state of 9 to 15-year-olds and found no increase in emotional stress during adolescence (Larson and Lampman-Petraitis, 1989). Other research into this area tends to find that only about 5–15 per cent experience serious emotional disturbance at this stage (see Durkin, 1995: 515).

The so-called 'generation gap' is also found by a number of research studies to be largely mythical. There *is* increased conflict between parents and adolescents, but both sides usually seem to see their differences as being confined to specific spheres rather than being a global breakdown of understanding. A very large survey of ten countries carried out by Offer and others (1988), for example, found that 91 per cent of teenagers denied holding a grudge against their parents or feeling that their parents were disappointed in them or ashamed of them. It is, however, the case that certain kinds of deviant behaviour – crime and drug abuse for example – do become prominent in adolescence, albeit only for a minority.

Autonomy and the peer group

One of the changes that normally occurs in adolescence is that young people are given, and expect, more autonomy. Again, this is a cultural matter to some extent. There are considerable cultural variations – and indeed probably class variations – in the amount of autonomy that smaller children are given. On the other hand there are cultures where even adults expect much less autonomy from their elders than do adults in Western industrial society, as was illustrated by the quote from a Samoan teenager earlier in this chapter. Nevertheless it is a fact that adolescents simply can't physically be controlled by adults in the way that small children can be and that there is therefore inevitably something of a shift in the balance of power.

But there are several kinds of autonomy, which don't necessarily go together. Steinberg and Silverberg (1986), looking at levels of autonomy among 12 to 16-year-olds, thought it would be more useful to break the idea of autonomy into several categories. These were:

- **emotional autonomy**, in which the individual relinquishes childhood dependence on her parents;
- **resistance to peer pressure**, in which the individual becomes able to act upon her own ideas, rather than conform to those of peers;
- **subjective sense of self-reliance**, in which the individual feels free of excessive dependency on others, takes initiatives, and has a feeling of control over her life.

What these researchers found in their survey of young people was that as 'emotional autonomy' increases, 'resistance to peer group pressure' decreases. There seemed to be a kind of trade-off. Young people become more reliant on their peer group as they become less reliant on their family of origin.

This begs the question as to whether the adolescents in this survey really were becoming more emotionally autonomous or simply transferring their emotional dependence from their parents to their peer group. Some other researchers, Ryan and Lynch (1989), used Steinberg's and Silverberg's categories and obtained similar findings in a survey of young people, but they decided that what Steinberg's and Silverberg's first category really measured was not emotional *autonomy*, but emotional *detachment*. Their view was that children who scored high on this measure are actually lacking in emotional support at home and so tend to compensate by relying heavily on their peer group. In their view securely attached adolescents were actually better placed to achieve genuine autonomy than emotionally detached ones, who would tend to be easily led by their peers rather than genuinely determining their own course in life.

The fact that these two sets of researchers could draw quite different conclusions from the same survey results does illustrate the difficulty of carrying out objective research in areas of this kind. But it seems clear that young people do somehow have to balance pressures and demands from family on the one hand and from their peer group on the other, as they attempt to find their own identity and try and obtain necessary support from both those sources without becoming excessively reliant on either.

Incidentally, as well relating it to attachment theory we could equally well link this question of peer group versus parental influence to social learning theory. You may recall that social learning theory suggests a variety of factors that influence our choice of role model.

One commentator (Kegan, 1982) has even suggested that an extra stage should be added to Erikson's eight, covering early adolescence and before the 'identity versus role confusion' stage. The characteristic struggle of this stage would be 'affiliation versus abandonment'. As Kroger (2000) observes, 'themes of affiliation and abandonment, of being accepted or left behind by others, appear to be prevalent identity concerns among many adolescents'.

I should add that 'autonomy' and 'identity' are not necessarily the same things. Certainly there is a view of identity that does indeed equate it with autonomy. We might call this the 'I did it my way' model, on the lines of the famous Sinatra song. But this is only one way of looking at identity, and some would argue that it is a characteristically 'masculine' way. Identity could equally well be defined, this argument goes, in terms of the way we link to and relate to others, and this is perhaps a more typically 'feminine' way of looking at it. It is interesting to note, incidentally, that Steinberg and Silverberg found that girls scored consistently higher than boys of the same age on all three of their measures of autonomy.

Gender differences

Stage models of development (at adolescence and other stages) are sometimes guilty of offering male development as the 'norm', and either ignoring female development or tagging it on as an afterthought. Freud's Oedipus complex is much more famous than his Electra complex, which is supposed to be the female equivalent. In Erik Erikson's *Childhood and Society* (1995), which came out originally in the 1950s, he called his chapter on the stages of psychosocial development 'The eight ages of *man*' (my italics). And Erikson suggested that girls might postpone the issue of identity development (which was central to his model of adolescence) in favour of finding a partner as a means of defining their identity.

You may at this point feel like saying something like 'What a sexist attitude! Seeing women as dependent on men for their identity!' But before dismissing it out of hand, you may like to consider the following question: is it possible that girls and women really do define their identity more in terms of *relationships* (not just with men, but in general), while men define it more in terms, say, of things like their occupation or their leisure interests?

Carol Gilligan (1982) suggested that because of differences in the assigned roles of boys and girls, we'd expect a preoccupation with *intimacy* to be central to girls at an earlier stage than boys. She suggests that girls link intimacy and identity while boys are more prone to link identity to *role* and to ideas of *autonomy*. Gilligan comments that stage theorists looking at male development tend to assign an awareness of the importance of intimacy and relationships to adulthood. For example, in Erikson's model, 'intimacy versus isolation' is the characteristic conflict in *early adulthood*. But Gilligan suggests that, in the case of girls, these thing are central from the outset. She suggests that there is a fundamental difference in perspective in the way men and women look at the world: women seeing it characteristically in terms of *connectedness* (and avoiding isolation), men characteristically placing a high value on *autonomy* (and avoiding intimacy). She saw the distinction as being rooted in the fact that women are usually the primary caregivers of small children, both boys and girls. Girls are thus able to identify more closely with their primary caregiver than boys, so that the boundary between self and others is from the outset less pronounced for girls than it is for boys.

Other researchers (Dyk and Adams, 1987) have proposed that girls follow several different paths. Some, who adopt a more traditionally 'feminine' route, do tend to fuse identity and intimacy in the way that Erikson proposed. Others, who adopt a more stereotypically 'masculine' route (more orientated to career and other such goals) work on identity before intimacy, which is also the pattern with men.

Attitudes to sex

An obvious area of gender difference is in the area of sex. Research shows (if we need to be shown) that boys and girls are still given very different messages about sex. To give an instance: a German study of teenagers asked boys whether their parents would allow them to have a girlfriend to stay overnight. Only 15 per cent thought their parents would forbid this. But 32 per cent of girls thought their parents would forbid them to have a boyfriend overnight (Neubauer and Meltzer, 1989).

The contrasting attitudes of teenage boys and girls to sex were illustrated by a study (whose ethics you may find slightly questionable) done in the USA (Clark, 1990). Male and female research assistants were sent out to ask college students of the opposite sex for a date, in some cases with the added suggestion that this would be followed by sex. Quite a high proportion of students of both sexes agreed to the date. While nearly 50 per cent of the boys agreed to the sex also, not one of the girls did.

A darker part of the same picture is perhaps provided by a finding of one US study in 1977 that 20–25 per cent of female college students reported having been the victim of attempts by male college students they have been out with to force sex on them (Kanin and Parcell, 1977).

The reasons for these differences are complex. It does seem that boys and girls get different messages about sex in adolescence: girls perhaps being given the message that they should not have sex, or should be selective, boys being given – covertly if not explicitly – the message that they must have sex in order to prove themselves. But where do these messages originate and why? This is a broad sociological and political question, and a question about the relation between biology and social structures, which I cannot do justice to here.

For both boys and girls, though, coming to terms with new sexual feelings and new social pressures about sex is, of course, integral to adolescence and a driving force behind the changes that occur during this stage. As one writer observes: 'Adolescents . . . cannot simply add new sexual feeling to an old self' (Cobb, 1995). These new feelings (and, I would add, the new social expectations that go with them) require a new self to be found.

Adolescence is of course the time that some individuals become aware that they are gay, with all the resulting additional pressures of the business of trying to find a new identity for themselves in the adult world, given that even now gay young people will pick up the message from many different sources that being gay is not an acceptable identity, that it is not compatible with being a 'real' man or a 'real' woman – and so on.

Identity, Race and Culture

Establishing an identity in adolescence, can present particular challenges for young people who are members of ethnic minorities. One reason for this is that they may be faced with competing – and very different – models of adult identity. A British Muslim teenager of Pakistani descent has to define her own identity not only in relation to the norms of the majority (white, Western, secular) culture, but also to those of her family's culture, which may subscribe to radically different values in relation to religion, sex, the role of women, marriage, family, authority, and so on. For ethnic minority teenagers, trying to establish a separate identity from their own parents, while at the same time taking pride in their identity as a member of a tradition which their parents represent, clearly is a more complex exercise than for children of the predominant culture.

Not surprisingly, therefore, ethnicity has been found to be a more important identity issue for those from minority cultures than it is for those from the majority culture (Phinney and Alipuria, 1990). And the same study found self-esteem among young people from ethnic minorities in particular to be correlated with their interest in and commitment to their own ethnic identity. Phinney (1989) has also proposed a model of ethnic identity development, based on Marcia's categories which we discussed earlier, in which there is a move from 'unexamined ethnic identity' to 'ethnic identity search' to 'achieved ethnic identity'.

An additional challenge faced by adolescents from minority ethnic groups must be, to varying degrees, racism. There must surely be extra challenges involved in establishing an adult identity in a society if one is given messages that one's membership of that society is not welcome or is in question in some way. And actual opportunities may be restricted by discrimination. Occupational role, for example, is generally accepted as being an important part of adult identity. And, if this is so, then we must acknowledge that the task of establishing such an identity is more difficult if you face racial discrimination in the job market.

Adolescence and Deviance

As we have seen, the stormy and rebellious stereotype of adolescence can be overstated, but nevertheless it is the case that a number of problems come to the fore in adolescence, or peak at that time. Suicide – very rare in childhood – sees an abrupt rise in adolescence, as does drinking and drug use. Unwanted pregnancies become an issue. The onset of schizophrenic psychosis rarely occurs before adolescence. It is a peak time for anorexia nervosa. It is also a peak time for certain categories of crime. There is evidence that criminal careers tend to start in adolescence and that, if you get through adolescence without graduating into crime, then you are much less likely to become criminal later. One American study (Wolfgang et al., 1987) found that of young people who had not offended in adolescence, 81 per cent still had no criminal record at 30. Only 19 per cent had offended as adults, in other words. But of juvenile offenders, 45 per cent were still chronic offenders in adulthood.

There are different ways of looking at the emergence of deviant behaviour in adolescence and researchers have identified and explored links both with socio-economic factors and with familial factors. Barber (1992) suggests that a developing individual needs psychological autonomy on the one hand and behavioural boundaries on the other. Young people whose parents have difficulties with allowing them psychological autonomy will tend to be more likely to withdraw and have internalised problems. Young people whose parents have difficulties with setting behavioural boundaries will tend to have external problems, such as delinquency. This seems to connect with the findings of Adams and colleagues cited earlier that 'identity diffused' young people tend to come from rejecting or detached families; while 'identity foreclosed' young people come from 'conformist child-centred families'.

But then again, if deviant careers begin in adolescence, this is not so different from any other kind of career. You would probably find a large proportion of doctors showed some sort of interest in medicine as adolescents, for example. So the choice of a criminal career (or any other 'deviant' career) may not necessarily differ much in pattern from socially approved career choices. Adolescence is the time when we establish an identity, deviant or otherwise. Indeed, many writers on the subject would say that the choice of a deviant career is in fact an attempt to establish some sort of adult identity. Jessor and Jessor (1979), for example, saw deviant behaviours as 'functional'. They were attempts to obtain some autonomy and control. Reicher and Emler (1986) likewise argued that delinquency can be a positive choice, a way of establishing a reputation and proving oneself. After all, many of the things that adolescents do which worry adults – smoking, drinking, having sex – are in fact attempts to feel more adult by doing the 'things that adults do'. In the absence of other alternatives, criminal activity too may really be a way of achieving the things that adults are supposed to do in the world: developing skills, providing for oneself and others, showing courage. . . .

Some adolescent girls perhaps choose to become pregnant at a very early stage for similar reasons. Being a parent is, after all, a recognised adult role, an adult *identity*, and for some it must seem like the only adult identity that is available.

Adults and Adolescents

The purpose of this book is to provide a tool-kit of ideas about human development for those actually working with people in a practical way. For this reason it seems appropriate to conclude this chapter by bringing together some pointers for adults dealing with adolescents. Before going any further you may want to reflect on your own thoughts on this, using the following activity:

✶ Activity 6.4 ✶

In Activity 6.1 I asked you to reflect on the way that adults dealt with you when you were an adolescent. Drawing on your thoughts then, and on any further thoughts resulting from reading this chapter, what would you suggest might be key points for parents and others working with adolescents as to how to approach this task?

Comments on Activity 6.4

What I have suggested in this chapter is that the primary task of adolescents is to find a new identity for themselves, taking into account new biological and social realities, in order to equip them to enter the adult world. We have seen that this is a difficult task, which can be side-stepped both by foreclosure on the one hand and by diffusion on the other, depending partly on parental styles adopted. The goal of adults working with adolescents is to provide both the support and the freedom needed to press on into moratorium – and then to the stage of identity achievement. You may have suggested, for example, that what is required is a balance between setting clear boundaries when necessary and yet accepting that adolescents need to explore, to have independent views and to find their own way in life. Following are a few more thoughts on this.

What researchers have consistently found is that factors that make for a successful adolescent transition to a confident adult identity, include:

- Parental involvement and connectedness with young people. 'Diffused' young people have been found to score lower on the scale for emotional attachment to parents than other young people and lower on independence (Perosa et al., 1996; Willemsen and Waterman, 1991). Seeking autonomy is not about ending close relationships with parents and family, but actually takes place most effectively within the context of close relationships with both parents.

- Parental acceptance of conflict and of their children's own emotions. 'Absence of conflict has characterised the family environment of foreclosed family relationships', writes Kroger (2000: 108 – citing Perosa et al., 1996; Willemsen and Waterman, 1991) while Bronstein et al. (1993) conclude that where parents accept and support non-hostile expressions of emotions by their children this is linked with their greater ability to cope with the transition from childhood into adolescence.
- Parents' ability to set firm boundaries, without being controlling or unresponsive. As Kroger (2000: 52) puts it, referring to work by Baumrind (1991) 'An authoritative (in which warmth and nurturance are coupled with firm control) rather than an authoritarian or permissive parental style has been associated with greater self-reliance, social responsibility and achievement motivation in later childhood and adolescence.'

Really what this seems to confirm is that the adolescent transition takes place best within the context of a *secure attachment* and that young people with an insecure attachment to their parents or carers (whether that is avoidant or ambivalent) will find it harder to establish a secure adult identity, just as attachment theory would predict. You may recall Bowlby's concept of the *secure base*, which the securely attached child is able to internalise and carry forward as a source of confidence and security in adult life, or Winnicott's idea that it is a parent's 'mirroring' of a child's needs and emotions which allows a child to develop a secure sense of self.

What we would also predict from attachment theory is that those adults who themselves experienced insecure attachments to *their* carers as children, will find it harder to provide this kind of security to others, perhaps particularly during the challenging and testing time of the adolescent transition. Parents who were themselves insecurely attached, for example, may find it difficult to reconcile being firm with being caring and supportive, and may attempt one at the expense of the other, or lurch unpredictably between the two. They may need help with striking a balance.

Chapter Summary

Who Am I Going To Be?

- In this chapter I began by looking at the relationship between biology and culture (a version of the nature/nurture question) with particular reference to puberty, which is both a biological change and a culturally determined one.

continued

- I then looked at another general topic with particular importance to adolescence, the psychology of transitions: the characteristic stages which human beings go through when responding to new circumstances of whatever kind.

- There is a general consensus that achieving an adult *identity* is the major challenge for young people going through adolescence and we looked at the various stages and factors in the development of a sense of identity.

- I looked at the changing nature of adolescents' relationships with their parents and with their peer group. I considered the 'rebellious' stereotype of adolescents and looked at the concept of autonomy and how it relates to identity. I looked at gender differences in relation to identity and at suggestions that the relationship between autonomy, identity and intimacy is different for girls and boys. And I considered the different ways in which boys and girls adjust to themselves as sexual beings.

- I considered the additional identity issues faced by young people who come from ethnic minorities.

- I then considered the increase in crime and other deviant behaviour that occurs in adolescence and how this relates to the discussion about identity.

- Finally I looked at different parenting styles and how the behaviour of adults impacts on the adolescent transition.

Many of these themes will be carried on into the next chapter where we look at early and middle adulthood and the changes and transitions that occur within the long period from the end of adolescence to the beginning of old age.

Suggested Reading

- Coleman, J. and Hendry, L. (1990) *The Nature of Adolescence*, 3rd edn (London: Routledge.)

  (An account of the whole range of issues relating to adolescence, put in a social context.)

- Durkin, K. (1995) *Developmental Social Psychology* (Oxford: Blackwell)

  (Gives a comprehensive overview of research studies dealing with both adolescence and adulthood – as well as other stages of life.)

- Kroger, J. (1996) *Identity in Adolescence* (London: Routledge)
- Kroger, J. (2000) *Identity Development, Adolescence through Adulthood* (London: Sage)
- Sugarman, L. (1986) *Life-Span Development: Concepts, Theories and Interventions* (London: Methuen and Co.)

7 Acting like a Grown-up

Challenges of adulthood

When does adulthood begin? As we saw in the last chapter some cultures view the onset of adolescence itself as the beginning of adulthood. But in Western industrial countries an adolescent is legally still a child and adulthood is a later and distinct stage. In Britain, for example, under the age of 16, a person cannot give legal consent to sex (although in many countries boys and girls may be married at 12 or 13) and it is compulsory to attend school. At 16 it is legal to marry with a parent's consent and to finish schooling, but the right to vote, drive a car and buy alcoholic drinks in a public bar are not granted by the law until the age of 18. In many American states it is illegal to buy alcohol until the age of 21. And, according to Kroger (2000), in New Zealand a person can vote at 18 but cannot enter into a legal contract until the age of 20. But still, roughly speaking, in industrial countries a boy or girl is legally recognised at around the age of 20 to have become an adult. This is a status in the eyes of the law which will last for the rest of an individual's life.

Though adulthood may be a single legal status, one might question whether it makes sense in psychosocial terms to see adults as necessarily having a great deal in common with one another. Does a young woman of

20 have more in common with an 80-year-old than she does with a girl of 15, for instance? And yet, on the other hand, if we try to divide adulthood up, like childhood, into several distinct developmental stages, this too can present problems because there are so many different routes through adult life, even within a single culture.

I am going to treat one part of adult life – old age – as separate by giving it a chapter on its own (Chapter 10). This is because it has a number of characteristics that mark it out as rather distinct, though I don't wish to imply that old people are not also adults. In the present chapter I am going to look at early and middle adulthood – the periods, roughly speaking, from 20 to 40, and from 40 to 60 – which themselves cover a total of forty years or so and the largest part of most people's lives.

What do we Mean by 'Adult'?

When we say 'let's sort this out like adults' or tell someone to 'grow up and stop acting like a child', what do we actually mean? What is the essential quality that marks out adulthood and prompts us to label some adults as childish, or adolescent, when they fail to conform to it? Before going any further, you may like to consider your own views on these questions by using the following activity:

Activity 7.1

With apologies to any younger readers, I am assuming that you are at some stage in your adult life. Looking back on your own experience, or at the experience of others:

At what point in your life did you start to think of yourself as an adult? Why? What had changed from how you were before?

If we divide adult life up into young adulthood, middle adulthood (middle age) and late adulthood (old age), which group do you belong to? How do you view adults in the other two groups? What is different about them and what do you have in common with them, that you do not have in common with adolescents or children?

Comments on Activity 7.1

Many adults would say that they don't actually feel like an adult to themselves. (Probably we all have times when we wish the real grown-ups would come along and solve our problems for us.) Nevertheless, there is a time in life when we stop thinking of ourselves as a boy or a girl and start thinking of ourselves as a man or a woman. This may or may not coincide with the time that the rest of the world starts to see us in that way.

As to the quality that distinguishes adult life from childhood or adolescence, I can't guess what you decided about this, but when I have discussed this with groups of adult students, the word that tends to come up is 'responsibility'.

In the end, all verbal categories are arbitrary. In English we have one word, 'adult', which covers people of a wide range of ages, but clearly there are big differences between the experience and outlook of, say, 80-year-olds with that of 21-year-olds. What does seem to be a common theme, though, is an expectation that, having reached adulthood, a person must take responsibility, for themselves and for others around them. This is reflected in the laws of Western countries, where such things as making legal contracts, giving consent to sex, driving cars, voting, marriage and alcohol consumption tend to be allowed to adults but are restricted or forbidden for younger people. It is also reflected in the use of the words 'childish', 'immature' or 'adolescent' to refer to adults seen as acting irresponsibly. This is not to say that children and young people cannot act very responsibly. In Britain alone, some 50,000 children and teenagers are estimated to be acting as carers for adults with disabilities. It is also the case that, for some adults, it may be a struggle to get society to let them take responsibility for their own lives (for adults with disabilities, or sometimes for elderly people, as we'll discuss further in Chapters 9 and 10).

But we would probably agree that young carers are in danger of 'losing out on childhood' if they are expected to take on too much responsibility, and that it is inappropriate to treat elderly people or disabled people like children. So it does seem to be the case that what marks out adulthood, at least in Western or industrialised societies is the expectation of responsibility.

In this context, it is interesting that the issues which Erikson suggested are paramount in early and middle adulthood (intimacy versus isolation, generativity versus stagnation) are both to do with relationships with others: firstly with other individuals, and then with the wider community.

Stages in Adult Life

There are rather more difficulties involved in trying to divide adult life up into distinct stages than there are in trying to do the same thing with childhood. (And even in the case of childhood, as we've seen in Chapter 4 in relation to Piaget, there are difficulties in trying to define clear and distinct stages.) The following activity may illustrate the problem:

⚒ Activity 7.2 ⚒

What would you say – in your own experience, and on the basis of your observations of others – are the major turning points in adult life? I am thinking here of events that seem to mark the end of one stage in development and the beginning of another.

Comments on Activity 7.2

The sort of events that you might have listed, I would guess, might include some of the following: marriage, divorce, the birth of a child, a child leaving home, career changes, house moves, bereavements, and retirement. You might also have mentioned certain milestone birthdays: 40, most likely, and perhaps also 30, 50 and 60.

You can see that, apart from the birthdays, only retirement is roughly linked to a particular age. (This is one reason why it seems feasible to separate old age into its own chapter in this book, though of course the age of retirement varies within and between societies.) Even if we leave out the unpredictable events such as bereavements, and the (possibly) relatively less important changes such as house moves and career changes, we are still left with parenthood, marriage and divorce as major turning points that can occur at any stage of adult life.

The difficulty with dividing adult life into stages, then, is that we pursue very different routes through adulthood. Some become parents in their twenties and have grown-up children and grandchildren by their forties, for example, while others do not embark on parenthood at all until their forties. And there is no biological event comparable to puberty with which to mark the division of adulthood into separate stages.

Nevertheless, not only Erikson, but others too, have attempted to offer some sort of stage model of adult life, and these models can help to provide a framework for looking at this period of life, if we do not attempt to apply them too rigidly. The branch of psychology which looks at development across the whole of life, and not just childhood, is known as 'life-span psychology'. As Leonie Sugarman (1986: 3) observes, a basic tenet of lifespan psychology has to be that 'developmental trajectories are socially and historically situated . . . [so] it becomes inappropriate to place great emphasis on searching for a developmental theory with predictive capacity across generations'. She might have added that not only do 'developmental trajectories' vary between one society and another and at different times in history, but they even vary substantially from one individual to another at the same time and in the same society. So life-span psychology cannot offer a universal blueprint but it can try and provide ways of making experience more intelligible.

For the purposes of organising the material in this chapter, I am going to look at the early adulthood period as the period up to 40 and the middle adulthood period from 40 onwards. I have done this because, although there are clearly wide variations between individuals, the early forties do represent a turning point of sorts for many people. And there are also some biological changes at this stage, as we'll discuss, though obviously they are not as marked as those of puberty.

Erikson's stages of early and middle adulthood

Erikson saw life stages as marked by a crisis or struggle which the individual must confront – and must resolve if she is to make a successful adaptation to the new demands being made of her. He differs from Freud in seeing this process continuing throughout the life-span, and in placing emphasis on social factors as well as sexual ones. I will discuss his early and middle adult stages separately below. (Table 2.1 on page 43 illustrates how they fit into the whole model).

Levinson's seasons

Daniel Levinson (1978) produced a stage model of adult development in a book called *The Seasons of a Man's Life* (a book which popularised the concept of the 'mid-life crisis', which I will discuss later). Levinson's model originally described transitions for men, not for women (though other researchers have explored its relevance to women too, and Levinson himself is co-author of a follow-up study on women in 1996). It was based on a wide-ranging and multidisciplinary study of forty men drawn from four different occupational groups – industrial workers, business executives, university biologists and novelists – who were interviewed extensively on a variety of topics. Levinson proposed that adult life for men typically unfolded through a series of stable (structure-building) stages and transitional (structure-changing) phases, and suggested that, while each individual was different, a typical man might pass through stages something like those summarised in Figure 7.1.

We will look in more detail at Levinson's stages below.

Young Adulthood

There are a number of features of early adulthood which, if not universal, do apply fairly widely to this age-range in modern industrialised societies:

- It is the peak time for human physical performance in most areas. Muscle tone and physical strength, for example, peak at around the ages of 25–30.
- Most people leave their parental home during this period and set up home separately.
- Most people marry or set up a living-together relationship during this period.
- Careers tend to be established in this period.
- Many people have children during this period.

(Most of these things are of course culture-specific. In traditional, pre-industrial cultures, the idea of a career may be unknown in the Western sense. Marriage and leaving the parental home may take place in a very different way.)

While there is no qualitative change in thinking comparable to those which occur in childhood, there may also be some cognitive changes as adulthood progresses. You will remember from Chapter 4 that Piaget's four

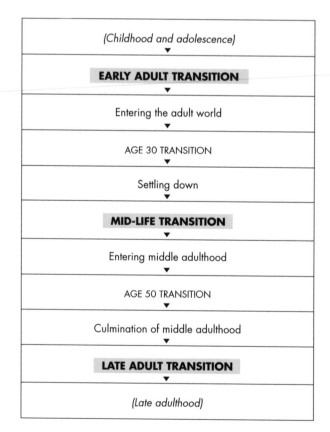

FIGURE 7.1   *Levinson's 'seasons of a man's life' (Levinson et al., 1978)*

stages of cognitive development concluded with the 'formal operations' stage, which was supposed to be attained in adolescence. But some psychologists have suggested that there may be further cognitive changes in adulthood. You can find a more detailed discussion of this in Sugarman (1986: 64–9), but for the present purposes I'll simply note that in adult life there are often specific tasks to perform, at work or at home, so that cognitive development may become more specialised and focused on particular areas.

Intimacy versus isolation – and identity

Erik Erikson saw the challenge of early adulthood as being the establishment of intimate relationships with other adults, following on from (and building on) the earlier adolescent struggle to establish one's own identity:

> The strength acquired at any stage is tested by the necessity to transcend it in such a way that the individual can take chances in the next stage with what was most vulnerably precious in the previous one. Thus the young adult, emerging from the search for and the insistence on identity, is eager and willing to fuse his identity with that of others ... even though [this] may call for significant sacrifices and compromises. (Erikson, 1995: 237)

His suggestion was that only when we are secure and confident in our own identity can we take the risks involved in genuine social and sexual intimacy of a lasting kind. He went on to say that 'the avoidance of such experiences because of a fear of ego loss may lead to a deep sense of isolation and consequent self-absorption'.

Some empirical support for his view that identity achievement is an important prerequisite for successful adult relationships is provided by an extremely long-term study by Kahn et al. (1985) who looked at the progress of a group of male and female college students over an eighteen-year period from late adolescence to their late thirties. The researchers found that those who seemed to have established a strong sense of their own identity during college also had the more enduring marital relationships eighteen years on. Men who seemed to lack a well-developed sense of identity in late adolescence were more likely to remain single into mid-life. But women who had likewise had difficulty in establishing a secure identity in late adolescence had usually gone on to marry, but then typically had had problems in maintaining stable marital relationships.

As this study illustrates, it clearly is not the case that everyone enters adulthood having successfully resolved the issues of adolescence and, as Kroger (2000: 151) comments, 'a number of existing longitudinal studies of adolescent identity development have produced samples with fewer than half of subjects attaining the status of identity achievement by young adulthood'.

This illustrates again that we must be wary of seeing stage theories as a neat progression from one stage to the next. Erikson himself made no such claims for his model and objected to writers who tried to make an *achievement scale* out of his stages, or made the assumption that at each stage 'a goodness is achieved which is impervious to new inner conflicts or to changing conditions' (Erikson, 1995: 247 [footnote]).

The task of identity formation, then, may well continue into adult life, like other tasks associated with earlier stages of development. Probably most people would agree with Erikson that establishing intimate adult relationships is an important theme in early adulthood. What seems to be the case is that this is more likely to be successful when an individual has already developed a confident sense of their own identity. Erikson added that some partnerships amounted to 'an isolation *à deux*, protecting both parties from the necessity to face the next critical development – that of generativity' (1995: 239).

Generativity in early adulthood

Generativity versus stagnation is, in the Eriksonian scheme of themes, associated not with early adulthood but with middle adulthood. However, this presents some problems when we see that, for Erikson, generativity is closely associated not only with involvement in the wider community but with parenthood:

> Generativity, then, is primarily the concern in establishing and guiding the next generation, although there are individuals who, through misfortune or through special and genuine gifts in other directions, do not apply this drive to their own offspring. (Erikson, 1995: 240)

The fact is of course that most people do not wait until middle adulthood to have children. It makes sense that intimacy precedes generativity in psychological development (just as sex precedes childbearing in a purely biological sense), but clearly they are not two distinct stages. Some researchers, however (for example Peterson and Stewart, 1990, who analysed the collected diaries and letters of one woman writer), have found that generativity themes increasingly predominated towards middle adulthood, while intimacy themes were more prominent in early adulthood and then diminished.

Such research is based on Erikson's view of generativity as something associated with participating in society and working towards goals beyond one's own immediate needs, as well as just with the bringing up of children. He made the connection, for example, between generativity and work. (This link is paralleled, as he noted, in Marxist thinking where both 'production' and 'reproduction' are seen as the means by which a particular social system perpetuates itself.)

But again, occupational role is as important to many in early adulthood as it is in middle adulthood. One writer, Vaillant (1977), went so far as to suggest an additional stage of 'career consolidation' between the intimacy versus isolation and the generativity versus stagnation stages. My own suggestion, however, would be that to attempt to make stage theories more elaborate is unlikely to be helpful, since even in a very simple and general form they have real difficulties in capturing the complexity and diversity of adult life. In particular, the concept of 'career' seems to me not only to be very culture-specific but even *class*-specific within a single culture.

Seasons of early adulthood

Levinson's model (1978) was based, as mentioned above, on a survey of an all-male sample covering four different occupational groups. It is interesting, particularly in view of the discussion in the last chapter on gender and intimacy, that Levinson does not seem to have seen intimacy as being the central concern of his male subjects during early adulthood. He and his colleagues suggested that the early adult period (20–40) typically went through the following phases:

- The *Early Adult Transition* is a bridge into the status of adulthood in which separation from the family of origin is a key theme.
- Then follows the phase of *Entering the Adult World* during which the young adult needs (a) to develop life goals (the 'Dream' as Levinson termed it) and (b) to establish a reasonably stable, organised life. It was suggested that too much emphasis on (b) might lead to options being closed too early. In other words, it would result in foreclosure, as when career or marriage choices are made prematurely. Too much emphasis on (a), on the other hand, might lead to a life with a transient, rootless quality (a form of identity diffusion, to return once again to Marcia's terminology as discussed in the previous chapter).
- The *Age Thirty Transition* then followed. Levinson and his colleagues found that most of their male subjects experienced some sense of crisis at this stage: a sense that now was the time to change your life, or it would be too late. It was a time for adjustments to the provisional plan made at the first stage.
- This was followed by the *Settling Down Phase*, a time to settle for a limited number of key choices in life and to invest in them. According to Levinson, there were two tasks at this stage: (a) consolidation and deepening of roots and (b) progression and advancement on the basis of the solid ground achieved.
- Following this phase came the *Mid-Life Transition*, which we'll discuss presently.

Levinson et al. also identified five main tasks in early adulthood. These were:

- *Forming and living out a 'Dream'*. By 'Dream' is meant a kind of vision that a young man has of what his life – and himself as an individual – is going to be about. Many of the men in their sample reported that there was some conflict between following their 'Dream' and meeting external demands on themselves.
- *Forming 'mentor relationships'*. Levinson found that it was typical for men in early adulthood to establish a relationship with someone older, but not old enough to be a parent (half a generation older, perhaps), to provide support and guidance. (I have found that many people, including myself, find this a surprising assertion at first, but are in fact able on reflection to identify important mentor figures in their own lives.) An older sibling can for some people be a mentor figure, or perhaps a more senior work-mate.
- *Forming an occupation*. Levinson saw this as something more than just finding a job, which may be a short-term decision. It is more about what kind of work identity one is going to seek to establish in the longer term.
- *Forming love relationships*. Here is Erikson's intimacy, but given less prominence.
- *Forming mutual friendships*. What Levinson actually found was that a lot of the men his sample did not in fact have close mutual friendships with other men (or non-sexual friendships with women), but that this was felt to be a gap. So he suggested that this was another task of early adulthood.

Levinson's original study was about men and did not pretend to be universally applicable to men and women, but studies of transitions in adult life for women have been carried out (Roberts and Newton, 1987; Levinson and Levinson, 1996) which have suggested that broadly similar patterns exist for women as for men. One difference seems to be that, while Levinson's men tended to formulate their Dream in terms of individual career goals, women – even very career-orientated women – tended more to construct Dreams round family relationships.

Difficulties in young adulthood

One limitation with models such as the ones we have been discussing is that they are essentially descriptive. For those who are working with young adults and who are looking for practical tools to help them in their thinking, this may be frustrating. In rather the same way, a car mechanic seeking guidance on how a particular type of engine works and what is likely to go wrong with it, might not find it very helpful to be given purely descriptive information about how a sample of cars behaved over their working life. However, though there is not and never will be a human equivalent of a car service manual, nevertheless there are many people who are having difficulties with the demands made upon them as young adults, and who need help of one kind or another. So it may be helpful to consider some of the real problems that occur and to consider whether any of the ideas we have discussed so far are of any assistance.

The kinds of problems that young adults may experience, and which come to the attention of professional services of one kind or another, probably fall mainly into the following categories:

- relationship difficulties
- parenting difficulties
- offending
- drug or alcohol problems
- mental health problems
- learning difficulties, physical disabilities or chronic illness (the issues here will be discussed in Chapter 9)
- difficulties in coping as carers of other adults (these difficulties become more common in middle and late adulthood)

To what extent can we look at these problems as being caused by the specific challenges of early adulthood? The following activity is intended to explore this question.

✻ Activity 7.3 ✻

Karl

Suppose you are a community psychiatric nurse working in a drug and alcohol service, and that one of your patients is a man named Karl, aged 24. Karl left school at 16. He has never had a job that lasted longer than a few weeks. He has a long string of criminal offences (burglary, shop-lifting). He is a heroin addict and is believed to have been a heroin user since the age of 17. He has two children by two different partners. Both partners have said that he has been violent towards them. A child protection agency has established that Karl recently left his youngest child (Sarah – aged 6 months) on her own when he went out to obtain drugs. He is attending youth service at the insistence of the child protection agency, who have made it clear that they will take steps to prevent Sarah remaining in Karl's care if he does not address his drug habit. Sarah's mother, Liz, who is 17, is also a drug user.

If you look at Karl specifically as a young adult, within the cultural expectations of young adulthood that now exist, does this illuminate his problem in any way? (In other words: what is there about being a young adult in particular that may contribute to his problem?)

Supposing you yourself were 24 years old, what difference might this make to how you work with Karl? And how about if you were 54?

Comments on Activity 7.3

Clearly drug use, criminal activity and so on are not unique to early adulthood. But it may have struck you that the expectations which are placed on young adults may be a pressure for some which could lead to drug use, offending and so on. Whatever the limitations of models such as that of Levinson, it seems to me that most people would agree that tasks like establishing a 'Dream', forming love relationships, forming an occupation are indeed typically associated with early adulthood – and that not being able to manage them would be seen by many as a kind of failure.

Karl will be aware of these expectations, but in attempting to meet them (to establish intimate relationships, to become a parent, to enter the world of work . . .) he may in effect be trying to run before he can walk. The sense of failure that results may well be a contributory factor in his drug use and violence, even though the end result of such behaviour is to set him even further back.

The reason why these adult demands are so hard for him to meet, may well be because he has entered adult life without the necessary resources that would come from successful resolution of challenges earlier in life. He almost certainly did not achieve a secure identity in his adolescent years. He may very well have never acquired the capacity to trust that comes from having one's needs mirrored in infancy. Perhaps any work with him will need to start by helping him to feel less ashamed of having to learn to walk before he can run?

Additionally, we need to be aware of the social dimension which is sometimes missing from purely psychological models. Karl's problems may well be rooted in his personal history, but they may also be exacerbated by his social environment. For example, he may come from a community where there are few educational or employment opportunities. If Karl was black, racism could have put additional obstacles in the way of his entering the world of employment.

Finally, on the question of your own age and how this might affect your work with Karl. It may have struck you that if you were the same age as Karl, he might find this very threatening, since you have managed to achieve a position of responsibility and authority which has eluded him. This is something you might need to bear in mind. He might well find it less threatening if you were 54 (old enough to be his parent), though other difficulties might arise if he has difficulty relating to his own parents, or if part of his problem is that his own parents have not let him grow up (see Chapter 8 for further discussion of this).

You may also like to consider how your gender and ethnic background, as well as your age, might impact on your work with Karl.

Middle Adulthood

Go into a greetings card shop in Britain (and I daresay in the United States as well) and look under the category 'Special Birthdays'. You'll find special cards for 18th and 21st birthdays, of course, and some for 30, 50 and 60, but probably the next most popular age after 18 and 21 to have its own special cards is 40, which is seen as a turning point of some kind.

Levinson and his colleagues (1978) found in their sample of men that 80 per cent had been through a period of some personal turbulence about the 40 mark. Certainly the 'mid-life crisis' has entered popular mythology as a time when adults (especially, I think, men) go through a sort of second adolescence. As with adolescence itself, however, the reality may be rather less turbulent for most people than the myth. For example Farrell and Rosenberg (1981) found that only 12 per cent of adults questioned felt that they had experienced a crisis at this stage while other commentators have pointed out that *all* stages of life are potentially turbulent. But the 'birthday card test', as one might call it, does seem to indicate that 40 does have some particular significance.

Why should this be? As with all such transitions, there are both biological and social factors, so that the psychological changes that occur can be seen as a complex interaction (differing from one individual to another) between the two. And both at the biological and the social level there are major gender differences, as well as differences between different cultures and societies and different historical periods. (For example as Kroger [2000: 176] points out, in the USA in 1900, only 50 per cent of the population reached the age of 50 and only 5 per cent reached 65.) And at this time of life, perhaps more than any other, there is a huge diversity among the life-paths that are taken by different individuals. As I pointed out earlier, some may only just be embarking on parenthood in middle adulthood, others at the same age may already be grandparents.

But it does seem that there are some common themes, at least in the context of contemporary industrialised society, which do make the early forties into a time of transition which necessitates – as do the changes in adolescence – a reappraisal of one's identity. You may remember that Erikson suggested that, at each transition, we may need to revisit un-resolved issues from earlier stages. If this is the case, it would explain why the mid-life crisis may not only parallel adolescence in some ways, but may also include elements of adolescent behaviour. If you have seen the film *American Beauty* you will remember, for example, how the hero got himself sacked by insulting his boss, bought himself a showy and expensive car, and developed a crush on one of his teenaged daughter's school friends, while his wife threw herself into a torrid affair with a work colleague.

Among the issues commonly encountered at this stage of life are the following:

- *Some physical decline.* This is not sudden, of course, but from this time onwards we are likely to become more aware of things such as greying hair, skin wrinkles and so on, as well as a gradual reduction in physical performance. Athletes, for example, will be past their physical peak. Clearly exercise and a good diet can slow this down, but the very need to be aware of such things may for many people be a change. We are also likely to become more aware of peers who have suffered serious health problems.
- *A decline in fertility for women.* During their forties, women's fertility reduces. What happens at a biological level is that the ovaries start to miss out on hormonal signals from the pituitary gland to release eggs. The pituitary then produces more hormones to compensate. (This is an example, incidentally, of a biological 'feedback loop' – a concept we will return to in the next chapter.) So hormonal balances change until, at around 50 or 55, the ovaries stop functioning and a woman reaches the menopause: the end of the reproductive phase of her life. Research tends to show (see for example Whitbourne, 1996) that the menopause is a transition whose impact has been somewhat exaggerated in popular mythology, but nevertheless it is an important and fundamental change to be adjusted to.
- *Adolescent children and the 'empty nest'.* Parents in middle adulthood and onwards have the experience of their children growing up and leaving home. As we've noted, this can fall at very different times for different people. Parenting an adolescent provides many new challenges and may bring up unresolved issues from the past. The impact of children actually leaving home is also likely to be an event which has very different meanings for different people. The impact on a woman who has devoted herself entirely to childcare and homemaking may be greater, for example, than the impact on men or women whose energies have gone into their career. Having devoted herself to building a 'nest', a fairly major adjustment may be needed on finding the nest empty – although of course this may also free her as never before to take on new challenges.
- *Fewer career options.* Career changes become more difficult, because, qualifications being equal, employers tend to favour suitably qualified

younger men or women to older ones. (One example of this attitude is provided by the information given on its website by the Australian High Commission in London to prospective skilled migrants: 'Please note that before you apply you must have had your skills assessed by the relevant Australian assessing authority . . . and that you must be under 45.')

- *Own parents entering old age.* The older generation getting old and dying becomes a fact of life from this point onwards. It may become necessary to provide care for parents or other elderly relatives. Or the death of parents may result in major reappraisals of one's own position in the world.

- *Letting go of dreams.* A man of 40 once remarked to me that from then on he was going to have to accept that he was just an ordinary person. Certain hopes and dreams that may have provided direction in earlier life may now have to be relinquished. If you haven't become a rock star yet, it is unlikely to happen now. In some cases, the dream to be relinquished may be the dream of becoming a parent.

- *The halfway point.* In modern times, in industrialised societies, one thing that men and women face at around 40 is that they are likely to have reached about the half-way point in their lives. This seems a natural point at which to review commitments made in earlier life and consequently also a time when men and women sometimes decide to end some old commitments, and strike out in new directions. (Levinson found, for example, that this was a common time for divorces and house moves.)

One could perhaps summarise the mid-life transition as a time of life when it becomes necessary to relinquish an identity as 'young'. Clearly, as with all such transitions, there is likely to be an element of grieving and denial involved in this. (You may like to refer back to Figure 6.1, p. 114.) However, if one can let go of young adulthood, new possibilities open up and there are in fact many benefits of this new stage. In Levinson's model, people move on from the Mid-life Transition phase, when their priorities change from re-appraising the past to building a new structure for the rest of their lives. At this point the individual is now in the 'Entering Middle Adulthood' stage.

Many of the new challenges associated with middle adulthood which I listed above have positive as well as negative sides. Children leaving home opens up new possibilities. Letting go of old dreams too can be a release from a pressure, as well as a source of sadness. In some cultures menopause itself is apparently positively welcomed (Neugarten et al., 1963). Even the death of parents, however sad in itself, is quite often experienced as a freeing from old ties, so that some people report, following the death of a parent, that they feel like an adult for the first time.

For many in middle adulthood, accumulated experience is a valuable resource. When recognised by others, this is a source of authority. (Most people in senior positions in politics, business and elsewhere, for example, are in middle adulthood.) Mallory (1984) found that 'identity achievement' increased with age (using Marcia's terminology which I discussed in the last chapter), while 'identity diffusion' decreased. Mallory found that identity achievement was higher for men and women aged 40–47 than for men and women aged 30–37 (for whom 'foreclosure' ratings were higher). This would suggest that, on average, the over-40s were more secure in their own identity than young adults.

Generativity

Summing up the concerns raised by adults aged 40–65 whom she interviewed, Jane Kroger writes:

> Although issues directly related to biological changes were not frequently mentioned, change in procreational and sexual capacities were clearly on the minds of some participants. However of greater interest for most seemed to be a new psychological awareness of their own mortality and how meaningfully to fill whatever time there was that remained for them. In addition, the wish to contribute to the welfare of the general community surfaced in ways not described by previous age groups. . . . And . . . community recognition of individual contributions was highly valued by many in the process of mid-life self-definition. (Kroger, 2000: 168)

Erikson's concept of generativity is quite difficult to pin down, and his proposal to link it to middle adulthood seems inappropriate when he also links the idea to parenthood. Nevertheless Kroger's comments perhaps illustrate a certain quality that is typical of middle adulthood (though not unique to it), in which there is a concern to contribute to – and be recognised by – the wider community.

Difficulties in middle adulthood

As I said earlier in relation to young adulthood, the ideas we have been discussing are quite descriptive and may seem to be of limited use when it comes to practical questions. Again, the best way of testing them may perhaps be to look at some examples of difficulties that might be faced in middle adulthood and consider how to approach them.

Of course the difficulties faced by adults in their middle years can come into all the same categories as the younger adults we discussed earlier, but the most common problems will change: specifically, adults in this age-range are more likely to be having difficulties with adolescent children, and far more likely to be caring for elderly relatives. Loss of career through redundancy, ill health or early retirement is also more likely in middle adulthood.

The following activity looks at two case examples of adults in their middle years:

✖ Activity 7.4 ✖

What themes do you notice in the following two cases?

- Jill (50) – Coming from a large African-Caribbean family, Jill incurred the anger of both her parents as a young woman when she chose not to start a family, in order to pursue a career in the Civil Service, her ambition being to become the first black woman to head a government department. She works extremely hard, and very long hours, and has always had a fairly limited personal life. As a result of her ability and efforts, she has risen to a senior post in the Department of Health, overcoming both sexist and racist obstacles. However, a few months ago she had a heart attack and had to take extended sick leave, with the possibility that she would not be able to return to her old job. She became very depressed during her enforced idleness and made an attempt on her own life. She is now in hospital being treated for depression.

- Sue (46) – The youngest of four, and the only girl, in a suburban white British family, Sue grew up with parents who pushed their sons to achieve, and seemed to value their daughter's achievements very little. Sue didn't leave home until the age of 24 when she married an older man and became a housewife and mother. She is proud of her two confident, well-adjusted children, both of whom have now left home. She has recently started a job as a learning support assistant in a local school, which she very much enjoys. But her mother has now died and her three brothers now expect Sue give up her part-time job to care for her father, pointing out that all three of them are the main breadwinners for their families, while Sue's income is small and she is supported financially by her husband. She agrees with them about her duty, but the prospect fills her with such dread that she has become ill.

Comments on Activity 7.4

Loss of a career and caring for older parents are both themes which become more common in middle adulthood. For both women, work was important to their identity and the loss of work – or the threat of it – was a blow. For both women, these typically middle-adulthood challenges may also interact with painful issues from earlier stages of life, as well as with gender and perhaps cultural issues.

In Jill's case, it would appear that she had to cut herself off from her family of origin to some extent in order to pursue her career. It is also possible that she may have had some regrets about not having children, but felt she had to make a choice between career and children (it would be more unusual for a man to feel that he had to make such a choice). Having made significant sacrifices in order to invest in her career, the possible loss of it must be a major blow. She has built an identity for herself around her career, rather than around personal relationships . On what is she now going to build a sense of meaning and purpose in her life?

Sue's family background seems to have resulted in her settling for 'identity foreclosure'. She never established herself as an independent adult as a young woman and perhaps only managed to escape the parental home by accepting a new parental figure in her much older husband. However she has gained some confidence from doing a good job as a parent and the 'empty nest' has for her been an opportunity to spread her wings and to begin to seek an identity of her own. This is now being placed under threat by the pressure from her brothers to once again subordinate her own needs to those of other people. This has brought up old struggles, never fully resolved, from her earlier years.

Many adults in middle years, as well as younger adults, will have had difficulties in dealing with the challenges of earlier stages, and this may make it more difficult to deal with the new challenges that they now face. And many, however well they faced previous challenges in their lives, will have extra challenges piled on them which they had not expected and which will force them to radically revise their expectations. In addition, the two things may come together: new challenges and old issues. Old unresolved issues may be brought to a head in middle adulthood by a new crisis that was unexpected but is nevertheless typical of middle adulthood: difficulties with adolescent children, loss of a valued career, the needs of ageing parents. This kind of interaction between old issues and new events will be explored further in the next chapter, when we look at family life-cycles.

New Challenges, Unfinished Business, Limited Opportunities

Stage models of development tend to turn out to be too simplistic – or perhaps too 'neat' – when applied to the real world. This was true in the case of Piaget's model of cognitive development. And it seems to me that Erikson's stages of adult life are (like Piaget's stages) a useful starting point for discussion but do not hold up if we attempt to apply them in too literal a fashion. The kind of identity development which Erikson consigned to adolescence does in fact continue into adult life, for instance, 'generativity' is clearly already an issue in early adulthood and not just in middle adulthood.

But I would suggest that what is most useful about stage theories is the insight that new developmental tasks become progressively more difficult if other developmental tasks have not yet been completed. Intimacy is more difficult if we have not established a secure sense of identity. It is perhaps harder to make a wider contribution to the community (generativity) if we have not yet mastered intimacy. This basic idea is common to all theoretical models in the psychodynamic tradition. In attachment theory, for example, establishing a secure base is seen as the necessary precursor to confident exploration of the world.

Thus, if we see life as throwing up new challenges (both predictable and unpredictable) at different stages, our ability to deal with them successfully will depend not only on the nature of the challenge itself but on the 'baggage' or 'unfinished business' we carry from earlier challenges. If we fail to master a new challenge, or find some way of side-stepping it rather than fully confronting it, then it in its turn will become part of the unfinished business which we carry forward into the future. If we succeed in meeting a new challenge, on the other hand, then this will equip us with new skills that will help us deal with other challenges in the future.

In addition to new challenges and unfinished business from the past, however, there is a third factor which, it seems to me, is often underestimated. This is *opportunity*. Life, after all, is rather like a Monopoly game in which the rules have been changed so that some players start with thousands and others start with almost nothing. Depending on your social class, your ethnic background, your gender and where you were born, there are huge variations in the options that are available. Building a secure adult identity presents very different challenges for those for whom there are no realistic prospects of any kind of 'career'. A child or a sick relative requiring constant personal care is a very different prospect for those who can afford to hire outside help than it is for those who have little choice but to take it all on themselves.

So I would suggest that as individuals our progress through life will be shaped by three distinct sets of factors:

- the nature of the challenges that we face
- the legacy of the past
- the opportunities available

The first of these three is often the only one that is visible. This means that, when working with people in difficulties, we have to bear in mind the other two. They may in reality, like the submerged part of an iceberg, be the largest part of the problem. We also have to bear in mind that present challenges, and how they are dealt with, will in turn become part of the legacy that a person carries into the future. This surely means that it is important not to try and solve other people's problems for them, but to try and help them resolve problems for themselves.

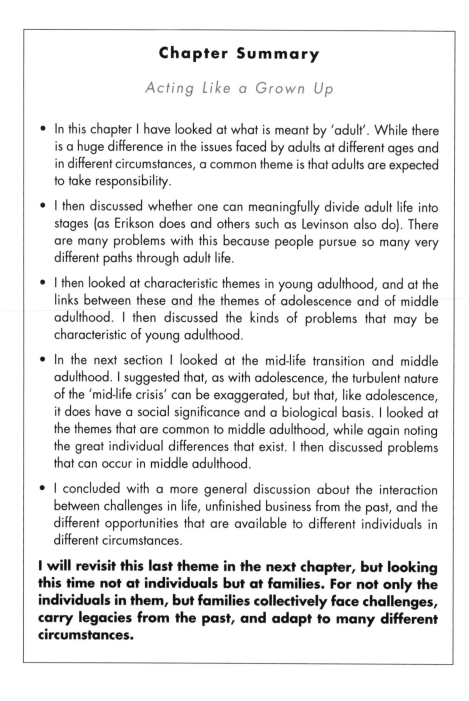

Chapter Summary

Acting Like a Grown Up

- In this chapter I have looked at what is meant by 'adult'. While there is a huge difference in the issues faced by adults at different ages and in different circumstances, a common theme is that adults are expected to take responsibility.

- I then discussed whether one can meaningfully divide adult life into stages (as Erikson does and others such as Levinson also do). There are many problems with this because people pursue so many very different paths through adult life.

- I then looked at characteristic themes in young adulthood, and at the links between these and the themes of adolescence and of middle adulthood. I then discussed the kinds of problems that may be characteristic of young adulthood.

- In the next section I looked at the mid-life transition and middle adulthood. I suggested that, as with adolescence, the turbulent nature of the 'mid-life crisis' can be exaggerated, but that, like adolescence, it does have a social significance and a biological basis. I looked at the themes that are common to middle adulthood, while again noting the great individual differences that exist. I then discussed problems that can occur in middle adulthood.

- I concluded with a more general discussion about the interaction between challenges in life, unfinished business from the past, and the different opportunities that are available to different individuals in different circumstances.

I will revisit this last theme in the next chapter, but looking this time not at individuals but at families. For not only the individuals in them, but families collectively face challenges, carry legacies from the past, and adapt to many different circumstances.

Suggested Reading

- Durkin, K. (1995) *Developmental Social Psychology* (Oxford: Blackwell)

  (He gives a very comprehensive overview of research studies dealing with adulthood.)

- Kroger, J. (2000) *Identity Development, Adolescence through Adulthood* (London: Sage)
- Levinson, D.J. (1978) *The Seasons of a Man's Life* (New York: Ballantine)

  (Looks at the transitions within adulthood, including the 'mid-life crisis'.)

- Sugarman, L. (1986) *Life-Span Development: Concepts, Theories and Interventions* (London: Methuen & Co)

8   No One is an Island

Family systems and their life-cycle

Human beings do not develop in isolation. Our growth is shaped in large measure by others around us and by the society of which we are part. Attachments in childhood, for example, can have far-reaching effects on the way we relate to others in adult life. The actual physical growth of children can be stunted in some instances by severe emotional neglect. In Chapter 10, I will discuss evidence that old people's physical health can be directly affected by the extent to which others let them have control over their own lives. As the seventeenth-century poet John Donne famously put it:

> No man is an *Iland*, intire of it selfe; every man is a piece of the *Continent*, a part of the *maine* . . .
>
> (Donne, in Potter and Simpson, 1959–62)

People form parts of larger systems, pieces of a continent. It is within that context that we become the individuals who we are.

What I haven't dealt with so far, though, is the fact that these larger systems themselves are subject to growth and change: relationships change, families change, communities and societies change. So in this chapter I am going to look at the growth and development of systems –

specifically at *family* systems – and at how one can view the growth and development of families as entities in themselves rather than just looking at the growth and development of the individuals within a family.

I have included this chapter because this seems to provide a useful perspective on child development, and a perspective which is necessary in any account of psycho*social* development. But in fact systems theory rarely seems to be mentioned in the developmental literature to date. Accounts of systems theory and its application to families are found mainly in the family therapy literature, which is naturally orientated more towards the practical task of working with troubled families than towards advancing knowledge of psychosocial development. There are many different approaches within the family therapy literature and there is no single 'founding father' or 'founding mother', as with some of the other theoretical models we have discussed, though Gregory Bateson (see Bateson, 1973) is described by one recent author as 'arguably the most important early theorist' (Barnes, 1998: 18).

Systems Theory

Derived originally from the work of Ludwig von Bertalanffy (1971), systems theory comes via mathematics, biology and cybernetics and deals with the way that parts come together in larger wholes. A system is a complex of interacting elements. An example of a very simple system is a room with a heating system controlled by a thermostat. The elements within this system – the room, the heating system and the thermostat – are linked together in a circular relationship: the temperature of the room affects the thermostat, the thermostat switches the heating on or off, the heating affects the temperature in the room and so on, as is illustrated in Figure 8.1.

Our bodies are systems like this. They are far more complicated, of course, consisting not just of three elements but of a large number of organs and tissues but, as in the example of the room and the thermostatically controlled heating, the different elements interact together. Heart-rate and rate of breathing, for example, are affected by the level of oxygen in the blood, and the level of oxygen in the blood is in turn affected by heart-rate and rate of breathing.

If you look at it on a smaller scale, each organ is a system made up of a large number of cells. And if you look inside a cell, that itself is a system of interacting parts. Going to the other extreme, human beings are themselves part of larger interlocking and overlapping systems; families, communities, organisations, countries, the biosphere.

Systems can be closed or open. A closed system is one which does not interact at all with the surrounding world. In open systems there is an

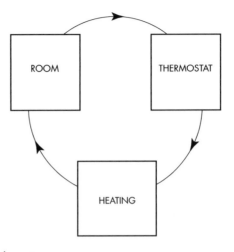

FIGURE 8.1 *A simple system*

interaction with the outside world across the boundary of the system. A system has to have some sort of boundary to exist as something separate from its surroundings, but that boundary may be permeable.

Living systems characteristically are open systems. They have a semi-permeable boundary but manage to maintain some sort of equilibrium with the outside world. The amoeba, for example, is a single-celled organism which has a semi-permeable membrane round it. Without the membrane, the contents of the amoeba would simply dissolve into the surrounding water, but if the membrane was completely impermeable the amoeba would not be able to take in the water, nutrients and oxygen that it needs, or get rid of waste products.

A feature of systems in general is circularity. The sequence of cause and effect does not just go in one direction. In my thermostat example, one could say that the thermostat controls the temperature in the room (because it is the thermostat that turns the heating on and off), but it would be equally true to say that it is the temperature in the room that controls the thermostat (because the thermostat is a mechanism that responds to changes in temperature). The relationship between thermostat and room in this example is what is called a negative feedback loop. That is to say: an increase in temperature results in the heating being switched off, which then of course leads to the temperature dropping down again. A positive feedback loop, on the other hand, would exist if the thermostat was wrongly wired up so that an increase in temperature had the effect of turning the heating up. You can see that a positive loop would result in the room getting hotter and hotter indefinitely, while a negative feedback loop has the effect of maintaining temperature at a more or less constant level. This is of course the purpose of a thermostat – the word thermostat comes from the Greek words for 'heat' and 'standing'.

Negative feedback loops are characteristic of living things, which try and maintain a state of equilibrium (we feel hungry, we eat; we stop feeling hungry, we stop eating) – or homeostasis as it is known, from the Greek for 'same' and 'standing'. Indeed our bodies have their own remarkably efficient thermostatic mechanisms which, unless we are ill, keeps our blood within half a degree or so of 37° C, the optimum temperature for our particular body chemistry, in summer or winter alike.

Systems and Families

But what does all this have to do with families? Well, as I've said, not only is every individual a biological system, made up of numerous sub-systems, but we ourselves participate in larger systems. A group of people sharing the same environment interact and influence one another in many different ways. And, as Franklin and Warren write:

> if there is . . . a sufficient level of contact between them, a global structure emerges that influences each of the actors in ways that cannot simply be explained by the impact of one individual on another; the whole is greater than the sum of the parts and cannot be explained completely by breaking it down into parts. . . . Thus a system is born. (Franklin and Warren, 1999: 401)

This applies to all kinds of groups of people. Most of us are familiar with the way that a sporting team or a team at work gradually 'gels together' into some kind of an entity, but of course the members of families in particular typically have a high level of contact over a long period of time. You may well have experienced the powerful and complex feelings, positive, negative, or both at once, that are set in train when the members of a family reunite at an occasion such as a wedding or a Christmas dinner, and the way that old patterns of behaviour, and old rivalries and alliances, reassert themselves, even after many years. Here, surely, is an entity that is greater than the sum of its parts.

To look at this entity which we call a family, and to consider it as a system, has the following implications, which have been found useful in practice in therapeutic work with families:

- If families are systems, they have properties which are more than the sum of their parts. So we cannot fully understand the behaviour of an individual in isolation, without looking at the system of which she is part.
- If they are systems, families will operate to try and maintain a reasonably steady state. So if a certain member of the family is habitually behaving in a certain way, this behaviour is likely to be serving the purpose of maintaining a steady state, even if the family members themselves do not recognise this.

- Communication and feedback between the parts of the system (that is, the members of the family) are an important part of the functioning of the system. So that, if we want to understand the family, we have to look at the way members communicate with one another, and not just at each individual in isolation.
- If you want to understand the behaviour of an individual in the family, you usually understand them better as examples of *circular causality*, rather than *linear causality* – that is to say: the behaviour of an individual is not simply the cause of other events in the family, or simply the effect, but is linked to the rest of the family in a feedback loop. As with the thermostat and the temperature of a room: each one both controls and is controlled by the other.
- All systems are made up of smaller systems and are themselves part of larger systems.

Proponents of a systems perspective argue that when we think about human problems and try to solve them, we often fail to bring about change because we focus too much on individuals and not enough on the system of which they are part. A probation officer, for example, might work very hard with a young offender, and feel that she was making real inroads with him. But then, for no obvious reason, he seemingly throws it all away and goes out and offends again. There could be many reasons for this, of course, but one possibility is that the probation officer has neglected to look at the family context in which the offender is operating. Perhaps the family is always criticising him and telling him he is no good, regardless of whether he offends or not. Perhaps it serves some purpose for the rest of his family to see this young man as an incurable ne'er-do-well, so in the end he feels he may as well offend as not. Or perhaps there is a culture within the family that a man must commit crimes to prove his manhood.

To return to the analogy of the thermostat: if you were to come into my house and find it rather cold, you might notice a small fireplace in the front room and a few bits of wood – and decide to light a fire. You might possibly be puzzled to find after a time that, far from warming up, the house as a whole was colder than ever. The reason for this is that there is a thermostat in my front room and if you light a fire in there, the thermostat will turn off the central heating for the rest of the house. In order to heat up the house as a whole, you'd need to know about the thermostat and know how to adjust it. Just stoking up the fire without adjusting the thermostat will only generate a local heat, which is not enough to offset the loss of the central heating over all the rest of the house.

To give another analogy: if a group of people are playing poker and one player starts playing rummy, he won't get very far. The rest of the group will stop him from carrying on, or they will evict him from the game. If he wants to play rummy he needs to persuade the rest of the group to play a different game.

Social workers, marriage counsellors and others who deal with family problems will often find that a particular member of a family – often a child – is identified as 'the problem'. But if they look at it more closely from a systems perspective they may well find that the problem lies in the whole group, and that the person identified as the problem may actually be performing a *helpful* role for the group, either by providing some kind of safety valve or by attracting outside help. The other family members may complain about this person's behaviour, but it may still turn out that in some way the family *need* this behaviour to continue.

If you are not accustomed to thinking about systems, this can seem quite a puzzling idea. The following activity may help to clarify it:

⚒ Activity 8.1 ⚒

In an otherwise apparently orderly family one child ('Ricky') is presenting serious behaviour problems (he is stealing, perhaps, or is soiling himself, or perhaps he is refusing school). As a result the father, who normally works very long hours, is having to take time out from work just to help the mother to cope, even though this means a significant loss of income.

Everyone else in the family sees Ricky as 'the problem' – and everyone is extremely angry with him – but what purpose may Ricky's behaviour serve for the whole system?

Comments on Activity 8.1

You probably noticed that one effect of Ricky's behaviour has been to bring his father home more. Children's problem behaviours frequently seem to serve some function for the marital relationship of their parents. Difficult behaviour can bring together parents who are drifting apart by giving them a task which they have to work on together. Or, by drawing their anger on to himself, a child can prevent them from taking it out on one another. If you have a partner and are a parent, you may well have noticed for yourself how one of your children becomes more demanding when you and your partner are not getting on.

Having his parents so angry and rejecting with him cannot be pleasant for Ricky, but it may well be less scary for him than having them angry and rejecting of each other. It may well be less scary for the parents and the rest of the family too.

If you are involved in social work or some other profession which involves working with families having problems, you will doubtless have noticed how preoccupied people often seem to be with the question of 'whose fault is it?' or 'who started it?' or 'who is to blame?' Indeed you may have noticed this within your own family or your own personal relationships. You may also have noticed that arguing about this rarely, if ever, seems to result in a solution.

From a systems perspective these are simply the wrong questions. They are *linear* questions, applied incorrectly to *circular* systems, which means that arguing about them is a bit like arguing about which came first, the chicken or the egg (or about whether the thermostat controls the room temperature or vice versa.) It is the whole system that needs to be looked at if change is going to come about.

The Family Life-Cycle

If we look at family systems rather than at individuals, not only do we need to jettison linear explanations for behaviour in favour of circular ones, we must also set aside linear models of development in favour of cyclical ones. By linear models I mean models such as that of Erikson which sets out life in ascending stages beginning with birth and ending with death. Individuals *are* born and grow older and die in that order but a family is not born and does not die. Death and birth are events which happen to individuals within the family, and they are events to which other individuals within the family must adapt and adjust, but they are not events (except in catastrophic circumstances) which happen to the system as a whole.

Nor do they happen in a specific order. In an individual life, birth necessarily precedes death. But in a family death and birth both precede and follow one another. Indeed it is perfectly possible for a family to be dealing simultaneously with the death of one of its members and the birth of another, and it is a certainty that any family will be dealing with several of Erikson's stages all at the same time. It is commonplace, for example, for a family to be dealing with the transitions involved in adolescence, those involved in mid-life and those involved in the onset of old age, because parents are typically at the mid-life stage when their children reach adolescence, and grandparents are typically at or past retirement age.

When we look at families as systems, growth and development are a cycle and not a line. In fact even to describe them as a *cycle* is a simplification, because events do not follow one another round and round in order like the cycle of the four seasons. In a family, winter, spring, summer and autumn may all be happening at the same time.

Betty Carter and Monica McGoldrick (1989) have produced an outline of the family life-cycle seen from a systems perspective which I will now describe in order to show how this approach differs from any that we have discussed so far. Carter and McGoldrick start from the assumption that a family is usually at least a three-generation system and nowadays often a four-generation one and that at any point in time different members of the system will be dealing with different challenges, as we have just discussed, which in turn become challenges for the system as a whole. And they suggest that a family is also somewhat unusual among human groupings in that people can join it in a variety of ways (birth, marriage, adoption) but they can't really leave it except by death. Attempts by family members to cut themselves off from the rest of the family do not really constitute leaving the family, in their view, as we will see. Even if we cut ourselves off from our family of origin we still carry the legacy of that family inside us. They suggest, in addition, that families, and individuals within them, can be subjected both to 'horizontal stressors' and 'vertical stressors'.

Stressors and system levels

Horizontal stressors are stress factors which come with the passage of time. This includes both *predictable* events – like the birth of a child or the onset of adolescence – and *unpredictable* events, like an illness, or redundancy, or divorce, or the discovery that a child has a disability.

'Vertical stressors' are a sort of inheritance that is transmitted down through the generations of a family. Some families have a history of mental health problems, some are unable to talk about sex, some are preoccupied with educational achievement, some have strong religious or political allegiances stretching back for many generations which individual family members cannot easily challenge, some have a pattern of absent fathers, or of powerful matriarchs, or of difficulties in coping with adolescence. The possibilities are perhaps as numerous as families themselves.

This division into 'horizontal stressors' and 'vertical stressors' is really the same distinction I made in the last chapter between new challenges (horizontal) and the legacy of the past or 'unfinished business' (vertical). But *with this important difference*: Carter and McGoldrick envisage that the issues from the past which make up the vertical stressors, are not just issues from an individual's own past. They suggest that these unresolved issues may be carried by a family, sometimes for many generations. And the challenges in the present likewise do not belong to one individual alone, but to the whole system. Adolescence, to give an obvious example, is not just a challenge for the individual concerned, but for her parents, and perhaps for siblings and grandparents as well.

But, as well as these life-cycle events and inherited patterns, people have to deal with their social circumstances: the family is part of wider systems – it is part of a community, a social class, a culture – and will have to deal with different issues, depending on their particular circumstances. People from poor communities, or from disadvantaged minorities, may have additional challenges to deal with which are not to do either with specific events (horizontal stressors) or with their family history (vertical stressors). These issues which arise from other 'system levels' correspond to 'opportunities available' in the three-part distinction I made at the end of the last chapter between 'new challenges', 'the legacy of the past' and 'opportunities available'.

'The family' is itself, of course, a particular system level. Just as it is part of wider systems, so within a family there are smaller systems, namely individuals, who have of course been the system level under discussion for most of this book so far. If you look back at Freud's idea of the ego as being assailed on the one hand by real events and on the other by the demands and constraints of the superego, you will see that we could equally well describe this as the interaction of horizontal and vertical stressors at the individual system level.

Figure 8.2, based on an illustration in Carter and McGoldrick's book, illustrates the interaction between horizontal stressors, vertical stressors and system levels.

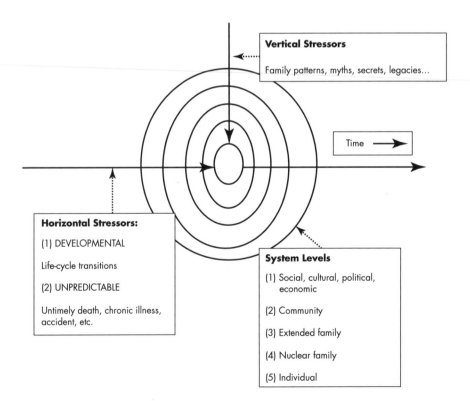

FIGURE 8.2 *Vertical and horizontal stressors (from Carter and McGoldrick, 1989)*

Now, according to this model, the *real* stress points in a family's life come when a horizontal stressor interacts with a vertical one. There is then, these writers argue, a 'quantum leap' in the level of anxiety in the system.

For example:

- If you come from a family with a history of anxious or ambivalent parenting, the birth of a child will produce heightened anxiety, far above the level of anxiety which this new event would produce in other families.
- If you come from a family where sexual abuse occurred, there are likely to be anxieties through the generations about physical contact and sex – even assuming that sexual abuse itself doesn't recur through the generations (which, sadly, it frequently does).
- If your childhood experience was that teenagers were put into care or sent to boarding school, then, as your own children approach adolescence, there is likely to be heightened anxiety in the family about this.
- If you come from a family where great store was placed on intellectual achievement, then there will be high anxiety around exams and so on. The discovery that a child has learning difficulties might cause particular problems for such a family.

Often the same theme will emerge in different ways in different generations. A family with problems around the issue of *control* may in one generation be obsessively controlling, and in the next generation have problems with setting boundaries at all. Both these patterns, though apparently opposite, are problems with control. For example, one may sometimes encounter drug addicts who have had great difficulty in controlling their habit or any other aspect of their lives, whose parents are very highly controlled and controlling. While the drug-using child and the controlling parent may seem poles apart, they are both exhibiting difficulties around the question of control.

Probably the best way to look at this question of horizontal and vertical stressors is to consider how they might work in practice. The following activity may help with this:

Activity 8.2

Looking at your own family of origin, can you think of any examples of vertical stressors that seem to have been passed down the generations? You may be able to identify these stressors by looking at the kinds of events that your family seems to find particularly difficult, as these would be the occasions when horizontal and vertical stressors interact.

> Or consider the following case example and ask yourelf what horizontal and vertical stressors are interacting here?
>
> Janice is 42. As a child, she was abused by her stepfather, sexually and physically. Her mother could not cope with her and at the age of 13, she entered the care system. She had several moves within the care system and suffered further abuse there at the hands of a male residential social worker.
>
> She is now a single mother of three sons, each by a different father.
>
> The two older sons are both teenagers and are now completely out of her control. They are not attending school. They are both offending regularly and using drugs. They come and go from the house as they please. They are aggressive and abusive to their mother if challenged.
>
> Janice has asked for professional help with the two boys: she says she has lost it completely with them and she thinks they should be in care.

Comments on Activity 8.2

I don't know what vertical stressors you noticed in your own family but in Janice's case, I would suggest that there may be vertical stressors do to with:

- Adolescence. Janice's mother could not cope with her as an adolescent, and she has no confidence in her own ability to cope with her teenage sons. Further exploration might well reveal that a history of children being evicted from the family at adolescence goes back for several generations. It is not hard to imagine that the two boys in turn will find it hard to cope assertively with their own adolescent children when they themselves become parents.
- Male sexuality and aggression. Janice was abused by her stepfather and by a male worker in care. She has not had a stable relationship with a man. She is finding it hard to cope with her sons now they have reached the age of sexual maturity. Again, the history of abusive men might well turn out to have gone back further into the past. And again it is easy to imagine that the two boys will grow up to become men who are abusive to women and girls.

Changing patterns

Carter and McGoldrick have produced a stage model based on a two-parent American family but they emphasise that this is not intended as a blueprint for all families and that in fact the American family itself has changed considerably in modern times. Some of those changes are:

- The idea of a phase of independent adulthood (between leaving the family of childhood and forming a new family) is a relatively new concept, particularly for women who in many societies today – and in our own society until recent times – were formally handed over from father to husband without any independent stage in between.
- The longer life-span means that the stage of retirement and the 'empty nest' may be a third of a person's life, or more.
- Marrying and having children is far from universal. Carter and McGoldrick cited figures which predicted that of women in the USA in 1989 12 per cent would not marry, 25 per cent would never have children, 50 per cent would enter marriages that would end in divorce, and 20 per cent would go through two divorces.

Stages in Family Life

We've looked at several stage models in this book. What is distinctive about this one is the fact that each developmental stage is seen as embracing the whole family, and posing tasks for the whole family – and this is what I suggest you focus in on as much as the details of the model (which, as the authors themselves acknowledge, will vary according to cultural norms and so on). In their terminology a successful transition into a new phase normally requires not only a 'first-order' change, but a 'second-order' change: a rearrangement of the whole system itself. (One person can't unilaterally change the rules of a game of cards – any rule change has to be negotiated between all the players.)

The following are some of the stages. I am purposely not summarising them in a chart as I did with the stage models of Erikson, Piaget or Levinson (although Carter and McGoldrick do so) because I want to emphasise that this model is not a linear one. And I have not presented all the stages in the same order as Carter and McGoldrick present them. Like chickens and eggs, the process has no beginning and no end, and any number of stages can be taking place at the same time.

Young single adults leaving home

The young adult needs to separate from the family of origin without, as Carter and McGoldrick put it, 'fleeing to a substitute emotional refuge' (which would be a kind of foreclosure, to go back to Marcia's terminology which we discussed in Chapter 6). If they do the latter they will never give themselves a chance to sort out emotionally what they are going to take along from their family of origin, and will miss the chance to reduce the number of 'vertical stressors' they carry along with them.

Successful change involves a transition for the whole family. Not only does the young adult have to revise his or her role, but the parents and grandparents will need to redefine theirs in relation to the young adult and to the other parts of their lives. Many families find this hard. Some parents encourage the young person to remain dependent. Some young people do indeed remain dependent while others rebel by breaking off contact with their family of origin, thus denying themselves the possibility of genuinely renegotiating the relationship, so they may remain stuck with a sort of adolescent attitude towards their parents.

A genuine transition to adult status requires that both the young adult *and* the parents make a transition to a new mutually respectful form of relating in which young adults and their parents appreciate each other for what they are, rather than trying to make them into what they are not. The typical problem for young women at this stage is short-circuiting their definition of themselves in favour of finding a partner. The typical problem for men is going for a pseudo-independent identity based on work.

Sometimes young adults find it difficult to leave the parental home at all. To understand the reasons for this fully we'd need to see what was going on for the other family members, as well as for the young person and the parents. It may be that there is a general anxiety throughout the system about the parental marriage after the 'nest is empty', and the young person staying at home may well be the system's attempt to shore this up. We might find, for instance, that there is pressure of various kinds from parents and from older siblings, which makes it difficult for the youngest to leave home.

It may be useful to measure these ideas against your own experience:

✂ Activity 8.3 ✂

How did you yourself negotiate your own departure from your parental home? (If you are still living with your parents, ask yourself how you might deal with this transition in the future.)

How were you helped or hindered by your parents and other members of your family? Looking back on it, how easy did you make it for them to change their role in relation to you?

What 'vertical stressors' existed/exist in your family that might have added to the difficulties of this particular transition?

What aspects did you/will you/would you find difficult as a parent dealing with your own children making this transition?

Comments on Activity 8.3

Everyone's experience will of course be different, but the sort of stressors that exist in some families might be:

- a history of parental marriages breaking down following the departure of children;
- a history of depression on the part of one or both parents, following the departure of children;
- a history of young adults entering into unhappy relationships soon after departure from home.

Marriage and divorce

Marriage is usually seen as the joining of two individuals but if we look at families as systems then marriage involves changing two entire systems which overlap, to develop a third system.

Carter and McGoldrick go as far as to maintain that a failure to renegotiate this new family status is the main cause of marital problems, even though this may not be recognised by those involved, who may be more likely to focus on problems around money, sex, chores and so on, which are the normal currency of marital discord. (Although I am speaking of marriage, the same kinds of issues also apply to couples who live together but choose not to marry.) The following are some illustrations:

- In-laws may be too intrusive and the new couple may be afraid to set limits (that is: to create a boundary around their own sub-system). For example, if a mother expects to have the same relationship with her son as she had when he was living at home, and he is afraid to hurt her feelings by resisting, this may create difficulties in his relationship with his wife. Solving the problem may involve not only husband and wife changing their behaviour, but his mother accepting that she now has a different role.
- On the other hand, the new couple may have difficulty relating with the extended family system as a married couple, and may cut themselves off as an isolated twosome. This could come about, for example, as a result of the older generation being too intrusive and refusing to deal with the couple as autonomous adults. Their attempted solution may cut them off from support which they actually still need and may create difficulties between them. A real solution might involve not only the two of them but also the wider family making, or accepting, changes.
- One or both of the members of the couple may still be too enmeshed in their family of origin to be able to create a real new system or to accept the implications of the new arrangement. For example, if a married man

continued to spend much of his free time with his mother, and regarded his mother as his first point of contact when he wanted to discuss problems and triumphs in his life, he might be effectively excluding his wife from feeling that they are really married. If the wife stopped wanting to have sex with her husband as a result, you can see that it would probably be fruitless to try and deal with this in isolation as a purely sexual problem. The underlying problem would be to do with the son and his mother failing to make the adjustments necessary to allow the new married system to get off the ground. The sexual difficulty is merely a symptom.

Just as marriage requires adjustments of whole systems and not just of the individuals involved, so do divorce and remarriage, when they occur. There are certain tasks which the members of the marriage and the system as a whole need to complete in order to move on. Somehow the system needs to achieve an 'emotional divorce' (retrieving hopes, dreams, expectations from the failed marriage) without a complete cut-off because, particularly if there are children, the old marriage cannot completely cease to exist as a system, but must radically be renegotiated to take into account the new realities.

Carter and McGoldrick suggest that if this work isn't done, families can remain in some ways 'stuck' for years, or even for generations. I would add that families can perhaps also remain stuck for equally long periods when, so to speak, a 'secret divorce' takes place between the parents, even though they remain physically together, because this doesn't offer any scope at all for addressing fears and openly renegotiating the system.

Family members growing old

When members of a family reach old age, further adjustments are required in the family system for it to be able to cope with the new circumstances. Difficulties in making the adjustment may result in older family members refusing to relinquish power (trying to hang on to it through manipulation, for example), or alternatively opting for a passive, dependent role. Or they may result in younger family members on the one hand refusing to accept the lessening powers of the older ones and continuing to make the same demands on them as ever, or, on the other, treating them as completely incompetent and refusing to accept that they are capable of doing anything.

Family members becoming parents

Again, this requires a change in the whole multigenerational system and Carter and McGoldrick suggest that the need here is for the new parents to 'move up a generation' within the family system so there is space within the system for them to become caretakers of a younger generation. Difficulties at this stage may be due to parents having difficulty in making the transition to this new role, and this is likely to reflect a problem with the whole system, and not just with the couple. When parents complain that their four-year-old is 'impossible to control', or expect their child to behave like an adult, it is almost as if they have not realised their own size and strength as adults. And *this* may well be because the previous generation has had difficulty in letting them grow up and cease to be children. Grandparents who have had difficulty in giving up their own role as the parental generation can fail to support their children in their new role as parents, and may even actively undermine them.

Adolescence

When children in a family reach adolescence a new phase begins, in that fundamentally different boundaries need to be established. Adolescence is not just something that happens to an individual. Once again it is relationships within the entire family that need to be renegotiated. In particular, parents at this stage need to change their attitude to control. It is no longer desirable or realistic to attempt to control every aspect of their child's life. Failure to make this shift will lead to either:

- the adolescent 'withdrawing from her own development' (that is, not beginning to take responsibility for her own life), or
- the adolescent refusing to accept control, and parents getting frustrated at what (to them) feels like impotence.

This phase commonly coincides with the 'mid-life' of the spouses, which (in common with Levinson) Carter and McGoldrick see as a time of intense re-negotiation of the marriage and when sometimes a decision is taken to divorce. They note also that, at this stage, focusing on parent–child problems can be used to mask marital secrets: an affair going on, perhaps, or a secret wish on the part of one party to divorce. So not only can different stages of the cycle occur at the same time, but they can have a direct effect on one another.

The systems model of development

For a model of this kind it is not necessary to insist that a particular sequence of steps is the only one possible (in different cultures very different sequences may occur, and within a single culture there will be many different patterns). What is central to a systems model, though, is the idea that, whatever the transitions to be gone through, their successful negotiation is a task for the whole system, not just the individual – and that problems that occur are problems with the whole system too.

Each family system negotiates or fails to negotiate these transitions partly as a result of the absence or presence of vertical stressors, some of which may be unique to that family, some of which may be pervasive in society generally. The implications for practical work with families are that it is important to be aware of the family as a whole, its culture, its vertical stressors and the pattern of relationships that exist within it. Successful transitions require the participation of as much as possible of the wider family system.

Larger Systems

As I've said, the application of systems theory to families is something that is usually discussed in books on family therapy, rather than in textbooks on human development, and it has been tested in the therapy room rather than in the psychological laboratory. (This is true also of psychodynamic theory, though the latter has spawned a much larger theoretical literature and has found its way into all the textbooks on psychological development.) The fact remains, as I hope this chapter has shown, that it offers a developmental model which illuminates areas which are neglected by the psychological models discussed so far.

This model does itself have limitations, however. One criticism that can be made of systems models of the family is that, by taking away responsibility from individuals and locating it in the group as a whole, it is in danger of ignoring the question of power differentials. This is particularly apparent when the model is applied to abusive family situations where, as White et al. (1993: 58) point out, 'taking a supposedly "neutral" stance in therapy sessions tacitly supports the power imbalance which exists in the family resulting in the continued oppression of the victims'.

This has led to some rethinking in systemic family therapy:

> A debate has been created in which a wider discussion of power and coercion in social systems has enforced the need for more distinctions in systemic thinking as it relates to therapy with families and intimate human relationship groups. The way in which people become drawn into habitual patterns that may not be to their individual liking, for reasons of economic survival or protection of their young, requires a different lens for examining theory. . . . Choice will also be dependent on relative power related to age. . . .
>
> Systemic therapy has therefore adopted a number of different lenses through which to consider the relevance of interconnection through choice and interconnection through circumstance. (Barnes, 1998: 17)

(For discussion on gender and power issues in particular, see also Perelberg and Miller, 1990.)

These comments on the political context in which families operate leads me on to a second limitation of focusing on family systems – and indeed on to a limitation of this book. The question must be asked: why families? Just as proponents of the family systems model can object to a focus on the individual as being too narrow, so a focus on the family can be criticised for failing to take into account larger systems. Communities are also systems, as are whole societies and nations. And these bigger systems, like families, themselves grow and change and themselves have enormous importance to individual human development. I noted in Chapter 5, when discussing the learning of gender roles, how difficult it was for one or two adults in isolation to change their child's perception of gender-appropriate behaviour, because of the pervasive influence of the wider society. This is an example of the larger system being more powerful than the family.

That this is the case is acknowledged in the Carter and McGoldrick model in their idea of concentric 'system levels'. (And no doubt bigger systems than families have horizontal and vertical stressors. If you look at recent events in nations such as Israel or Ireland, you can see how whole societies have to deal not only with the day-to-day 'horizontal' issues that every nation faces, but have to do with the 'vertical' legacy of fears and aspirations that comes from their particular history.)

In a longer book than this, it might be appropriate to follow this chapter on family systems with a chapter on society and development, which would look at the subject matter of this book from the perspective of sociology, because sociology as a discipline looks at the individual as the product of society as a whole.

The next chapter is on disability, where, I hope to demonstrate in discussing disability and its impact on development, that what at first sight may seem a physical, biological problem confronted by individual human beings, is in fact something whose impact and meaning is determined both by the family context and by the wider context of society.

Chapter Summary

No One is an Island

- In this chapter I have introduced some basic concepts from systems theory and suggested that these ideas can be applied usefully to human groups, and particularly to families.

- I have suggested that by looking at families in a systemic way, a new perspective is gained, which can be lost by more 'linear' and individually focused models.

continued

- I then looked at a systemic approach to the family life-cycle, contrasting it to earlier stage theories. In the system model, development is part of a cycle. (From the point of view of a family, birth follows death just as much as death follows birth.)

- Finally I suggested some limitations of a family systems perspective. I suggested that it was in danger of ignoring power differentials within a family. In addition, I argued that the family itself, just like a human individual, can be seen as a component of still larger systems. I acknowledged that the sociological perspective, which is not separately addressed in the book, is a viewpoint that looks at the much larger systems within society as a whole.

In the next chapter I will look at disability, how disability is approached by families and by society at large, and how this impacts on development.

Suggested Reading

- Barnes, G. (1998) *Family Therapy in Changing Times* (Basingstoke: Macmillan)
- Barker, P. (1998) *Basic Family Therapy* (4th edition). (Oxford: Blackwell Science)
- Carter, B. and McGoldrick, M. (eds) (1989) *The Changing Family Life Cycle* (Boston/London: Allyn & Bacon)

9 Access to Adulthood
Growing up with a disability

In a delivery room in a maternity hospital, a mother is about to give birth after an eight-hour labour. There are four people present: the mother herself, the baby's father, a midwife and a doctor. Everyone is trying to encourage the exhausted mother ('Keep pushing!' 'You're almost there!' 'Don't forget your breathing!')
   Then the father shouts out excitedly 'I can see its head!'
   Suddenly a fifth human being is in the room . . .

This account of a birth is so far identical to that at the beginning of Chapter 1. But let us suppose now that, as the baby emerges into the world for the first time, the four adults present become aware of a birth defect which for some reason had not previously been picked up by ante-natal tests: the baby's fingers are missing perhaps, or she has no eyes. Imagine how different the reaction will be to what it would otherwise have been.

Many abnormalities are picked up ante-natally, and many others do not become apparent until some time after birth, so this is only one of a number of possible ways in which parents find out that their child has an impairment of some kind. But it does illustrate a point that we will keep coming back to in this chapter: disability is not just about physical abnormalities, but also about the reactions of others. In other words, while disability may seem to be about the absence of a limb or of a functioning sense organ, or about a difficulty with learning, in fact it is about the way these things impact upon and are dealt with by whole systems: by families and by society as a whole.

One thing that systems can do to individuals is to 'infantilise' them, to treat them as infants. Old people are often infantilised ('Are we going to eat up all our pudding today, Mr Jones?'). So are women ('Don't you worry your pretty head about this'). So, at least in some contexts, are men ('He's just a big kid . . .'). Black people have been infantilised in all kinds of ways in recent history. Even children are infantilised, although it might sound odd to put it that way, when they are treated as if they didn't have minds and feelings of their own, or as if the big issues of life were somehow beyond them.

Disabled people are certainly often infantilised. In all kinds of ways disabled people can find themselves prevented or impeded – by society at large, by particular organisations, by anxious and overprotective loved ones – from moving through the stages of development which we have been discussing in the previous sections.

People with disabilities may find themselves permanently in a dependent status. They may face formidable obstacles to having a satisfying work career, or of making a contribution to the community. They may also be discouraged from having sex, or forming relationships or having children. So, not only do people with disabilities often have difficulty gaining access to a whole range of things, from buses to toilets to public buildings, they may even have to struggle to gain access to the pleasures and responsibilities of adulthood itself. For this reason it seemed important, in a book about psychosocial development, to devote some space to looking in particular at the developmental issues faced by people with disabilities.

Social and Medical Models

There are really two aspects to the problems faced by people with a disability:

- The purely physical or organic aspect (which might be a missing limb, a non-functioning sense organ for example). This I am going to call *impairment*.
- The aspects resulting from the attitudes of the rest of society. This I will call *disability*.

So, to give an example, the fact that a person has no legs is, in the terms I am going to use, an impairment. The fact that this person can't use public transport is a disability, and would be more or less of a disability depending, for example, on the kinds of doors that were fitted on trains and buses and the staff that were available to assist.

But terminology can be confusing in this area. You will find that some writers use the word *disability* to refer to the actual physical difficulties encountered by the person with an impairment (the inability to walk, for example, in the case of a person whose impairment is having no legs) and *handicap* to describe the social restrictions resulting from that. In common parlance, 'disability' or 'handicap' are often used interchangeably to cover all these different meanings, though handicap is now thought to have negative connotations. Actually many terms that have been used in the past to describe different impairments have acquired – or have always had – deeply negative connotations: 'spastic', 'idiot', 'moron', 'imbecile', 'cripple'.

The definitions which I am using – those of the Union of the Physically Impaired Against Segregation (UPIAS, 1976) – reflect what is called a *social* model of disability, as opposed to a *medical* model. The social model is based on the idea that it is normal for a society to contain individuals with mental and physical impairments. Disability is a consequence of *society's* failure to recognise this and to make provision for the inclusion of such people in mainstream activities.

In contrast to the social model, which sees disability as being something created by society, the medical model sees the disability as being purely to do with the individual concerned. (You will notice a similarity in this discussion to that in the previous chapter about individuals and systems.) The World Health Organisation defines a disability as 'the restriction or lack (resulting from impairment) of ability to perform an activity in the manner or range considered normal for a human being' (WHO, 1980). You can see that the WHO definition makes no mention of society. Yet whether or not an impairment results in a disability does in fact depend on the social context.

Short-sightedness or long-sightedness, for example, are undoubtedly impairments, but one could argue that they are not disabilities, or not very serious ones, in our society, as there are few areas of society to which access is denied or restricted for spectacle wearers.

In the American island of Martha's Vineyard there was for a period such a high incidence of congenital deafness among the population that it ceased to be regarded as abnormal and even most hearing people learned to use sign language. This is an instance where profound deafness, while still clearly an impairment, was not a serious disability (Quinn, 1998).

Once again we find – as we have already found in relation to gender roles in Chapter 5 and puberty in Chapter 6 – that when something appears at first sight to be an essentially physical or biological matter, it then turns out to be only the starting point. The biological fact exists, but its impact on the individual depends on the social context and on the meanings that society assigns to the biological fact.

Impairments and Developmental Pathways

Impairments vary very greatly both in kind and degree and one must be careful not to generalise about them as if they were all the same. The principal areas are as follows, though within these categories there are still large differences, and many people have more than one type of impairment:

- learning impairments (impairments that affect cognitive ability);
- motor impairments (which affect mobility and/or other abilities involving muscle control such as speech or use of the hands);
- sensory impairments (which in practical terms means blindness and deafness – the lack of the ability to smell would also be a sensory impairment, but would not result in serious disability, because for human beings smell is not of primary importance either for communication or for finding our way about).

Although disability is in large part a socially constructed phenomenon, an impairment in itself can constitute an obstacle to an individual developing along the same path as people who do not have impairments, even if given all possible support. A person with learning difficulties will not necessarily be able to move through all the stages of intellectual development envisaged by Piaget, even in optimum conditions. And there are certain skills that a blind person could never acquire, simply by reason of being blind. (A blind person could not be an airline pilot, for example.) However, it is often difficult to tease out whether developmental problems are due to the impairment itself or to social and environmental factors.

Hodapp (1998) suggests that, if we compare the development of children with impairments to that of children who do not have impairments, we can look at several different aspects:

- *rate*
- *sequence* (does development progress through the same stages, or does it progress in a different order?)
- *structure* (do developments in one area relate to developments in other areas in the same way?)

Not surprisingly, research shows that the rate of development does vary, as it does in the general population, but interestingly it appears that the sequence of stages is broadly the same. All children seem to move along analogous paths, albeit at different rates, contrary to a widely held stereotype that children with learning difficulties in particular are somehow static.

When it comes to structure there are differences. You may remember that Piaget's model envisaged that development occurred across a broad front, with analogous stages being moved through, across a wide range of areas – language development, spatial understanding and so on. In fact, though, there do seem to be important variations in the structure of development depending on the type of impairments.

Learning impairments

Among children with learning impairments, there are differences in the structure of development depending on the nature of the impairment. Children with Down syndrome, for example, are strong on social skills but slow on language and mathematical skills. Children with Williams syndrome are strong on language skills and social skills, but weaker on skills such as drawing and other spatial skills (see Hodapp, 1998: 54).

But while children with specific impairments will experience particular problems in particular areas, the extent of developmental delay in these areas is also undoubtedly linked to context, the type of encouragement or discouragement that is offered, and the extent to which compensatory input is offered in particular areas of difficulty.

Motor impairments

Studies of the development of children with motor impairments (such as Cione et al., 1993) have found that these children tend be behind other children developmentally in a general sense, but fall behind in particular areas such as development of the concept of 'object permanence' (as discussed in Chapter 4). This is not a surprising finding given that motor impairments will make it more difficult to explore and manipulate physical objects.

The heading 'motor impairments' covers a wide variety of different things. Motor impairments can result from *cerebral palsy*, for example, which is caused by brain damage at an early stage of development – and can result in learning as well as motor impairments. Or they can result from hereditary conditions such as *spina bifida*, which is a spinal problem and can lead to muscle weakness in the lower half of the body, including sometimes problems with bowel control. It is often associated with *hydrocephalus*, which is caused by a fluid build-up around the brain. *Thalidomide*, a drug once prescribed to pregnant women, caused some children to be born with defective or absent limbs. Other motor impairments are the result of physical injury.

Just as with learning impairments, the *structure* of development has been found to differ from one type of motor impairment to another. Children with *spina bifida–hydrocephalus* often have verbal abilities well in advance of their performance abilities, while children with cerebral palsy seem to develop their abilities more evenly, though on average they are behind children who do not have impairments (see Hodapp, 1998: 150–4).

Sensory impairments

Blind children tend to be slower at developing skills in the areas of object permanence than do sighted children (Warren, 1994). Without sight, a blind baby has far fewer cues than a sighted baby to tell her that an object still exists when it is out of reach, and often no cues at all, unless the object makes a sound, or gives off heat or a smell. So it is not surprising that blind children take longer to grasp this concept. And it seems to be the case that lack of sight leads to delays, or at any rate to *different* pathways, in a number of other areas of cognitive development. Motor skills and spatial skills are slower to develop, as are skills such as 'classification'. Language skills also develop in slightly different ways. Blind children are apparently slower in grasping the difference between 'this' and 'that' (Anderson et al., 1993). They are also apparently less prone than other children to 'overgeneralise', for example by using the word 'dog' to refer to all animals, but *more* prone to 'undergeneralise', for example by using the word 'dog' as if it referred to one particular dog only (see Hodapp, 1998: 132). Without sight, presumably, a child is less well placed to notice similarities between objects with which she is familiar and other objects in the world at large.

In the case of deaf children, as one might expect, it is language development that takes a different course from that of hearing children. But here there are some interesting complications which again serve to illustrate the pervasive role of context and culture in human development. These arise because, in the case of deaf people, there are distinct and separate languages. In the USA, the main sign language used by deaf people is American Sign Language (or ASL), in Britain, BSL. Apart from being signed rather than spoken, these languages have their own quite distinct grammar and sentence structure. 'ASL does not resemble English or BSL [British Sign Language], but relies on agreement and gender systems in a way that is reminiscent of Navajo or Bantu' (Pinker, 1994: 36). But deaf children, in Britain and the USA, when they learn to read and write, learn English, and they will have to use English in some form to communicate with most hearing people. This means that when studying the language acquisition of deaf children it is necessary to bear in mind that they may be working simultaneously on acquiring two quite distinct language systems. Researchers have found that deaf children who are exposed to sign language from an early age acquire it in much the same way – and in the same time scale – as hearing children acquire speech. The deaf babies of deaf parents even apparently 'babble' in signs at the age of 10–14 months (Petitto and Marentette, 1991).

There is also evidence (Greenberg and Kushe, 1989) that children who are deaf and whose parents are also deaf progressed educationally more rapidly than children who are deaf but whose parents are hearing. This is likely to be due to a number of factors. Deaf parents would understand without having to think about it, the particular needs of deaf children (for example, the need to find visual ways of getting a deaf child's attention). Deaf children of deaf parents are also able to acquire sign language in the same informal way that hearing children acquire spoken language, whereas deaf children of hearing parents tend to be behind in all aspects of language development.

This is an another illustration of the way that context determines how much an impairment becomes a disability. Rather like the deaf inhabitants of Martha's Vineyard in the past, deaf children of deaf parents grow up in a family environment where deafness is 'normal'.

Emotional development

This discussion on impairments and developmental pathways has so far related to issues to do with the acquisition of specific skills. But if impairments may result in children taking different developmental routes in respect of cognitive development, is it possible that impairments can also result in different pathways in respect of emotional development or the development of personality characteristics? You may remember that I argued in Chapter 4 that there was necessarily a close relationship between cognitive development and emotional development.

The following activity is intended to help you think about the particular challenges faced by people with disabilities:

Activity 9.1

Below are the favourable outcomes which Erikson proposed for each of his eight stages of development:

1 trust in the environment
2 sense of autonomy and self-esteem
3 ability to initiate activities
4 a sense of competence and achievement
5 ability to see oneself as a consistent and integrated person
6 ability to experience love and commitment to others
7 the ability to be concerned and caring about others in the wider sense
8 a sense of satisfaction with one's life and its accomplishments

What obstacles might stand in the way of achieving these outcomes for:

- a person with a sensory impairment?
- a person with a learning impairment?
- a person with a motor impairment?

Comments on Activity 9.1

The following are a few suggestions:

In the absence of appropriate help, a child with a sensory impairment such as blindness, attempting to find her way in a world designed for sighted people, might well have difficulty establishing a sense of trust in the environment.

Similarly, in the absence of appropriate support, a person with cerebral palsy, who was unable to do things such as walk, dress herself or use the toilet, might have difficulty with a sense of autonomy.

A child with learning difficulties, in the absence of appropriate help, might well have difficulty in developing a sense of competence, when comparing herself with other children.

All of us, whether or not we are disabled, carry 'unfinished business' from the earlier stages of our life, and all of us find it hard at times to meet the challenges made on us in the here and now. People who have disabilities may have to carry additional emotional baggage from the past as well as dealing with exceptional challenges in the here and now.

Commenting on the high incidence of mental illness among people with learning impairments, Howells (1997) observes that:

> a disadvantaged life-style coupled with lack of contact with non-disabled peers restricts emotional development. They [people with learning impairments] have few opportunities to exercise choice, their expectations are low and they suffer from overprotection. Little scope exists to develop social networks beyond the family and paid carers. The result is too great an emotional investment in too few people. This, in turn, increases the significance of loss through bereavement and changes in staff. (Howells, 1997: 77)

On the other hand it may be a mistake to attempt to apply models such as Erikson's to people with disabilities. Stage models impose a particular pathway. For example Erikson, like Freud, speaks of toilet-training as a very basic way in which children learn about taking control of their own lives. Clearly this is not an option for someone whose impairment means that she will never be able to control her bowels. But this should not be taken to mean that she cannot develop a sense of being in control, merely that she needs to find other pathways in order to give her that experience, and help with finding those pathways may be one of the things she needs.

I don't think that this is a point that Erikson would disagree with, since he was well aware that different cultures assigned different meanings to different events and therefore followed different developmental pathways. How crucial bowel control as such is in a child's emotional development would depend on 'whether the cultural environment wants to make something of it' (Erikson, 1995: 71. He wrote that the Sioux, for example, placed little or no emphasis on toilet-training in the sense that it is understood in European culture.) Once again, context is as important as biology.

Families, Children and Disability

The birth of a child with an impairment is an event to which a whole family has to adjust. To use the terminology from Carter and McGoldrick (1989) which I introduced in the last chapter, the event itself is a 'horizontal stressor', an event that poses a challenge. But how the family copes with this challenge – and the extent to which the child will be welcomed, supported and helped within the family, will depend on the wider social context, and upon the 'vertical stressors' that exist within that particular family. The vertical stressors might also operate at several 'system levels'. At the societal level, they might include widely held cultural beliefs (in some cultures, the birth of a child with a disability is viewed as a punishment from God), while at the family level they would include the family's own unique beliefs and ideas about disability, and about many other related questions. Some families might set great store by sporting achievement, others by intellectual achievement, and these families might be differently affected by the birth of a child with physical or intellectual impairments. You may remember that in the Carter and McGoldrick model, it is when vertical and horizontal stressors intersect that things become especially difficult for a family.

For a long time, one of the most influential models of what occurs at the point that a mother gives birth to a child with a disability was that offered by Solnit and Stark (1961). They proposed that the birth of a child with an impairment was in some senses a bereavement. Parents had to go through a period of mourning for their dreams of a perfect child and this would involve going through the stages associated with grieving: shock, denial, sadness and anger, adaptation and reorganisation. Modern thinking has moved away from this grief model somewhat, as we will see, but nevertheless (and however much one might wish it were different) an element of grief is surely a not untypical response to the birth of a disabled child.

It is worth thinking for a moment about what it means for a *child* if her birth, instead of being a joyful event, is the occasion for mourning. It is not an ideal start in life.

It is also worth noting that, even if thinking has moved away from an approach which describes the birth of a disabled child as a bereavement, there can be no doubt that such a birth involves a major adjustment. As I discussed in Chapter 5, when looking at transitions, any major adjustment – whether it is a bereavement or not – does seem to involve going through the same sorts of basic stages.

The reaction against the Solnit and Stark model has been towards models that are focused on stress and coping, rather than on mourning. The presence of a child with a disability is undoubtedly frequently a *stressor* on the family system, to varying degrees, and the capacity of the family to cope depends on a number of factors. Minnes (1988), looking in particular at families with children who had learning impairments, categorised these factors under the following headings:

(a) The child's own characteristics
The families of children with Down syndrome seem to cope better – on measures of stress and depression – than those with children with some other kinds of intellectual impairment. This is probably due in part to the fact that Down children tend on average to be affectionate and sociable, and to be less prone to difficult and challenging behaviour patterns than some other learning-impaired children. But it is perhaps also because the syndrome is well known and there are well-developed support networks.

(b) The resources of the family
Minnes broke this down further into 'internal' and 'external' resources.

- By 'internal' resources are meant the personal characteristics of the family members and of the family as a whole. In particular, coping strategies that are focused on solving practical problems seem to be more adaptive than 'emotion-focused' coping strategies. According to Hodapp (1998: 81) 'In virtually every study, mothers who were focused on actively solving problems seemed better off than those focused primarily on their own emotional reactions.'

- By 'external' resources are meant such things as the family's financial resources and/or the availability of financial help, and the services and support networks that are available.

(c) The family's perception of the child
The family's beliefs are also important. As Hodapp observes (1998: 81) some families may view a child as a special burden or responsibility

placed upon them by God. Others may view the additional demands of a child with learning impairments as being 'unfair', and a brake on achieving what they saw as their legitimate aspirations in life. Family perceptions of *specific* impairments are also a factor. Returning to the case of the Down child, the widespread *perception* that Down children are affectionate and lovable may be helpful, as well as being in fact the case.

You will see that, although the terminology is different, the different kinds of factors which Minnes has tried to tease out, could also be categorised under the headings of 'vertical' and 'horizontal' stressors, acting at various 'system levels', to use the terms of Carter and McGoldrick's model. Carter and McGoldrick viewed all developmental challenges as being challenges for the whole family, and not just for the individual concerned, and clearly this is very much the case with disability. A family with a disabled child may in some cases have a radically different life-cycle from other families. What Carter and McGoldrick called 'the launching of children into the world' may not occur in a family where a child has serious learning impairments.

In fact the presence of a child with a disability can be a cause of family breakdown. Gath (1977) found a higher incidence of divorce or marital dissatisfaction among parents of children with Down syndrome, while Hodapp and Krasner (1995) found the incidence of divorce among parents of school-age children with visual impairments to be 25 per cent, as against 15.3 per cent among a sample with non-disabled children.

But the presence of a child with a disability can also result in positive growth. Marriages can be strengthened by the arrival of children with disability, as well as broken, and extended families can be drawn together into a strongly mutually supportive system. Grossman (1972) carried out a study of older siblings of children with disabilities and found an almost exactly even split between predominantly positive and predominantly negative feelings. Feelings of resentment and frustration were reported by 45 per cent, while another 45 per cent described the experience of having a sibling with disabilities as being on balance a rewarding and enriching one. You will remember that, from a family systems perspective, a family's ability to adapt successfully to new challenges depends on its members' capacity to renegotiate the family structure to take on board the new reality. Perhaps the second group in Grossman's study came from families which had been able to renegotiate successfully their structure in order to take on the particular tasks involved in bringing up a child with a disability. Perhaps the families of the first group had become 'stuck', unable to resolve and move on from their initial negative reactions.

Failing to resolve initial negative reactions is a danger for families of children with disabilities and therefore a danger to the child herself, because healthy emotional development is not assisted by negative or ambivalent feelings on the part of one's parents. Another danger is that parents may become so preoccupied with managing the particular special needs of a child with a disability, perhaps out of a desire to make the child become as 'normal' as possible, that they lose sight of the fact that the child has the same universal emotional needs as any other child. Such needs might include needs for fun, cuddles, exploration and so on and also needs for consistent care. If you work with families of children who have disabilities – or are the parent of a child with a disability, or have a disability yourself – you will be aware of the difficult balance to be struck between a family's needs for 'respite' and a child's need for continuity of care.

Before moving on, you may find it useful to go through the following activity to check out your own thinking about families of children with disabilities.

⚒ Activity 9.2 ⚒

In the family life-cycle model discussed in the last chapter, 'horizontal stressors' were new events (predictable or unpredictable) with which a family had to deal. 'Vertical stressors' referred to the 'baggage' from the past which families carry, and which might in some cases interact with horizontal stressors to create particular problems for the family system. These stressors could also operate at different 'system levels': at the individual level, or at the level of society.

Looking back over the discussion so far on the impact on a family of a child with a disability – and at your own experience – can you think of:

- horizontal stressors that might result from the presence of a child with a disability;
- vertical stressors that might exist in particular families which might make successful family adaptation more difficult;
- stressors that might exist at the system level of the wider society.

Comments on Activity 9.2

A child with a disability may place extra stress on a family for the entirely practical reason that she requires more care than other children, and therefore makes more demands and takes up more time. The need for care may also go on for longer than for other children. As well as demands on time, there may be additional demands on the family's money, its space, its capacity to ask for outside help.

Vertical stressors would include particular concerns, preoccupations or anxieties which might be triggered by the presence of a child with a disability. I earlier suggested that these might include a preoccupation with intellectual or sporting achievement, but many other issues might be brought to the fore. For example, issues about responsibilities for providing personal care might be highlighted. (Consider a family where, up to now, it has been accepted in practice that personal care is a woman's job, although there has been some resentment about this on the part of the women in the family. What would be the impact of a child who requires enormous amounts of personal care?). Or in some families where there are anxieties on the part of family members about getting enough care or attention, the arrival of a child with considerable needs for personal care might well increase anxieties and tensions. You will no doubt be able to think of many other instances such as these.

Moving to other system levels, you might have considered the different social context that exists in societies such as some Scandinavian countries, where there is a high level of public provision for children with disabilities, as against societies where there is none, and where making provision is the financial and personal responsibility of the family concerned. You may also have considered the different beliefs, values and prejudices about disability that exist in different social contexts.

Another 'system level' is of course that of the individual person with a disability – and this will be the focus of the remainder of this chapter.

Adolescence and Disability

The developmental task of adolescence is widely agreed to be the construction of a new identity with which to enter the adult world. Components of this identity, at least within modern industrialised society, may differ from one individual to another, and also vary between boys and girls, but is likely to include elements of the following:

- *Autonomy*: increasing independence from one's family of origin, which may include physically leaving home, as well as making one's own decisions and taking responsibility for one's own needs. This also includes the increasing importance of a peer group as a source of support.
- *Sexual identity*: a sense of oneself as a sexual being, which arises from learning to successfully negotiate sexual relationships.
- *Occupational identity*: a sense of oneself as competent and able to provide for oneself and others, which comes from acquiring skills and work habits.

Clearly there are enormous differences between, say, a young person of above average intelligence who is deaf, and one with Down syndrome, or between a young person who is quadriplegic (with limited movement in all four limbs) as a result of cerebral palsy and one who is blind, and it would be wrong to generalise about all young people with disabilities as if they were a single homogeneous group. Nevertheless there are some themes which do seem to run through the experience of many adolescents with disabilities. I will discuss these under the three headings above, but before going on to this discussion, you may like to use the following activity to consider the issues:

Activity 9.3

What particular obstacles might stand in the way of adolescents with disabilities in the areas of:

- taking steps towards increasing autonomy
- exploration of oneself as a sexual being, and
- starting to develop some sense of one's future work or career identity?

Comments on Activity 9.3

The obstacles that you thought of probably included some which are societal (for example, the absence of transport arrangements and social facilities for young people with disabilities), some which are familial (protectiveness on the part of parents), and some which are biological or physical (limited language acquisition for some young people with learning impairments, or physical obstacles to sex). As ever, development seems to hinge on the interaction at a number of different levels.

Autonomy

Young people with disabilities may have their peer-group involvement limited or curtailed in various ways. They may attend special schooling, separate from other young people. In some ways this may promote peer-group involvement, by allowing young people to mix with others who share the same kinds of experience, but it does also have the effect of isolating young people with disabilities from young people generally. In cases where young people with disabilities attend residential schools, or are bussed to schools at some distance using special transport services, this problem may be particularly pronounced. They miss out on getting to know young people in their own neighbourhood.

Mobility problems may also make street-corner type socialising more difficult or impossible, as can intellectual impairments (some young people with Down syndrome may lack the necessary linguistic or cognitive abilities) and visual impairments. There may be problems with gaining acceptance from non-disabled peers – or even reluctance to admit that they are peers – and difficulties with access, for physical or other reasons, to social and leisure facilities used by non-disabled young people in the same age group.

Becoming independent from one's family of origin may also be complicated – or made impossible – if one is dependent on one's family for basic physical care, such as dressing, bathing or going to the toilet. Whether these needs can be met in other ways will depend on financial resources and/or the availability of publicly funded services. Parents may also be in a position to hold on to control which they simply would have had no choice but to relinquish with an able-bodied child. For non-disabled children, establishing autonomy typically involves an element of wresting power from adults, as well as being granted it. Young people with disabilities may find this more difficult.

As Quinn (1998) observes, not only parents, but also adults in the caring services may be tempted to impose their own views on young people with disabilities in a way that might not be possible with non-disabled young people:

> There is a definite tendency for social service and medical personnel to empower people with disabilities to do what the professionals think they should do rather than what the clients themselves would choose. (Quinn, 1998: 103, referring to Sobsey, 1994)

Sexual identity

Exploration of sex and sexual relationships is complicated for young people with disabilities for all of the reasons given above. Even access to information about sex may be more restricted, because adolescents typically acquire sexual information from their peers as well as from adults and, as we've seen, some young people with disabilities have more restricted contact with their peers.

Lollar (1994) makes the point that young people with spina bifida (and this would apply to some with other conditions also) have been subjected throughout their life to highly intrusive examinations and therapeutic interventions, so that they will not have developed the same boundaries about their bodies as other young people, and may need particular help with this. Some young people with spina bifida may also have limited sensation in the genital area or, in the case of boys, be unable to have an erection.

Protectiveness on the part of parents and other adult carers may also result in lack of sexual opportunities, although protectiveness may be justified in the case of young people whose limited cognitive abilities may otherwise place them in situations which they are unable to control or understand.

Occupational identity

Depending on the nature of the impairment, and on the social environment, a young person with a disability may also have difficulty finding an occupation and acquiring skills that will allow her to earn her own living and participate in the work of society. This is as likely to reflect the shortcomings of society generally, including prejudice against people with disabilities and a lack of facilities which would allow them to participate in work or training, as much as the young person's own potential, though limited abilities, whether cognitive, sensory or motor, do obviously preclude some occupations.

There are many instances of people with disabilities who have been highly successful in their careers: the blind British politician David Blunkett, the hearing-impaired percussionist, Evelyn Glenny, and the physically disabled theoretical physicist Stephen Hawkins are three famous examples.

Establishing an identity

So the routes by which people typically establish a separate identity during adolescence may be more restricted, or even closed in some cases, to young people with disabilities. The challenge for these young people and their supporters seems to lie both in challenging unwarranted obstacles and in finding alternative pathways to establishing a secure adult identity.

Disability and Adulthood

You will remember that Erik Erikson (1995) proposed that the central issues for early, middle and late adulthood respectively were intimacy, generativity and integrity. I argued in Chapter 7 that in practice it is not possible to divide adulthood up neatly into stages and that, in particular, the issues of intimacy, generativity and identity are closely intertwined. However, we can probably agree that in Western industrial society at any rate, adult life is seen as typically including at least some of the following:

• moving out of the parental home and becoming responsible for one's own care;

- engaging in sexual relationships and establishing a long-term sexual partnership (Erikson's 'intimacy');
- becoming financially independent;
- raising children (part of Erikson's 'generativity');
- leaving school and full-time education and moving into a career or occupation;
- contributing to the community (also seen by Erikson as part of generativity).

Of course, many people with impairments of all kinds achieve and excel in all these areas. And doubtless many do not pursue all these goals because of free choice, and not because of their impairments. Disabled and non-disabled people alike may choose not to marry or to have children. However it is also the case that many people with impairments will have difficulty achieving some or all of these goals not because of choice, but because of difficulties created by their impairment and by the attitude of society to that impairment. In some cases the disability that results can amount to a denial of access to adulthood itself. People with learning difficulties in particular are infantilised by the language that is used about them: 'He is 50, but really his mental age is 5.'

Moving out of the parental home

In the last chapter I suggested that transitions such as the departure of a young adult from the family home are not just issues for the individual concerned, but for the whole family system, and indeed for society in general. This is well illustrated by the case of adults with disabilities. Some people with disabilities remain with their parents into adulthood. While this is sometimes a free choice, nevertheless where the disabilities are severe, negotiating this stage may present serious challenges to both the young person concerned and to their families. It will be particularly difficult if the alternatives are not satisfactory.

Historically, even when young adults have moved out of the family home, they may have moved into institutional environments where they continued to be treated as dependent children. This applied particularly to adults identified as having learning difficulties. As Sperlinger reminds us about the situation in the UK:

> When the national health service was set up in 1948, the colonies or institutions which were built originally in the nineteenth century to segregate people with learning difficulties from the rest of society became 'hospitals' in which people were 'nursed' (all of their lives) and their problems were defined in medical terms. People with learning difficulties were seen as sick and in need of treatment. (Sperlinger 1997: 6–7)

In the 1970s I worked in a ward in such a hospital in the west of England. In this institution adults with learning difficulties, many in their forties and fifties, were uniformly referred to by themselves and staff as 'boys' and divided into 'high-grades' and 'low-grades'. They were offered no opportunities for sexual relationships, other than furtive ones. They had no choice about when and what they had for meals. They slept in dormitories and had no safe place for personal possessions. They had to ask for toilet paper when they needed it. Cigarettes were issued to them from the ward office. Privileges were withheld as punishments. Yet some of these men were of high enough intellectual ability to be able to read and write fluently. It was a tribute to the human spirit that many of them were still able to maintain a great deal of personal dignity and some very caring long-term relationships. There are no longer hospitals in Britain quite like this, but the underlying attitude which they represented, does, I would suggest, still exist.

Historically, many adults with learning or physical impairments would also have remained with their parents throughout their adult life. In the past, life expectancy for people with Down syndrome or cerebral palsy was considerably shorter than it is now, so that parents could generally expect to outlive their children. This is no longer the case, so that we now have people with Down syndrome or cerebral palsy, who have lived with their parents into middle or late adulthood, having to move on into other accommodation at a time not of their choosing, but dictated by their parents' deteriorating health, or their parents' death. Clearly, if adults with disabilities are to be given comparable opportunities to other adults, they would need to be given opportunities to choose the time of their departure from their parental home, and to move into environments where they would have choice and control of their living arrangements.

Intimacy, generativity and independence

The difficulty faced by people with disabilities in acquiring what is normally recognised as an adult status is not just a question of living independently, as against living with parents or in an institution. As Quinn (1998) helpfully pointed out, few people, disabled or otherwise, are really independent:

> Each person depends on others for food, electricity, transportation, postal services and many other components of daily life. A more appropriate goal is that of *responsible interdependence*. . . . In this case, each person does what she does best and negotiates with others for the goods and services she needs to fill the gaps. (Quinn, 1998: 160; my italics)

The difficulty experienced by some people with disabilities, then, is not the lack of independence (for none of us is really independent), but the lack of opportunity to experience responsible interdependence, as opposed to childlike dependency. When people with disabilities find themselves faced with obstacles to forming sexual relationships, to becoming parents, to entering the world of work, it is not just their 'independence' that is at stake but their opportunity to work through the issues of intimacy and generativity which are part of adult development.

Disability and old age

I will conclude by noting that, in later adulthood, disability of course becomes much more prevalent. Those of us who are fortunate enough not to have to confront the challenges of disability in earlier life, may well have to do so in old age. Nearly half of those over 75 in Britain in the mid-1980s had mobility problems, a third had hearing loss, and over one-tenth had impairments of intellectual functioning. The comparable figures for those in the 16–59 age-range were, respectively 0.1 per cent, 1.7 per cent and 2 per cent (Martin et al., 1988).

Chapter Summary

Access to Adulthood

- In this chapter I have looked at the interaction of physical and environmental/social factors that together constitute 'disability' (I have used 'impairment' to refer to the purely physical/biological aspect). The restrictions that result from disability can in some circumstances amount to a restriction in access to the status of adulthood itself.

- I then looked at different types of impairment – learning impairments, motor impairments and sensory impairments – and considered the particular developmental challenges that each poses. As discussed in previous chapters, there are dangers in imposing a certain developmental pathway as 'normal' and this is apparent in the case of people with disabilities.

- I looked at the family context of children with disabilities. I looked at the initial reaction of a family to the arrival of a child with disabilities and at the impact of disability on a family system (which, it would appear, can be both disruptive and strengthening).

---

continued

- I then moved on to look at the particular issues faced by adolescents with disabilities, bearing in mind that adolescence is normally viewed as a time of establishing a separate identity.

- I concluded by looking at issues for disabled adults.

In the next chapter, I will look at the particular issues of late adulthood, or old age.

Suggested Reading

- Hodapp, R.M. (1998) *Development and Disabilities: Intellectual, Sensory and Motor Impairments* (Cambridge: Cambridge University Press)

  (Summarises a large number of research findings and covers, the Solnit and Stark and subsequent models on the birth of a child with a disability.)

- Quinn, P. (1998) *Understanding Disability – a Lifespan Approach* (London: Sage)

  (Covers each stage of the life-span in a separate chapter.)

- Davey, B. (ed.) (1995) *Birth to Old Age: Health in Transition.* (Buckingham: Open University Press)

  (Chapter 1 discusses medical and social models of disability. There is also a chapter on disability in later life.)

10 Coming to a Conclusion

Themes in old age

Physical and cognitive impairments of one kind or another are more common in old age than at other stages of life. Many old people will have to deal with specific impairments of various kinds – and will be disabled by them to varying extents depending on social attitudes and social provision – but old people also have to operate within the context of society's prevailing attitudes towards old age. These may include preconceptions that old people will be unable to cope, or that they are incapable of making decisions for themselves. There is the notion of late old age as a 'second childhood', and even in an academic textbook you may find a discussion about the age at which adulthood ends (see Sugarman, 1986: 101, though Sugarman rightly adds that 'People in their 80s might, with some justification, object to being thought of as no longer adult').

The changes that take place in old age are, like all such changes I have discussed, the results of a complex interaction between biology and specific circumstances. The transitions that have to be made are both biological and cultural, and are usually a mixture of the two. Thus, while there are certainly physical changes in old age, and psychological adjustments to these physical changes which have to be made in any culture, different cultures may offer different ways of doing so.

And other adjustments are *entirely* cultural in origin. Compulsory retirement or eligibility for a pension are completely culture-specific. They are unknown in some societies and, in societies where they do exist, they take various different forms.

As well as biological changes, changing social expectations and changing social options, old age also brings new existential issues to the fore. By 'existential issues' I mean the fundamental questions of existence which every human individual and every human culture has to face in some way or another. In old age we may be faced with new questions about the purpose of our lives, when we no longer have work to keep us busy and make us feel useful. And in old age everyone must face the fact of their mortality, just as in early childhood everyone must come to terms with finding themselves in a strange new world. Death is a possibility at any time of life, but for most of us, most of the time, it can be pushed to one side as something that happens to other people, or something very remote. In old age, death in the not too distant future is a certainty, something to be prepared for and something that plans must take into account. More than ever before, it is possible to look back on a long road travelled, but it is not possible to look forward any more to a long road ahead (or not, at any rate, in this world).

I will now look in more detail at the changes involved in old age, but you might first like to consider the case example in the following activity. I should add that this example is not meant to represent a *typical* old person, but is intended to give an instance of the kind of issue that can arise for professionals working with old people:

Activity 10.1

Consider the following case study and ask yourself what position you might take, if you were a professional involved in the situation it describes – the general practitioner, a member of the hospital staff, or a social worker asked to look into the case:

Miss Kipling (aged 82) lives in a house on her own with a large number of cats. She is very isolated, venturing out once a week for her shopping, but avoiding almost all social interaction with her neighbours. A niece, Mrs Yeats, who lives some way away, visits her a few times a year. Miss Kipling is physically quite frail. On several occasions, neighbours have had to call out the police on hearing her shouting, to find her lying on the floor where she has fallen and been unable to get up. On these occasions the police and neighbours have always been concerned about the dirty conditions in the house, and its poor state of repair.

A recent fall resulted in a broken leg, and Miss Kipling is now in hospital. Mrs Yeats has been summoned as next of kin, and there is a strong feeling on the part of Mrs Yeats and the neighbours that Miss Kipling should not return to her own house, but should be found a place in a residential care home. The arguments given for this are that:

- Miss Kipling is clearly not safe, and could fall and lie for a long time without being found. It would be irresponsible to allow her to return, since it could easily result in a fatal accident.
- Miss Kipling's house and her cats are now a health hazard.
- Miss Kipling would be happier with company and others around her.
- It is not fair on Mrs Yeats or the neighbours to have the worry of her – and it is difficult for Mrs Yeats to keep coming at short notice.
- Miss Kipling is increasingly confused. According to Mrs Yeats, Miss Kipling showed no sign of recognition at first when she visited her in hospital, and seemed unsure as to where she was. It is suggested that she is growing 'senile'.

Having considered this case, and decided what stance you would take on it, ask yourself whether your thoughts would have been different if Miss Kipling had been aged 32?

Comments on Activity 10.1

You may have noticed that Miss Kipling's physical safety was assumed by the neighbours not to be Miss Kipling's own responsibility, but a responsibility that is being placed, unreasonably, on themselves. It seems to me that with younger people, we are more ready to accept that the taking of risks is a matter of personal choice.

It may have struck you too that, if Miss Kipling had been a young woman, the health hazard allegedly posed by her cats and living conditions might be a matter that neighbours would deal with by complaining to Miss Kipling herself, or by taking the matter up legally. They would be less likely to suggest that Miss Kipling is not fit to have a home of her own.

Finally, it may have struck you that the neighbours are very quick to assume that Miss Kipling is growing 'senile'. A younger person might well be confused in similar circumstances – a fall resulting in a broken bone, a long wait to be discovered, and then a hospital admission – but this would not, anything like so readily, be considered to be evidence of permanent mental decline.

Changes in Old Age

When 'old age' begins is a debatable question, but in industrialised societies retirement age represents a key transition, in that there is an expectation that most people will stop working at this stage, and there is often entitlement to some financial help from the state. Clearly there is a big adjustment to be made here, although its timing is social rather than biological in origin. It can represent a change in financial circumstances, the loss of an important role and the opening up of enormous amounts of time for other activities. Some people welcome retirement, for others it represents a frightening loss of purpose. Either way there is a transition to be negotiated – and you may remember from the discussion of transitions in Chapter 6 that essentially the same process seems to apply to both positive and negative changes.

Retirement is only one of a number of changes that have to be adjusted to in late adulthood. Among the others are declining physical strength – and quite probably physical or sensory impairment, resulting in increased dependency on others – the loss of friends and loved ones through death, and the approach of one's own death.

These changes affect old people not only as individuals. From a systems perspective, a successful transition into old age requires adjustments from the entire family system. Elderly couples will need to renegotiate their relationship if they are to cope comfortably with changing roles and more time together. And the wider family too needs to make changes. An ideal adjustment would be one in which the members of the extended family were sensitive to the possibility that it might be necessary to reduce their demands on ageing family members, and to offer them additional support when necessary, yet without at the same time characterising them as more helpless or incapable than they really are. But whether the wider family is actually able to make this adjustment will depend on family history (vertical stressors) and on the other challenges now facing the family as a whole (horizontal stressors).

The following activity looks at an instance of a family struggling to cope with some of the problems of old age.

⚒ Activity 10.2 ⚒

What horizontal and vertical stressors can you identify in the family described in the following case example?

Mr and Mrs Patel (aged 80 and 75) came to Britain in the 1970s as refugees from Uganda, where Mr Patel ran a chain of grocery shops.

When they arrived they had no money, because their home and property in Uganda had been confiscated during the Idi Amin era. However they were able to set up a new business (a convenience store), which is now run by their two daughters. Mr and Mrs Patel have no sons.

Mr Patel has always been reliant on his wife to provide for him in the home, and she is no longer really able to do this as she suffers from severe arthritis and is in fact physically much frailer than Mr Patel.

He is suffering from mild dementia as a result of arterio-sclerotic illness, with the result that he forgets things after even a few minutes and is often muddled about who he is talking to. He sometimes imagines that he is back in Uganda, or even in India where he was born. He constantly imagines that his wife and daughters are plotting against him. He also requires pretty constant supervision from a safety point of view. He has turned a gas fire on without lighting it and has been picked up wandering in the street, not knowing where he is.

Mr and Mrs Patel have never had a very happy marriage. Both of them are rather 'highly strung', volatile people, and Mr Patel in particular can be domineering and 'bullying'. He has always found it difficult to come to terms with what happened in Uganda.

Mrs Patel's daughters say that she is being made ill by the worry and stress of trying to cope with Mr Patel and she is now on anti-depressant medication. Neither of the daughters is willing to have Mr Patel living with them, though they do try and provide support to Mrs Patel. Both daughters insist that for his own safety and his wife's health, Mr Patel should now be in residential care.

However, confused as he is, Mr Patel is still able to state, absolutely adamantly, and tearfully, that he does not want to have to leave his home. His one supporter in the family is his son-in-law Sanjay (now separated from Mr and Mrs Patel's older daughter), who says that Mr Patel has worked hard all his life to provide for the family, has had to cope with the constant nagging and attempts to undermine him of his wife and daughters – and he does not deserve to be pushed out.

Comments on Activity 10.2

Among the possible vertical stressors you may have noticed are marital problems and a possible tendency for the family to polarise into male and female camps. The family's expulsion from Uganda, associated with a loss of property and prestige, may well also be relevant here, and may make the suggestion of giving up his family home especially distressing for Mr Patel.

Among the horizontal stressors you might have included: Mrs Patel's arthritis, Mr Patel's arterio-scelerotic illness, the current marital difficulties between the daughter and son-in-law, and perhaps the demands of running the family business.

Although this is only a small 'snapshot' of a case, it may illustrate how much more is at stake in these situations than the immediate care needs of a given old person.

I have been speaking of changes in old age. As the discussion so far has already indicated, these changes are not so much a matter of transitions *into* old age as transitions *within* old age. In fact, as with any other 'stage' which I've discussed, old age is itself an arbitrary category which lumps together a very wide range of different human experiences. There is clearly a very big difference between a fit, healthy, recently retired person, and a very frail person twenty or thirty years older. Kroger (2000) suggests for this reason that we could look at two distinct phases within old age: younger old adulthood (66–79) and very old adulthood (80 and over). But any division based on ages will of course miss out on the very substantial differences between one individual and another.

Health

Poor health is not inevitable in old age. One American survey (Suzman et al., 1992) found that a majority of the over-eighties continued to live in the community and that, of these, one-third described their health as either 'good' or 'excellent'. Nevertheless, the likelihood of having to cope with illness or a number of disabilities does of course increase with old age. Although Suzman et al. found that a good number of their over-80 sample were in good health, the fact remained that over half of the old people in their survey had some sort of impairment.

It is important, however, to avoid having an expectation of poor health in old age, because such an expectation can be a self-fulfilling prophecy. A negative message to old people ('Well, what do you expect at your age?') can actually discourage them from remaining active, resulting in a deterioration in their fitness. There are social factors too which may contribute to ill-health in old age. In Britain old people are on average worse off financially than other age groups. In 1992 the state pension for a single person was worth less than 16 per cent of average male earnings before tax (Walker, 1993).

Cognitive changes

Some old people suffer memory loss as a result of specific conditions such as Alzheimer's disease and arterio-scelerotic illness (neither of which, incidentally, is unique to old people). However, psychological research confirms what most old people report: there is generally some deterioration in memory in old age. The problem seems to lie particularly in the area of retrieving items from memory. That is to say, the memories are still there, but are harder to locate, so that old people are more prone to the experience 'I know I know it, but I can't put my finger on it.' This is demonstrated by the fact that old people fare less well – in comparison to younger people – on tests of recall than they do on tests of recognition.

This difficulty with retrieval may reflect a more general slowing down of some cognitive processes. Old people do less well on tests of 'fluid intelligence', which are tests involving finding solutions to problems not previously encountered, as opposed to tests of 'crystallised intelligence', which involve problems that draw on accumulated knowledge (this distinction was made originally by Cattell, 1971). One researcher in this area has argued, though, that intelligence tests themselves may become less and less valid as tools as their subjects grow older, due to the increasing diversity of people's life experiences. The more diverse the experience of those tested, the less likely that a standardised test will do justice to their abilities (Dittman-Kohli et al., 1990).

One type of intelligence is traditionally associated with old age, the kind that is known as 'wisdom'. It is likely that if you were asked to call to mind an image of a 'wise man' or 'wise woman', then that image would be of an older person. Wisdom is a hard quality to define, however, with the result that it doesn't lend itself very readily to psychological tests, with their characteristic multiple-choice questions and puzzles. Nevertheless, some researchers have attempted to do so, by posing problems to subjects involving long-term issues and complex and ambiguous situations open to more than one interpretation. Interestingly, while not all old people did better on these tests, old people were more highly represented than other age groups among those who did do well (Baltes et al., 1992).

While there is a biological basis for some cognitive decline, external pressures also have a major effect on old people's cognitive functioning. Most professionals who work with elderly people will probably have noticed how old people can become dramatically more 'confused' (like 'Miss Kipling' in Activity 10.1) as the result of an admission to residential care or hospital – a form of psychological defence at a time of frightening loss of control over one's own life. This question of loss of control is a topic that we'll return to below.

Personality

Psychologists have also tried to explore the personality changes that take place in old age. Using personality tests that are supposed to measure how introverted or extroverted people are, researchers have found that there is a shift in old age from extrovert to introvert. It has also been suggested (by Eysenck, 1987) that there is a gender difference here: at younger age-ranges men tend to score as more extrovert than women. In old age both men and women tend to become more introverted, but the change is more pronounced in men, to the extent that they become the more introverted gender.

This inward shift seems to be reflected in approaches to life in general. Older people may be more inclined to deal with a stressful situation by adapting their own life to work round it, rather than attempting to confront the cause of the problem.

The inward shift also reflects Erikson's view (which we'll discuss shortly) that this is a stage of reflection and consolidation, aimed at achieving internal integrity. But it could also be argued that it reflects resignation to the reality of declining power and influence in the external world. We will come back to the latter possibility later in this chapter when I discuss the concept of 'disengagement'.

Tasks and Challenges in Old Age

Late adulthood – old age – is the last of Erikson's eight stages (see Table 2.1, page 43) and he assigns to it a sort of summing-up task. As Bond et al. (1993) observe:

> In order to understand people in later life it is necessary to see them in the context of their whole life history with the problems both successfully and unsuccessfully resolved from earlier periods of life. (Bond, Briggs and Coleman 1993: 30)

This would be true also of people at earlier stages. What is different about old age is that, if we fail to negotiate *this* stage successfully, there will not be further opportunities later. Hence *Integrity versus Despair* is what Erikson (1995) identified as the 'crisis' of this particular stage. A successful outcome would include: acceptance of one's life for what it has been, freedom from the burden of regret that it had not been different, and acceptance that one's life is one's own responsibility. Erikson referred to this as the achievement of 'ego integration'. An acceptance of one's own small place in the scheme of things could be said to be part of what is commonly referred to as 'wisdom', a quality which, as I noted above, is commonly associated with old age. So perhaps Erikson's 'ego integration' could be seen as the achievement of a kind of wisdom.

This statement from the British politician Lord (Dennis) Healey at the age of 83, seems to illustrate what might be entailed in achieving 'ego integration':

Personally, I did not notice much change until I was 75. From that age on, I have found my memory deteriorating and my senses getting less acute. . . . I can distinguish between different vowels, but all consonant sounds are the same to me. I can fail to see something I am looking at when it is staring me in the face.

There is a saying that when you are old, you either widen or wizen. . . . Physically I have wizened; I lost two stones in weight between the ages of 75 and 77. I can no longer run upstairs as I used to do. I find travel very tiring. Psychologically I have widened. I am much more interested in people as human beings and can imagine them at every age from childhood onwards when I see them.

I have lost all interest in power and position and no longer worry about making money. I still enjoy my work, but only what I want to do. . . .

I am much more sensitive to colours, shapes and sounds. My eye will automatically compose a clump of flowers or a corner of a landscape into a picture. . . . I get greater pleasure out of the sound of different instruments.

I have become exceptionally sensitive to sunlight, which immediately moves me to pleasure. . . . I love my wife, my children and my grandchildren more than ever. . . . (Guardian. 'Society', 27/9/00: 3)

But Lord Healey has many advantages. He is no doubt comfortably off financially, he clearly has a caring family around him and he can look back on a distinguished career in which he had many interesting experiences, met many interesting people and had ample opportunity to develop and use his talents. Not everyone adjusts so contentedly to the final stage of life. And for those who do not reach the state of 'ego integration', Erikson suggests, there can be despair, a sense that life has not been as it should have been and that it is now too late to change it.

Old people show this despair in different ways. It may be expressed as a contempt for people, institutions or the world in general. Other old people retreat into a passive, helpless role. 'Many people simply do not complete the life-cycle', Clayton (1975) observes. 'They die uncommitted, unresolved and frustrated, never having arrived at the stage where they could fully integrate and utilise their accumulated years of experience and knowledge.'

Successful ageing depends on the satisfactory resolution of issues raised earlier in life, but it also depends on external factors: the opportunities and encouragement available in a person's environment. And one of the aims of those who work with the elderly must surely be to maximise those opportunities, and to recognise the scale of the task that is involved in growing old.

As Coleman et al. (1993) comment:

In old age we are often left alone without support, without a partner, without a job, a role or money to spend. We may face infirmity and considerable isolation. It is no wonder that adjustment difficulties appear enhanced. In fact of course many older people are reasonably well adjusted. But because of our lack of imagination we do not appreciate their achievement. It is a shame that we have to grow old ourselves before we realise. (Coleman, Bond and Peace 1993: 15)

Old Age and Society

Old age is, like adolescence, adulthood, or childhood, as much a social construction as a biological fact. So what old age means to an individual will depend not only on factors like physical health and level of cognitive functioning, but on the messages she receives from those around her and from society at large. As ever, these cultural and biological factors interact. Even physical health and cognitive functioning are themselves directly affected by external circumstances and messages received from others. So it is important not to assume that, because old people happen to behave in a certain way under certain circumstances, that behaviour is in some way inevitable. The debate about 'disengagement', which I'll describe shortly, illustrates this point very well.

Having noted that the way old people perceive themselves will be shaped by the world around them, one must bear in mind that that world is also changing. For instance:

- Demographic changes resulting from a declining birth-rate and longer life-spans mean that old people are a larger proportion of the population than in most other periods of history, particularly in the industrialised world. Differences in the average life-span of men and women also mean that there are more elderly women than men.
- Rapid social and technological change in society generally, as well as longer life-spans, means that the world in which old people find themselves is vastly different from the one in which they grew up. This would not have been true to anything like the same extent in many pre-industrial cultures, where technology and social mores might remain relatively unchanged for generations.
- Compulsory retirement means that many old people are deprived of a role in the economy whether or not it is their wish. This results for many in a large drop in income and in dependency on others and the state. (You may remember the discussion in the previous chapter on dependency, independence and 'responsible interdependence'.) Of course, we should also acknowledge that retirement is very welcome to many people.

Disengagement

The term 'disengagement' was coined in the 1960s by Cumming and Henry (1961), to describe the generally reduced involvement of old people in the outer world. Models of ageing tended at that time to be *medical* models expressed in terms of deteriorating functioning, and the term 'disengagement' was supposed to provide a more positive way of describing – and thinking about – the process of letting go of external involvement that is typical of many old people.

Cumming and Henry suggested that this disengagement from external interests – along with other personality changes such as a preference for simple and familiar situations – does not represent any sort of reduced functioning, but rather a way of preserving energy for other tasks which have become more important. These tasks are really of the kind envisaged by Erikson, to do with reflecting on, reviewing and coming to terms with one's life as a whole.

But critics of the idea of disengagement, such as Estes et al. (1982), have pointed out that disengagement is often forced upon old people, for example by compulsory retirement or by institutional care. Old people do not necessarily *want* to give up their involvement in the world. The theory of disengagement, according to this view, simply lends legitimacy to a process by which society chooses to marginalise its elderly people and, so to speak, to tidy them away out of sight.

There is no reason, incidentally, why both Cumming and Henry *and* Estes should not be right. Disengagement could indeed be a normal and necessary psychological characteristic of old age, and yet also be exploited as a concept for political ends. You may remember from Chapter 3 that Bowlby's attachment theory may likewise have been taken on board by those wishing for political reasons to get women out of the industrial workforce, but this does not invalidate the theory itself.

Control

In the discussion of learning theory in Chapter 5, I considered evidence that ability to control events in the environment is linked directly to indicators of stress. I also discussed the idea that passivity and helplessness can itself be a form of behaviour that is learned in situations where we have no control. Many old people do experience a sense of reduced control over their environment for a variety of reasons, and this can lead to anxiety, depression and low self-esteem, and even to reduced physical health.

One study (Langer, 1983) demonstrated the importance of a feeling of control in a residential home setting. A group of residents was addressed by the home administrator with speeches that placed an emphasis on their responsibility for their own lives. The speaker encouraged them to make decisions and gave them actual decisions to make as well as asking them to take responsibility for things in the home environment other than themselves. Another group of residents was addressed by the same person with speeches that emphasised the responsibility of the staff of the establishment to provide care for them and meet their needs. Of the latter group, 71 per cent were found to become more debilitated in a period as short as three weeks, while in the former group, 93 per cent showed overall improvement.

The fear of losing control of one's own life is common in old age, but it is not an inevitable feature of old age. After all some of the most powerful people on earth have been old people (see box below). Just as disability is not only a result of impairments but also of society's attitude to people with impairments, so the feeling of losing control is a product of society's attitude to old people. Langer's study could be said to have demonstrated how this works, since it shows that the old people concerned felt more or less in control of their lives *purely because of the messages they were given.*

📖 **Powerful Old People** 📖

- Indira Gandhi was the Prime Minister of India, the world's second most populous country, when she was assassinated in 1984 at 67.

- Nelson Mandela became president of South Africa in 1994 at the age of 76, having spent twenty-five years of his life in jail.

- Golda Meir became Prime Minister of Israel in 1969 at the age of 71. She was 75 when she resigned.

- Deng Xiaoping, who died in 1997 at the age of 93, was the most powerful man in the most populous country on earth until well into his eighties.

Langer's experiment illustrates how a feeling of losing control – even if the feeling is as a result of no more than different *words* – can have a very dramatic effect on general well-being. Old people experience many difficulties which can lead to a feeling of loss of control. They may have limited financial resources, compared to people in work, and limited life choices as a result. Some, though not all, have to deal with physical impairments. All will be aware of at least some loss of their physical power, and be aware that younger people around them are physically more capable (old people may feel more vulnerable to crime, for example). And even if they are mentally and physically in very good shape, old people may have to deal with the *assumption* that this is not the case. Indeed in some contexts they are treated as if they are not adults at all (infantilised) and spoken to as if they were dependent children ('Have we been to the toilet yet, Mrs Jones?').

Socio-economic position

Financial hardship is more common in old age than it is for other age groups. If you look at the poorest 20 per cent of the population in Britain you find that 27 per cent of them are over 65, although the 65+ age-range represent only 13 per cent of the population as a whole (Slater, 1995: 160). This means that old people have on average to spend a higher percentage of their income than the rest of the population on basic essentials such as food, rent and fuel. And thus, though they suffer the highest risk of hypothermia, they are the age-group least able to afford to keep their accommodation warm enough.

Elderly women are, on average, financially worse off than men and a higher proportion of women than men face mobility problems in later life. A higher proportion of women than men also live on their own or live in institutions. This is largely because women constitute the largest part of the elderly population. In Britain, for instance, there are 123 women for every 100 men in the age-range 65–74 and this ratio rises to 289:100 in the 85+ age-range. Old people on low incomes experience significantly higher health problems than those from more prosperous backgrounds.

Ageism

'Ageism' is a word coined by analogy with 'sexism' and 'racism' to mean *the unwarranted application of negative stereotypes to old people*. Certain qualities are often assumed to be characteristic of old age, although it is the case that there are many old people whom they simply do not fit – or indeed many younger people who they *do* fit. In one study, Carp (1969) compared 350 elderly people with 350 college students, and found that some of the personality characteristics associated with old age were actually *more* common among the students than among the old people.

I do not wish to portray all old people as necessarily victims of oppression and injustice. Many old people would not see themselves in such a light at all, and, as we have seen, there are positive as well as negative stereotypes of old age, powerful old people as well as powerless ones. But negative stereotypes do exist and they do have an effect on people. We know that negative stereotypes of black people or women can be internalised by black people or women themselves, so that in some respects prejudice may become a self-fulfilling prophecy. Indeed most of us have at some point probably noticed the way that we tend to become what others label us. Labelling theory was developed by Lemert (1972), Becker (1963) and others to describe the way that people tend to live up to deviant labels that are applied to them, and the concept is applicable in many areas, such as academic performance, or the acquisition of gender roles. By the same token if old people are labelled as 'bad-tempered', 'inflexible', 'senile' or whatever else, then they are likely to live up to the expectations created.

Certainly there *are* numerous negative images of old people. There are far more demeaning terms for old people than there are for other age groups. Think of 'wrinkly', 'fuddy-duddy', 'old dear', 'old fart', 'old crow' or 'old bat'. Indeed only children seem to be comparable with the elderly in having derogatory terms (like 'brat') which are specific to their age group, and even in their case, these terms are much less numerous. A number of unwarranted generalisations are also made about old people's health and mental capacity, though the majority of old people are *not* sick or demented and there is no medical condition that is exclusive to old age. Even in the 80+ age group four out of five do not suffer from severe or moderate dementia (Briggs, 1985) and, in a 1988 British survey, 20–40 per cent of people in the over-85 age group reported that they did not have a physical disability (Martin et al., 1988). An even higher proportion of old people under 85 are neither mentally nor physically frail.

Another common assumption is that old people are no longer sexually active. Given that sexual activity is generally seen as one of the prerogatives of adulthood, this is perhaps an instance of the way that old people are 'infantilised' as a result of ageism. In fact an American survey found that, among the over-seventies, 79 per cent of men and 65 per cent of women reported that they were sexually active (Brecher, 1984).

In the political arena, old people are sometimes characterised as an unsustainable burden on the public purse, because of the cost of pensions, social security benefits, health and social care. In fact, though some old people are heavy users of health services compared to the rest of the population, the majority are not. Old people consult their doctors less than other age groups for conditions such as headaches, colds and 'flu, according to Cox et al. (1987). And of course it is the state that determines that in most areas of work old people have no choice but to retire by 65, even if they wish to go on working.

Ageism is not just a matter of attitudes but of actual *treatment* of old people. As we've noted, in the welfare system old people are often infantilised, both in the way they are spoken to and about, and in the way that their options are taken from them. Taking away control can result, in a very direct way, in a deterioration of mental and physical health. Ageism can have a very direct effect on people's well-being, as well (rather cruelly) of once again having the effect of self-fulfilling prophecy – that is to say: if you treat elderly people as passive, dependent and unable to think for themselves, they start to act that way, and this seems to justify your original assumption and allow you to continue treating them accordingly.

Even some of ideas that are intended to be helpful and supportive to old people may reflect ageist assumptions. For example, reminiscence has come to be regarded as an important function in old age, and efforts have been made to facilitate it for old people in residential care. However, it seems possible that old people – particularly those in institutional care – may retreat into reminiscence because there is nothing much to talk or think about in daily lives that are all organised for them. The use of 'reminiscence therapy' in old people's homes, well meant though it may be, can actually in itself be patronising in that it makes the assumption that all old people share similar nostalgic memories. Would a group of 40-year-olds appreciate such an assumption being made about them? In fact, having lived the longest, old people are probably the most *diverse* of all the age groups.

If we contrast the active, positive attitude of famous and successful elderly people – such as Lord Healey quoted earlier – with that of those who seem to have accepted a passive, dependent, childlike role, we can perhaps get some sense of the impact of ageism on old people who do not have the same advantages.

Social attitudes to old people, however, are not fixed, and this is evidenced by the fact that in different societies old people are viewed in different ways.

Cultural differences

In Britain senior judges are often criticised for being too old and out of touch, and are quite often lampooned as being 'senile'. There is surely more than a little ageism in that common criticism. Perhaps we should ask instead why, if men and women of over 70 can continue to be active and effective as judges and politicians, they should be regarded as unemployable in most other areas?

Old people are traditionally seen as repositories of wisdom (and allowing judges to continue working into old age is perhaps a hangover of this view), but Western industrialised society does not place the value on the wisdom of old age that is, or was, given to it in other cultures. An anthropologist, David Gutmann (1987), who compared attitudes to ageing in industrialised societies with attitudes in the Middle East and Central America, suggests that in industrialised societies, we miss out on the strengths of old age. He argues that old age flourishes in a coherent culture with well-defined traditions. In such a culture, women become more powerful in the extended family as they enter old age. Older men tend to disengage from day-to-day decision making and action, but become custodians for the values of their culture.

The constantly changing circumstances of modern society make these roles much harder to play because old people are like time travellers, brought up in a society vastly different from the one in which they now find themselves. For instance 90-year olds in the year 2001, though born only a few years after the first ever powered flight, now live in a world in which communication satellites, charter-flight package holidays and intercontinental missiles are a fact of life. They will have adjusted to new developments over the years, but the values they were brought up with were the product of a world in which women did not have the vote, European empires ruled Africa and Asia, and the contraceptive pill, the domestic telephone and the mass-produced motor car did not yet exist.

But an assumption that the cultures of pre-industrial and developing countries place a higher value on old people, and that their families take more responsibility for caring for them, can in itself be unhelpful for old people from ethnic minorities within Western industrial societies. There is now a sizeable number of old people in Britain who are members of ethnic minority communities originating in Asia, Africa and the Caribbean, and there is a common assumption among caring professionals that African-Caribbean and Asian old people will not require the same level of support from public services as the white elderly because they will be cared for by their extended families. The assumption is not entirely ungrounded because there is evidence that such support really *is* more forthcoming for people from these communities than it is for the white elderly population. But nevertheless isolation in old age is by no means rare in these groups either, and the very fact that support from extended family is seen as the norm in a given community, may mean that much more stigma and shame is attached to those who do not receive it.

The following activity will give you an opportunity to reflect on the discussion so far about old age, and consider its practical implications:

Activity 10.3

Erikson described the central task of old age as resolving the 'crisis' of Integrity v. Despair.

Think of old people you've known or worked with, and try and think of instances of people who have managed to achieve some sense of integrity in old age – and others who have not. (The latter might be evident either as a resigned passivity or as a general hostility . . .)

What role can professionals and others play in helping old people accomplish this task?

Comments on Activity 10.3

You have probably been able to think of some examples, though of course many old people will fall somewhere in between the two extremes. Resolving any 'crisis' (in Erikson's sense) is ultimately something that a person can do only for themselves, but it may have occurred to you that the modern welfare system is full of attitudes which can hardly help old people to feel positive about the last stage in their lives. Perhaps you felt that if we treated old people as (a) human beings (rather than merely logistical problems), and (b) adults (rather than quasi-children) this might help.

It seems appropriate to conclude this discussion with the thought that our attitudes to old people are really our attitudes to our future selves. This means that, as Slater (1995: 159) warns,

> if you believe people should be discriminated against on grounds of age, rather than need – as [British] newspaper headlines in the early 1990s claimed was happening in the health service – then you cannot complain when you are on the receiving end of such prejudice when you grow older.

Chapter Summary

Coming to a Conclusion

- In this chapter, I've looked at the changes that occur in old age, including physical and psychological changes. While some common changes may be biological in origin, we should be careful not to assume that they apply equally to all old people. An assumption that all old people have poor health would not only be unwarranted by the facts, but could also have the effect of being a self-fulfilling prophecy.

- I then looked at the particular tasks and challenges in old age, using Erikson's idea of old age as a time when our principal task is to come to terms with, or reconcile ourselves to, our lives as a whole. I offered contrasting images of people who succeed and fail to achieve this.

- I then looked at old age in a social context. I looked at the idea of 'disengagement', relating it to Erikson's model, but also asking the question as to what extent an old person's disengagement from the world is a psychological necessity, and to what extent it is actually imposed by society. I looked at the diminished control over the rest of the world that commonly occurs in old age and its impact on the individual. I considered the socio-economic position of old people, the impact of prejudice against old people (ageism) and, finally, briefly considered cultural issues and particular issues facing members of ethnic minorities in old age.

In the next and final chapter we will consider dying and death.

Suggested Reading

- Bond, J., Coleman, P. and Peace, S. (eds) (1993) *Ageing in Society* (London: Sage)

  (A particularly comprehensive collection of writings on many different aspects of the psychology and sociology of old age.)

- Davey, B. (ed.) (1995) *Birth to Old Age: Health in Transition* (Buckingham: Open University Press)

  (This has two useful chapters on old age.)

- Fennell, G., Phillipson, C. and Evers, H. (eds) (1988) *The Sociology of Old Age* (Buckingham: Open University Press)
- Markides, K.S. and Mindel, C.H. (eds) (1987) *Ageing and Ethnicity* (London: Sage)

11 The End

Death and dying

I have put this chapter on death after the chapter on old age, so I should perhaps start by acknowledging that of course death is not the exclusive property of the old. We can die at any age and at any age we may have to cope with the death of others. However, as Sidell (1993: 151) observes 'Death has become increasingly unfamiliar to young people' in modern industrialised society. Most people live to old age and most people die in the relatively segregated environment of hospital with the result that many people, for much of their lives, have little direct exposure to death. Many adults, for example, have lived through their lives without ever actually seeing a dead person.

In Britain in 1998, more than 80 per cent of those who died were 65 or older, and more than 60 per cent had reached or passed their 75th birthday (Office of National Statistics, 2000). In Britain in 1991, 73 per cent of deaths occurred in hospitals or other institutions rather than at home, as against 53 per cent in 1960 (Seale, 1995: 179).

As with other events which we have discussed, death is both a biological event and a social one. Death occurs when the body ceases to function as a biological entity, but the meanings attached to it, both by the individual concerned and by those around her, are dependent on the complex web of personal and social circumstances in which the death occurs, as well as on the way of dying itself.

Indeed Seale (1998: 34) makes the point that biological death and social death need not necessarily coincide:

> The material end of the body is only roughly congruent with the death of the social self. In extreme old age, or in diseases where mind and personality disintegrate, social death may precede biological death. Ghosts, memories and ancestor worship are examples of the opposite: a social presence outlasting the body.

Currer adds that there is actually quite a widespread fear of social death prematurely preceding actual death: 'There is evidence in certain cemeteries ... of mausolea with bell-towers with a connecting wire through into the coffin to enable the allegedly deceased person to ring the bell in the event of waking' (Currer, 2001: 25).

Here I am going to look at death at three 'system levels' (to use a term which I discussed in Chapter 8). I will consider first death in the context of society as a whole, then (under the heading 'Death and others') death at the level of family and community, and finally death as an individual experience. But, as ever, dividing the subject up in this way is in the end an artificial device. All the topics under these headings could in fact be discussed with reference to each of these three levels. Religious belief, for example, can have a very direct impact on the individual experience of death, but religions are something developed and maintained at the level of society as a whole. Death itself is not just an event, but an existential question (see p. 20), one with which we struggle at every level and in every culture and social context.

Death and Society

Dying takes place in a social context and how we deal with it is shaped in part by the society in which we live. Among the many areas of difference between different cultures and different epochs, are the following:

- The extent to which death and dead people are a fact of everyday experience. (Many people in western industrialised society go through most of their lives without ever having seen a dead person.)
- Beliefs as to the existence and nature of an afterlife. (All the world's major religions include some conception of an afterlife, but its components vary greatly. Consider, for instance, the ideas of heaven, hell, purgatory and limbo in Roman Catholic theology, the widespread belief in ghosts, or the Buddhist idea of a soul being reborn again and again on earth in different human and animal forms. In modern secular industrial cultures, many people do not believe in any kind of continuation of personal existence after death. Davies (1991) suggested that

in England about half the population hold a belief in some form of immortality, while about a quarter believe there is no afterlife and the remainder are uncertain.)

- Cultural beliefs regarding acceptable and appropriate expressions of grieving. (In some cultures an extravagant display of grief is encouraged, in others restraint and containment of emotion are admired and seen as decorous.)
- Funeral rituals and the treatment of human remains. (The different practices that exist for the latter include cremation, burial, mummification and even 'sky burial', as practised in some Native American cultures, where human remains are placed on a platform to be consumed by birds.)
- The extent to which dying people are made aware of the fact that they are dying. (This is now the norm in Britain, for example, but is less common in Japan, apparently, where relatives may be informed about the fact that the dying person has a terminal illness, although this news is kept from the dying person herself, according to Seale, 1998: 111.)

I shall not attempt here to cover all these topics (for an overview of cultural differences, see Murray Parkes et al., 1997). What I will do now is look at two themes in current thinking about death.

The denial of death

According to one view of contemporary attitudes to death, we live in a society that denies death – and death is now a taboo subject in the way that sex once was.

According to this view, death is hidden in hospitals or institutions and we no longer know how to talk about death, or to help the bereaved, or to mourn properly for the dead.

A leading exponent of this perspective has been Ariès (1976), a French historian, who argued that in medieval times people were much more at home with death, which was visible all around them. He argues that in modern times medical science has led to the idea of controlling illness and controlling nature. Instead of believing in an afterlife, we comfort ourselves with the illusion that *this* life can be prolonged indefinitely by defeating death. So death becomes something to be battled against, as illustrated by the media cliché: 'X finally lost her courageous battle against cancer.' In modern times, it is argued, the doctor fighting disease has replaced the priest fighting for the salvation of the soul. But, as doctors ultimately cannot abolish death, death has become segregated, hidden away. People avoid others who are bereaved or dying. Dying people are isolated as a result and deprived of support which they might otherwise receive.

This idea can be extended also to our treatment of old people. In the previous chapter we discussed the concept of 'disengagement' (Cumming and Henry, 1961), and the debate as to whether disengagement in old age reflected a psychological need on the part of old people, or merely a need on the part of the rest of society to justify the marginalisation of old people. Kearl (1989) takes the latter argument further by suggesting that the purpose of disengagement is to remove from society those who are likely to die, so that the rest of us need not be confronted by the fact of death. There are two views on disengagement, and it is also possible to argue, as does Kalish (1985) that disengagement is a useful psychological preparation for dying, on the part of the individuals concerned. Kalish argues that disengagement is one reason that old people tend to find it easier to accept their own imminent death than do younger people: they have already begun the work of letting go.

This difference of view on disengagement reflects a difference of view on the whole 'denial of death' thesis. Many commentators would dispute whether the 'denial of death' in modern times is really as extreme as Ariès argues – or whether there has been such a fundamental change as he suggests in comparison with previous periods of history. Some degree of denial of death is surely inevitable – and probably always has been at any stage in history – to allow us to get on with our own lives. Indeed Seale (1998: 211) argues that our whole social and cultural life – the stories we tell ourselves about the nature and meaning of life – can be seen as defences against death:

> Social institutions which are reflected in the minutiae of conversational exchanges, are based on a successful but continuing active defence against disorder and decay, the root cause of which is the temporal nature of bodily existence.

On this basis the medicalised approach to death which Ariès characterises as 'denial of death' is just a new way of managing an old problem.

It is interesting to contrast Seale's suggestion that 'social and cultural life can, in the last analysis, be understood as a social construction in the face of death' (Seale 1998: 211) with the psychodynamic ideas I looked at in Chapters 2 and 3, which place an emphasis on *early* life experience as shaping how we relate to the world. We can look at our social relationships as existing in the shadow of our early childhood experiences, or we can look at them as having a shadow cast over them from the future.

Freud believed in the existence of a 'death instinct', an instinctive drive towards annihilation, alongside the sexual instinct which seeks to perpetuate and renew life. Kleinian theory in particular draws heavily on this concept. If we look at it this way death becomes, not just an external enemy to be kept at bay, but a drive within ourselves to be managed, as we have to manage our other drives and longings.

'Revivalist death'

Something of a reaction has occurred to the medicalised model of death so that we now also have what Walter (1994) calls a 'revivalist' model, in which death is seen as an important stage of life to be, if not celebrated, at any rate experienced to the full. There would seem to be a close parallel here with changes of attitude to childbirth where again, during the second half of the twentieth century, there has been a reaction against an excessively medicalised approach and towards a more personal one in which the individual concerned, rather than the professionals, is placed at centre stage. This changing view of death is reflected in the growth of the hospice movement.

In the 'revivalist' view the dying person herself is seen as choosing her own way of dealing with her own death, rather than subjecting herself to the control of doctors, and death is seen as a psychological process, rather than just a medical event – something to be worked through, rather than blotted out. Dying, in this model, is a process of coming to terms with the end of one's life, the final culmination of the process of integration which I discussed in the previous chapter. We should note, however, that the logical consequence of giving more choice to dying people about the manner of their dying means that some might actually *choose* the more medicalised model. The 'revivalist' approach is itself only one way of looking at things.

Society's attitudes to dying seem to fluctuate between several different perspectives. The practical implications of this for those working with dying or bereaved people, would seem to be that it is important to have thought through one's own attitude on these matters, but also important to be aware that there is no one 'right' approach, and that others may have very different views about the social context of death.

You may like to use the following activity to consider your own thoughts on this:

Activity 11.1

Should dying people always be informed that they are dying? And if not, under what circumstances should they not be informed, and who should take the decision not to inform them?

Suppose you are a doctor and your patient Mr J is dying of cancer. His daughter, who is his only surviving relative, has been told that the disease is terminal and untreatable. She insists that Mr J should not be informed of this, saying that it would be cruel and would cause him quite unnecessary distress.

On the other hand Nurse B, who is also caring for Mr J, feels very strongly that Mr J should be informed. She says that if it was her she would certainly wish to be informed and would be very angry if she was not informed, and was therefore deprived of the opportunity to say her goodbyes to life. Nurse B does not consider that her daughter, or anyone else, would have any right to deny her this information. To deny Mr J this information, she says, would be to deny him his right to be treated as an adult.

What would you do? Would it make any difference to you if Mr J came from another country, and if his daughter informed you that in their country dying people were not normally told the nature of their illness?

Comments on Activity 11.1

The question of whether or not to tell dying people that they are dying is not one that has a final definitive answer, because in different societies at different times, there have been different views about what is appropriate. Your decision might be simplified if you were able to establish what Mr J's own views on this matter had been in the past, or if you were able to establish what was the norm in the country from which he had come. (If Mr J came from a country where dying people were not normally told, it is likely that he himself would be aware that this was the norm, and would not himself expect to be told.) But there is no straightforward answer.

Death and Others

In Chapter 6, I discussed the psychological stages that are involved in transitions, moving from initial shock and incredulity through depression and self-doubt to eventual letting go. In Chapter 8, when I looked at the family life-cycle from a systems perspective, I presented the idea that every transition that occurs is not just a challenge for the individual but also for every other member of their family network. This is true of marriage, the birth of a child, puberty, retirement, and the onset of old age. All of these events require, to a greater or lesser extent, that a whole group of people have to find a way of letting go of an old and familiar order of things, and (whether they wish it or not) to re-establish themselves as best they can in new and unfamiliar territory. And this is also true of death.

There are a few very isolated people whose death has little significant impact on anyone else, and some unloved people whose death is not mourned. There are also some people who are loved but whose death is felt to be a welcome release by all concerned. But in most cases, for family and friends the corollary of a death is bereavement and grief. In the case of deaths which are predictable, that grief does not just follow on from the death, but includes the 'anticipatory grieving' which can also be experienced by the dying person herself.

Grief is a reaction to what can be a massive disruption in one's social world. When we grieve for someone we loved, we are also grieving for the part of ourselves that we invested in that person. More generally, Seale (1998: 211) suggests that grief

> is in fact an extreme version of an everyday experience of 'grief' which is routinely worked upon in order to turn the psyche away from awareness of mortality and towards continuation in life.

In other words, Seale is suggesting that it is in the nature of life that we are constantly struggling with the possibility of death and loss – an actual bereavement simply brings our worst fears to the fore. An analogy might be a flood in a landscape, such as the Cambridgeshire Fens, which is normally kept dry by constant pumping.

The nature and extent of grief, and the ability of the bereaved person to move on, will depend of course on a whole range of factors, including the personal history of the grieving person, the nature of the relationship and the manner and timing of the death (see the discussion below, on timely and untimely deaths).

Attachment and loss

In thinking about bereavement, it is useful to go back to attachment theory. You may remember that John Bowlby's major work was entitled *Attachment and Loss*, and it is of course sadly the case that the risk of loss is the inevitable price to be paid for the many benefits of forming an attachment. Attachment theory suggests that some people find it difficult to form secure attachments in adult life as the result of defences that they established in childhood against the pain of loss: 'the determination at all costs', as Bowlby (1946) put it, 'not to risk again the disappointment and resulting rages and longings which wanting someone very much and not getting them involves'.

According to attachment theory, people who as children had a secure attachment with their carers are able to internalise the security that came from that relationship (the 'secure base') and this will not only help them to form satisfactory adult relationships, but will help them to withstand the pain of loss in the future. Sable (1989) undertook a study of widows who had lost their husbands in the previous one to three years. She found that women whose early attachment histories had been relatively secure coped better with their bereavement than women with histories of insecure attachment, experiencing less distress and less depression.

Howe (1995) suggests that we can identify characteristic grieving patterns for the *avoidant attachment* style and for the *ambivalent attachment* style. Avoidant individuals are ones who show 'compulsive self-reliance' and often display delayed grief reactions.

> The typical attempts to be emotionally self-reliant and wary about forming intimate relationships means that the loss of someone close . . . triggers the usual defence mechanisms of emotional shut-down and distancing. In the short term at least the person suffering the loss may not cry or appear to be unduly upset. Those who fail to grieve remain vulnerable to future losses. Seemingly exaggerated grief reactions to a loss experience . . . can sometimes be accounted for when it is realised that the individual never really acknowledged or adjusted to the earlier loss of a significant attachment relationship. (Howe, 1995: 136)

On the other hand, *ambivalently* attached people experience relationships in which there are 'equal measures of desperate clinging and resentful anger'. As a result, if the other partner dies, the bereaved person may experience 'guilt and self-blame (because anger and hostility had been a constant feature of the relationship) and acute pain (because there is now no one emotionally available)' (Howe 1995: 136). In cases of *chronic grief*,

> individuals cannot seem to escape their feelings of despair and depression. It may be that their relationship with the lost other was characterised by deep feelings of ambivalence. . . . The simmering resentment that may have lurked beneath the surface of the relationship is still difficult to acknowledge and so the true range of feelings associated with the grief fail to receive proper expression and therefore remain unresolved. (Howe, 1995: 137)

(For more discussion on the relationship between childhood attachment and coping with bereavement in adult life, see Murray Parkes et al. 1991.)

Narratives of grief

From a sociological perspective, Seale (1998), as I've already mentioned, sees society constructing various discourses or narratives with which somehow to contain or combat the fact of death. This takes place at the system level of society as a whole. He suggests that 'in late modern society medicine and psychiatry offer one of a number of discourses that people have constructed as a sheltering canopy against the adverse consequences of embodiment' (Seale 1998: 211). ('Embodiment' refers to the fact that we are physical biological entities, the consequence of which is that we cannot avoid dying.) But he also describes ways in which individuals construct their own narratives to deal with their own feelings in particular circumstances. Each of us when bereaved has to deal with the fact that a loved or familiar person is no longer available, and to make some sense perhaps of the suffering and indignities that person may have suffered at the end. Often there is also guilt or regret about not having been there, or not having done more to help, or of having left things unsaid or unresolved until it was too late.

Moving on from a death may in part be seen as the construction of a narrative which in some way contains these things. You may remember from the discussion of transitions in Chapter 6 that the latter stages in the model I presented there were:

- *Letting go* of the old order of things as they existed prior to the new event (which have been clung on to up to now in defiance of the new circumstances).
- *Testing* and exploring the new circumstances, trying out new identities and starting to form new attachments.
- *Searching for meaning* by looking back at the past from the new viewpoint of it *being* in the past, reappraising it and trying to make sense of it.
- *Integration*, when the transition process is complete and we feel 'at home' in the new reality. New behaviours, new ideas about ourselves have become part of our sense of our own identity.

Many people who have lost someone to whom they have been very close would say that they never 'feel at home' in the new reality. But constructing a narrative, an explanation to oneself about what has occurred and how it makes sense in the scheme of things, would seem to be part of the work involved in being able to move on into a life in which the lost other person will no longer be a part, except in memory.

A very simple and rudimentary example of this process, perhaps, is the common custom in Britain in recent times of laying flowers at the site of fatal accidents and murders. The people who do this do not necessarily know the deceased person personally, but it is as if they are seeking to cover up the image of tragedy and violence associated with a particular spot, with a new image of beauty and growth.

Loss and restoration

Another account of the process of coping with bereavement is offered by a 'dual process model' (Stroebe and Schut, 1999). They suggest that two types of coping are involved in bereavement, which they call respectively 'loss-orientated' and 'restoration-orientated' (see Figure 11.1).

While other models imply a chronological sequence in which coming to terms with loss is followed by 'building a new life', these authors suggest

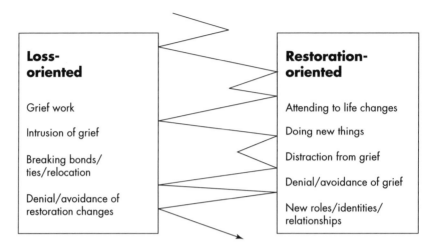

FIGURE 11.1   *Bereavement: oscillation between loss-orientated and restoration-orientated tasks (from Stroebe and Schut, 1999: 213)*

that a 'waxing and waning' occur and that grieving people typically oscillate between grieving and getting on with life. They point out that in reality bereaved people do take 'time off from grieving' (1999: 212), and have to address themselves to the practical adjustments that are required in the wake of a death (financial arrangements for example) and indeed to other matters.

Loss-orientation and restoration-orientation, then, are two separate kinds of work, or stressor, that bereaved people face, though the former is what is conventionally seen as grieving, and has received much more attention. It is interesting that the model illustrated above envisages that to get on with *either* of these tasks requires a degree of denial. Loss work involves turning away from the here and now, restoration work involves turning away from the pain of grief. This is a reminder that while denial (or 'defensive exclusion') can be harmful and counter-productive in its effects, it is also a very necessary psychological mechanism.

Stroebe and Schut suggest that there are individual differences as to how people allocate their time between loss-orientation and restoration-orientation, and that this can lead to conflict between survivors. For example, following the death of a child, the parent who focuses more on restoration may be seen by the other parent as not grieving, whereas in fact this person simply has a different *way* of grieving. These authors also suggest that typically men are more restoration-orientated when bereaved, while women are more loss-orientated. Female grief has, it seems, historically been studied more than male grief, in contrast to other areas that I have discussed in this book where generalisations have sometimes been made from a mainly male perspective.

Stroebe and Schut postulate that oscillation between loss-orientation and restoration-orientation is likely to be psychologically more healthy than going to either extreme. In one study (Schut et al., 1997) they tried out different kinds of grief counselling with widows and widowers. What they found was that:

'Teaching' bereaved men and women to cope in the way that the opposite sex usually adopts (teaching men to be more emotion-oriented and women to be more problem-oriented) was associated with a lowering of distress. (Stroebe and Schut, 1999: 219)

The Individual Experience of Death

People deal with the fact of their own death in many different ways, depending on their own personality, their culture and the actual circumstances.

Predictable and unpredictable deaths

Some deaths – such as death from cancer – can be predicted in advance by the person who is dying as well as by others. It is these deaths which the 'revivalist' model and the hospice movement, which I discussed above, really address. In such circumstances the dying person herself can go through a grieving process for her *own* life.

Kübler-Ross (1970) a psychiatrist who worked extensively with terminally ill patients, has described the reaction to news of a terminal illness as going through several stages:

* *denial* ('It can't be true. You've made a mistake . . .')
* *anger* (against doctors, family members, God . . . someone must be blamed)
* *bargaining* (the dying person attempts to make some kind of deal with fate: 'just let me live to see my grandchild . . .')
* *depression* (feelings of guilt, fear of dying, loosening of relationships, preoccupation with a sense of loss)
* *acceptance* (letting go, the end of the struggle . . .)

You can see that although not divided up in exactly the same way, this is very much the same pattern as the transition model which I discussed in Chapter 6.

Not all deaths can be predicted in this way. There are many sudden, unexpected deaths. About a quarter of deaths occur as a result of heart disease, often involving a sudden heart attack. Fatal accidents are another example, and in Britain are the commonest cause of death in the 1–30 age group (NAHA/RoSPA Strategy Group, 1990). There are also chosen deaths, not only suicides, but also less clear-cut choices made by elderly people to let go of life, perhaps after a long illness. And, though 'old age' *per se* is not a cause of death, many old people die as a result of a series of health problems, so that the actual cause of death is quite hard to define. In such cases there may not be a moment at which the dying person is clearly faced with the knowledge that she is dying. There are cases too where others may know that a person is dying but the knowledge has been withheld from the dying person herself. As I noted earlier this may be more common in some cultures than others.

Timely and untimely deaths

The way we experience death – and the way also that it is experienced by others – may be greatly influenced by whether we see the death as timely or premature. In the case of old people, death is often accepted as inevitable and even as 'fair'. In England, when a person dies at quite an old age, it is commonplace for others to remark: 'Well, he had a good innings.' (For readers who do not come from the cricket-playing part of the world, I should explain that the reference is to the game of cricket and a batsman's 'innings' is the time he lasts on the pitch.) We also speak of a 'ripe old age', where the connotations of the word 'ripe' are of fruit or corn that has reached the time where it is ready to be gathered or reaped. Death itself, of course, is traditionally the 'grim reaper'.

And dying does seem, in general terms, to be a rather different experience for the old person than it is for younger people. Young people who learn that they are dying may feel cheated of life, just as their friends and relatives may feel that they have been stolen prematurely from them. One study of attitudes to dying among old people found that older people most often personified death as 'gentle, well-meaning' (Kastenbaum and Alsenburg, 1976). 'Speaking generally, one of the many benefits . . . of living well into old age', write Young and Cullen (1996: 27), who interviewed dying people and their relatives in the East End of London, 'was that death was easier to accept.' As an 80-year-old interviewee of theirs remarked:

> When I was your age . . . I'd have been terrified of dying but not now. As you grow older it becomes inevitable. I'm not afraid of dying, no, nor the manner of dying. I just don't think about it. It doesn't trouble me at all. (Young and Cullen: 1996: 25–6)

One reason for this resignation seems to be that in old age, most people will increasingly have experienced the death of friends and loved ones.

'I do my book at Christmas and it's crossing out such a lot', said one old person (quoted in Sidell, 1993).

I do not wish to suggest that this degree of acceptance is characteristic of *all* old people. But, as Sidell puts it (1993: 155) many old people do not seem to follow the famous advice of the poet Dylan Thomas to his father:

> Do not go gentle into that good night,
> Old age should burn and rave at close of day;
> Rage, rage against the dying of the light.
>
> (Thomas, quoted in Larkin, 1973)

On the contrary, many seem to yield to the 'good night' of death without a fight. The implication of this is that old people tend to reach Kübler-Ross's stage of *acceptance* in relation to their own death more easily than younger people, if 'easily' can ever be an appropriate word when talking about this most fundamental of tasks.

People dying at a younger age, seem to spend more time at the earlier of Kübler-Ross's stages (*denial, anger, bargaining* and *depression*). For the younger people in Young and Cullen's study, 'their general inclination . . . was to struggle against the onset of death (or the unseemly acceleration of ageing that death implies) with all the vigour they could muster' (1996: 27).

> Whether a fighting spirit makes final death any easier or more difficult we do not know, and even those who are very close to the end can do no more than guess. But during the period which leads up to it, such a spirit certainly does give something to live for. (Young and Cullen, 1996: 36)

But we should be careful not to overgeneralise about younger people, any more than about older ones. Even for those who die before old age, the approach of death may be accepted, even if not welcomed.

'Things are both more trivial than they ever were, and more important than they ever were', said the playwright Denis Potter, dying at 59, in an interview with Melvyn Bragg, 'and the difference between the trivial and the important doesn't seem to matter – but the *nowness* of everything is absolutely wondrous' (Channel 4, 1994 cited by Seale, 1998: 129).

Death and the afterlife

I have already alluded to the fact that many people still believe in some kind of afterlife. As I mentioned earlier, one study suggests that about 50 per cent in England do so. The figure would doubtless be much higher in countries where traditional religion maintains a stronger hold.

Carl Jung considered that the belief in an afterlife was important for mental health, while Freud by contrast saw it an instance of unhealthy denial. Research seems to have supported Jung's position on the whole. Kalish and Reynolds (1976) found that people with strong religious convictions showed the least anxiety about death, though people with confused religious beliefs, interestingly, showed *more anxiety* than did atheists. So it would appear that a belief in the possibility of some form of afterlife, but a lack of clarity as to its nature, may be particularly worrying. Or perhaps convinced atheists have been forced to face up to their fears at an earlier stage.

Whether or not a belief in an afterlife is helpful to the dying, is of course a very different question than that of whether an afterlife actually exists. But this is a question that I will not attempt to address.

The End

I began this book with the image of a baby's birth, and so it seems appropriate to conclude it like this:

In a bed in a side room on a hospital ward, an elderly woman is drawing close to death. It is some hours since she last spoke and it is not clear whether she is entirely conscious. There are four other people in the room: a son, a daughter, a daughter-in-law and a nurse. They can all see that the end is very near. The son and the daughter are holding their mother's hands. The daughter is murmuring 'Dear mum, dear, dear mum . . .'

And then she stops. 'She's gone', she says, and they all know it is so. There were five people in the room a moment ago, but now there are only four.

Chapter Summary

The End

- In this chapter I have looked at the social context of death, drawing attention to the many cultural differences that exist in relation to death. I have drawn attention in particular to two approaches within secular industrialised society: the medicalised approach (which some suggest represents a 'denial of death') and the 'revivalist' approach which places an emphasis on dying as a part of life to be experienced by the individual concerned.

- I then looked at the impact of death on those around the dying person, discussing the nature of grief and bereavement.

continued

- Finally I looked at the ways that death is experienced by the dying person, looking at different factors and focusing in particular on the differences between deaths that could be predicted in advance and those that cannot, and between deaths in old age and deaths at other ages. Finally I mentioned the impact of different beliefs about the possibility of an afterlife.

Suggested Reading

- Seale, C. (1998) *Constructing Death: The Sociology of Dying and Bereavement* (Cambridge: Cambridge University Press)
- Walter, T. (1994) *The Revival of Death* (London: Routledge)
- Bond, J., Coleman, P. and Peace, S. (eds) (1993) *Ageing in Society* (London: Sage)

  (Useful chapters on death in old age.)

- Currer, C. (2001) *Responding to Grief, Dying and Bereavement and Social Care* (Basingstoke: Palgrave)

  (A book aimed specifically at social care workers with dying and bereaved people.)

References

Chapter 1

Bouchard, T.J., Lykken, D.T., McGue, M., Segal, N.L. and Tellegen, A. (1990) 'Sources of human psychological differences: the Minnesota Study of Twins Reared Apart', *Science* 250: 223–8.

Burman, E. (1994) *Deconstructing Developmental Psychology* (London: Routledge)

Crawley, A.C. (ed.) (1992) *Geoffrey Chaucer: The Canterbury Tales* (Everyman Edition) (London: David Campbell Publishing)

Dawkins, R. (1976) *The Selfish Gene* (Oxford: OUP)

Elster, J. (ed.) (1986) *Karl Marx, A Reader* (Cambridge: CUP)

Howells, C. (1988) *Sartre: The Necessity of Freedom* (Cambridge: CUP)

Sartre, J.-P. (1943) *L'Etre and le Néant* (cited in Howells, 1988)

Steen, R.G. (1996) *DNA and Destiny: Nature and Nurture in Human Behavior* (New York: Plenum Press)

Yolton, J.W. (ed.) (1977) *The Locke Reader* (Cambridge: CUP)

Watson, J.B. (1931) *Behaviourism* (2nd edition) (London: Kegan Paul, Trench & Trubner)

Chapter 2

Berne, E. (1961) *Games People Play: The Psychology of Human Relationships* (Harmondsworth: Penguin)

Erikson, E. (1995) *Childhood and Society* (first published 1951) (London: Vintage)

Freud, S. (1923) *The Ego and the Id*, Standard Edition, Vol. 19 (London: Hogarth Press)

Freud, S. (1933) *New Introductory Lectures in Psychoanalysis*, Standard Edition, Vol. 22 (London: Hogarth Press)

Freud, S. (1949) *An Outline of Psychoanalysis* (London: W.W. Norton & Co.)

Masson, J. (1984) *The Assault on Truth: Freud's Suppression of the Seduction Theory* (Harmondsworth: Penguin)

Plato (1973) *Phaedrus and Letters VII and VIII*, translated by Walter Hamilton (Harmondsworth: Penguin)

Rycroft, C. (1995) *A Critical Dictionary of Psychoanalysis* (2nd edition) (Harmondsworth: Penguin)

Segal, J. (1992) *Melanie Klein* (London: Sage)

Webster, R. (1995) *Why Freud Was Wrong: Sin, Science and Psychoanalysis* (London: HarperCollins)

Chapter 3

Ainsworth, M., Blehar, M., Aters, E. and Wall, S. (1978) *Patterns of Attachment: A Psychological Study of the Strange Situation* (Hillside, NJ: Lawrence Erlbaum)

Bowlby, J. (1951) *Maternal Care and Mental Health* (Geneva: WHO)

Bowlby, J. (1990) *Childcare and the Growth of Love* (first published 1953) (Harmondsworth: Penguin)

Bowlby, J. (1997) *Attachment* (London: Pimlico)

Bowlby, J. (1998a) *Separation* (London: Pimlico)

Bowlby, J. (1998b)*Loss* (London: Pimlico)

Burman, E. (1994) *Deconstructing Developmental Psychology* (London: Routledge)

Clarke, A. and A. (2000) *Early Experience and the Life Path* (London: Jessica Kingsley)

Harlow, H. (1963) in B.M. Foss (ed.) (1963) *Determinants of Human Behaviour* (London: Methuen)

Howe, D., Brandon, M., Hinings, D. and Schofield, G. (1999) *Attachment Theory, Child Maltreatment and Family Support* (London: Macmillan)

Jensen, G.D. and Tolman, C.W. (1962) 'Mother–infant relationship in the monkey, *Macaca Nemestrina*: the effect of brief separation and mother–infant specificity,' in *Journal of Comparative Physiological Psychology* 55: 131–6

Robertson, J. and Bowlby, J. (1952) 'Responses of young children to separation from their mothers', in *Courier of the International Children's Centre* 2: 131–42

Rutter, M. (1981), *Maternal Deprivation Reassessed* (2nd edition) (Harmondsworth: Penguin)

Rutter, M. and the English and Romanian Adoptees Study Team (1998) 'Developmental catch-up, and deficit, following adoption after severe global early privation', *Journal of Child Psychology and Psychiatry* 39(4): 465–76

Chapter 4

Baillargeon, R. (1987) 'Object permanence in 3.5- and 4.5-month-old infants', *Developmental Psychology* 23: 655–64

Burman, E. (1994) *Deconstructing Developmental Psychology* (London: Routledge)

Chen, Z., Sanchez, R.P. and Campbell, T. (1997) 'From beyond to within their grasp: analogical problem solving in 10- and 13-month-old infants', *Developmental Psychology* 33: 790–801

Cox, M.V. (1991) *The Child's Point of View* (2nd edition) (Hemel Hempstead: Harvester)

Donaldson, M. (1978) *Children's Minds* (Glasgow: Fontana)

Goswami, U. (1998) *Cognition in Children* (Hove: Psychology Press)

Mussen, P., Conger, J. and Kagan, J. (1974) *Child Development and Personality* (New York: Harper & Row)

Piaget, J. (1930) *The Child's Conception of Physical Causality* (London: Routledge)

Piaget, J., Montangero, J. and Billeter, J. (1977) 'Les correlats' in *L'Abstraction réfléchissante* (Paris: Presses Universitaires de France)

Vygotsky, L.S. (1962) *Thought and Language* (New York: Wiley)

Chapter 5

Bandura, A. (1977) *Social Learning Theory* (Englewood Cliffs, NJ: Prentice-Hall Inc.)

Berenbaum, S.A. and Hines, M. (1992) 'Early androgens are related to sex-related toy preferences', *Psychological Science* 3: 202–6.

Boswell, J. (1996) *The Marriage of Likeness: Same Sex Unions in Pre-Modern Europe* (London: Fontana)

De Shazer, S. (1985) *Keys to Solution in Brief Therapy* (London/New York: W.W. Norton)

Golombok, S. and Fivush, R. (1994) *Gender Development* (Cambridge: Cambridge University Press)

Herrnstein, R.J., Loveland, D. and Cable, C. (1976) 'Natural concepts in pigeons', *Journal of Experimental Psychology: Animal Behaviour Processes* 2: 285–302

Huxley, A. (1955) *Brave New World* (first published 1932) (Harmonsdworth: Penguin)

Langlois, J.H. and Downs, A.C. (1980) 'Mothers, fathers and peers as socialization agents of sex-typed play behaviors in young children', *Child Development* 51: 1237–47.

Perry, D. and Bussey, K. (1979) 'The social learning theory of sex difference: imitation is alive and well', *Journal of Personality and Social Psychology* 37: 1699–712

Seligman, M. (1975) *Helplessness: On Depression, Development and Death* (San Francisco: Freeman)

Skinner, B.F. (1953) *Science and Human Behaviour*, (New York: Macmillan)

Skinner, B.F. (1960) 'Pigeons in a pelican', *American Psychologist* 15: 28–37

Skinner, B.F. (1974) *About Behaviorism* (London: Jonathan Cape)

Tolman, E.C. (1951) *Collected Papers in Psychology* (Berkeley: University of California Press)

Watson, J.B. (1931) *Behaviourism* (2nd Edition) (London: Kegan Paul, Trench and Trubner)

Chapter 6

Adams, G.R., Gullotta, T.P. and Markstrom-Adams, C. (1994) *Adolescent Life Experiences* (Pacific Grove, CA: Brooks/Cole)

Barber, B.K. (1992) 'Family, Personality and Adolescent Problem Behaviours', *Journal of Marriage and the Family* 56: 375–86

Baumrind, D. (1991) 'The influence of early parenting style on adolescent competence and substance abuse', *Journal of Early Adolescence* 11: 56–95

Bronstein, P., Fitzgerald, M., Briones, M., Pienadz, J. and D'Ari, A. (1993) 'Family emotional expressiveness as a predictor of early adolescent social and psychological adjustment', *Journal of Early Adolescence* 13: 448–71

Clark, R.D. III (1990) 'The impact of AIDS on gender differences in willingness to engage in casual sex', *Journal of Applied Social Psychology*, 20: 771–82

Cobb, N. (1995) *Adolescence: Continuity, Change and Diversity* (2nd edition) (Mountain View, CA: Mayfield)

Durkin, K. (1995) *Developmental Social Psychology* (Oxford: Blackwell)

Dyk, P.H. and Adams, G.R. (1987) 'The association between identity development and intimacy during adolescence: a theoretical treatise', *Journal of Adolescent Research* 2: 223–35.

Elkind, D. (1967) 'Ego-centrism in adolescence', *Child Development* 38: 1025–34

Erikson, E. (1995) *Childhood and Society* (London: Vintage)

Gaddis, A. and Brooks-Gunn, T. (1985) 'The male experience of pubertal change', *Journal of Youth and Adolescence* 14: 61–70

Gilligan, C. (1982) *In a Different Voice: Psychological Theory and Women's Development Morality* (Cambridge, MA: Harvard University Press)

Hopson, B. (1981) 'Response to the papers by Schlossberg, Bramner and Abrego', *Counselling Psychologist* 9 (2): 36ff.

Jessor, R. and Jessor, S. (1979) *Problem Behaviour and Psychosocial Development: a Longitudinal Study of Youth* (New York: Academic Press.)

Kanin, E.J. and Parcell, S.R. (1977) 'Sexual aggression: a second look at the offended female', *Archives of Sexual Behaviour* 6: 67–76

Kegan, R. (1982) *The Evolving Self: Problem and Process in Human Development* (Cambridge, MA: Harvard University Press)

Kroger, J. (1996) *Identity in Adolescence* (London: Routledge)

Kroger, J. (2000) *Identity Development, Adolescence through Adulthood* (London: Sage)

Larson, R. and Lampman-Petraitis, C. (1989) 'Daily emotional status as reported by children and adolescents', *Child Development* 60: 1250–60

Marcia, J. (1993) 'The relational roots of identity', in J. Kroger (ed.), *Discussions on Ego Identity* (Hillsdale, NJ: Lawrence Erlbaum)

Moffit, T.E., Caspi, A., Belsky, J. and Silva, P.A. (1992) 'Childhood experience and the onset of menarche: a test of a sociobiological model', *Child Development* 63: 47–58

Neubauer, G. and Meltzer, W. (1989) 'The role of school, family and peer group in the sexual development of the adolescent', in K. Hurrelmann and U. Engel (eds), *The Social World of Adolescence: International Perspectives* (Berlin/New York: de Gruyter)

Offer T., Ostrov, E., Howard K.I. and Atkinson R. (1988) *The Teenage World: Adolescents' Self-Image in Ten Countries* (New York: Plenum Press)

Perosa, L.M., Perosa, S.L. and Tam, H.P. (1996) 'The contribution of family structure and differentiation to identity development in females', *Journal of Youth and Adolescence* 25: 817–37

Phinney, J.S. (1989) 'Stages of ethnic identity development in minority group adolescents', *Journal of Early Adolescence* 9: 34–49

Phinney, J.S. and Alipuria, L.L. (1990) 'Ethnic identity in college students from four ethnic groups', *Journal of Adolescence* 13: 171–83

Piaget, J. (1968) *Six Psychological Studies* (London: Harvester Press)

Reicher, S. and Emler, N. (1986) 'The management of delinquent reputations', in H. Beloff (ed.), *Getting into Life* (London: Methuen)

Ryan, R.M. and Lynch J.H. (1989) 'Emotional autonomy versus detachment: revisiting the vicissitudes of adolescence and young adulthood', *Child Development* 60: 340–56.

Simmons, R.G., Burgeson, R., Carlton-Ford, S. and Blyth D.A. (1987) 'The impact of cumulative changes in early adolescence', *Child Development* 58: 1220–34.

Steinberg, L. and Silverberg, S.B. (1986) 'The vicissitudes of autonomy in early adolescence', *Child Development* 57: 841–51.

Sugarman, L. (1986) *Life-Span Development: Concepts, Theories and Interventions* (London: Methuen & Co.)

Tupuola, A.M. (1993) 'Critical analysis of adolescent development – a Samoan woman's perspective', unpublished masters thesis, cited by Kroger (1996) (*see above*)

Willemsen, E.W. and Waterman, K.K. (1991) 'Ego identity status and family environment: a correlational study', *Psychological Reports* 69: 1203–12

Wolfgang, M.E., Thornberg, T.R. and Figlio, R.M. (1987) *From Boy to Man, from Delinquency to Crime* (Chicago: University of Chicago Press)

Chapter 7

Erikson, E. (1995) *Childhood and Society* (London: Vintage)

Farrell, M.P. and Rosenberg, S.D. (1981) *Men at Mid-life* (Boston: Auburn House)

Kahn, S., Zimmerman, G., Csikszentmihalyi, M. and Getzels, J.W. (1985) 'Relations between identity in young adulthood and intimacy at mid-life', *Journal of Personality and Social Psychology* 9: 117–26

Kroger, J. (2000) *Identity Development, Adolescence through Adulthood* (London: Sage)

Levinson, D.J. (1978) *The Seasons of a Man's Life* (New York: Ballantine)

Levinson, D.J. with Levinson, J.D. (1996) *The Seasons of a Woman's Life* (New York: Knopf)

Mallory, M. (1984) 'Longitudinal analysis of ego identity status', unpublished doctoral dissertation, University of California, Davis. *Cited by* Kroger (2000: 179–180)

Neugarten, B.L., Wood, V., Kraines, R.J. and Loomis, B. (1963) 'Women's attitudes towards the menopause', *Vita Humana* 6: 140–51.

Peterson, B.E. and Stewart, A.J. (1990) 'Using personal and fictional documents to assess psychosocial development: A case study of Vera Brittain's generativity', *Psychology and Aging* 2: 400–11

Roberts, P. and Newton, P.M. (1987) 'Levinsonian studies of women's adult development', *Psychology and Aging* 2: 154–63

Sugarman, L. (1986) *Life-Span Development: Concepts, Theories and Interventions* (London: Methuen & Co.)

Vaillant, G. (1977) *Adaptation to Life* (Boston: Little, Brown)

Whitbourne, S.K. (1996) *The Aging Individual: Physical and Psychological Perspectives* (New York: Springer-Verlag)

Chapter 8

Barnes, G. (1998) *Family Therapy in Changing Times* (Basingstoke: Macmillan)

Bateson, G. (1973) *Steps to an Ecology of Mind* (St Albans: Paladin)

Carpenter, J. and Treacher, A. (eds) (1993) *Using Family Therapy in the 90s* (Oxford: Blackwell)

Carter, B. and McGoldrick, M. (eds) (1989) *The Changing Family Life Cycle* (Boston/London: Allyn & Bacon)

Donne, John in G.R. Potter and E.M. Simpson (eds) (1953–62) *The Sermons of John Donne*, Vol vii, p. 369 (University of California Press, CA: Berkeley and Los Angeles)

Franklin, C. and Jordan, C. (eds) (1999) *Family Practice: Brief Systems Methods for Social Work* (Pacific Grove, CA: Brooks/Cole)

Franklin, C. and Warren, K. (1999) 'Advances in systems theory', in C. Franklin and C. Jordan (eds), *Family Practice*, pp. 397–425 (Pacific Grove, CA: Brooks/Cole)

Perelberg, R.J. and Miller, A.C. (eds) (1990) *Gender and Power in Families* (London: Routledge)

von Bertalanffy, L. (1971) *General System Theory: Foundations, Development, Application* (London: Allen Lane)

White, J., Essex, S. and O'Reilly, P. (1993) 'Family therapy, systemic thinking and child protection', in J. Carpenter and A. Treacher (eds), *Using Family Therapy in the 90s*, pp. 57–86 (Oxford: Blackwell)

Chapter 9

Anderson, E.S., Dunlea, A. and Kekelis, L. (1993) 'The impact of input: language acquisition in the visually impaired', *First Language* 13: 23–49

Carter, B. and McGoldrick, M. (eds) (1989) *The Changing Family Life Cycle* (Boston/London: Allyn & Bacon)

Cione, G., Paolicelli, P.B., Sordi, C. and Vinter, A. (1993) 'Sensorimotor development in cerebral palsied infants assessed with the Uzgiris-Hunt scales', *Developmental Medicine and Child Neurology* 35: 1055–66

Erikson, E. (1995) *Childhood and Society* (London: Vintage)

Gath, A. (1977) 'The impact of an abnormal child upon the parents', *British Journal of Psychiatry* 130: 405–10

Greenberg, M.T. and Kushe, C. (1989) 'Cognitive, personal and social development of deaf children and adolescents', in M. Wang, M. Reynolds and H. Walberg (eds), *The Handbook of Special Education: Research and Practice*, Vol. 3, pp. 95–129 (New York: Pergamon)

Grossman, F.K. (1972) *Brothers and Sisters of Retarded children* (Syracuse, NY: Syracuse University Press)

Hodapp, R.M. (1998) *Development and Disabilities: Intellectual, Sensory and Motor Impairments* (Cambridge: Cambridge University Press)

Hodapp, R.M. and Krasner, D.V. (1995) 'Families of children with disabilities: findings from a national sample of eighth-grade students', *Exceptionality* 5: 71–81

Howells, G. (1997) 'A general practice perspective', in J. O'Hara and A. Sperlinger (eds), *Adults With Learning Disabilities*, pp. 61–79 (Chichester: Wiley)

Lollar, D.J. (1994) *Social Development and the Person with Spina Bifida* (Washington, DC: Spina Bifida Association of America)

Martin, J., Meltzer, H. and Elliot, D. (1988) *The Prevalence of Disability among Adults* (London: HMSO)

Minnes, P. (1988) 'Family stress associated with a developmentally handicapped child', *International Review of Research on Mental Retardation* 15: 195–226

O'Hara, J. and Sperlinger, A. (eds) (1997) *Adults with Learning Disabilities* (Chichester: Wiley)

Petitto, L. and Marentette, P.F. (1991) 'Babbling in the manual mode: evidence for the ontogeny of language', *Science* 251: 1493–6

Pinker, S. (1994) *The Language Instinct* (Harmondsworth: Penguin)

Quinn, P. (1998) *Understanding Disability – a Lifespan Approach* (London: Sage)

Sobsey, D. (1994) *Violence and Abuse in the Life of People with Disabilities: The End of Silent Acceptance* (Baltimore, MD: P.H. Brookes)

Solnit, A. and Stark, M. (1961) 'Mourning and the birth of a defective child', *Psychoanalytic Study of the Child* 16: 523–37

Sperlinger, A. (1997) 'Introduction', in J. O'Hara and A. Sperlinger (eds), *Adults With Learning Disabilities*, pp. 3–16 (Chichester: Wiley)

UPIAS (1976) *Fundamental Principles of Disability* (London: Union of the Physically Impaired Against Segregation)

Warren, D.H. (1994) *Blindness and Children: An Individual Differences Approach.* (Cambridge: Cambridge University Press)

(WHO) (1980) *International Classification of Impairments, Disabilities and Handicaps* (Geneva: World Health Organisation)

Chapter 10

Baltes, P.B., Smith, J. and Staudinger U.M. (1992) 'Wisdom and Successful Ageing', in T.B. Sonderegg (ed.), *Nebraska Symposium on Motivation* 39, 123–67 (Lincoln, NE: University of Nebraska Press)

Becker, H. (1963) *Outsiders: Studies in the Sociology of Deviance* (New York: Free Press)

Bond, J., Briggs, R. and Coleman, P. (1993) 'The study of ageing', in J. Bond, P. Coleman and S. Peace (eds), *Ageing in Society* (2nd Edition), pp. 19–52 (London: Sage)

Bond, J., Coleman, P. and Peace, S. (eds) (1993) *Ageing in Society* (2nd Edition) (London: Sage)

Brecher, E.M. (1984) *Love, Sex and Aging: A Consumers' Union Report* (Boston: Little, Brown)

Briggs, R. (1985) 'Acute confusion', in M. Lye (ed.), *Acute Geriatric Medicine* (Lancaster: MTP Press)

Carp, F.M. (1969) 'Senility or garden-variety maladjustment', *Journal of Gerontology* 24: 203–8

Cattell, R. (1971) *Abilities, their Structure, Growth and Action* (New York: Houghton Mifflin)

Clayton, V. (1975) 'Erikson's theory of human development as it applies to the aged: wisdom as contradictive cognition', *Human Development* 18: 119–28.

Coleman, P., Bond, J. and Peace, S. (1993) 'Ageing in the twentieth century', in J. Bond, P. Coleman and S. Peace (eds), *Ageing in Society* (2nd Edition), pp. 1–18 (London: Sage)

Cox, B.D., Blaxter, M., Buckle, A.L.J., and Fenner, N.P. (1987) *The Health and Lifestyle Survey* (London: Health Promotion Research Trust)

Cumming, E. and Henry, W. (1961) *Growing Old: The Process of Disengagement* (New York: Basic Books)

Davey, B. (ed.) (1995) *Birth to Old Age: Health in Transition* (Buckingham: Open University Press)

Dittman-Kohli, F. and Baltes, P.B. (1990) 'Towards a neofunctionalist conception of adult intellectual development: wisdom as a prototypical case of intellectual growth', in C. Alexander and E. Langer (eds), *Beyond Formal Operations: Alternative Endpoints to Human Development* (Oxford: Oxford University Press)

Erikson, E.H. (1995) *Childhood and Society* (London: Vintage) (first published 1951)

Estes, C.C., Swan, J.S. and Gerard, L.E. (1982) 'Dominant and competing paradigms in gerontology', *Ageing and Society* 2: 151–64

Eysenck, H.J. (1987) 'Personality and ageing: an exploratory analysis', *Journal of Social Behaviour and Personality* 3: 11–21

Gutmann, D.L. (1987) *Reclaimed Powers: Towards a New Psychology of Men and Women in Later Life* (New York: Basic Books)

Healey, Lord Denis (2000) *Guardian*, 'Society' supplement (27/9/00: 3)

Kroger, J. (2000) *Identity Development, Adolescence through Adulthood* (London: Sage)

Langer, E.J. (1983) *The Psychology of Control* (London: Sage)

Lemert, E. (1972) *Human Deviance, Social Problems and Social Control* (Englewood Cliffs, NJ: Prentice-Hall)

Martin, J., Meltzer, H. and Elliot, D. (1988) *The Prevalence of Disability Among Adults* (London: HMSO)

Slater, R. (1995) 'Experiencing later life', Ch. 10 in B. Davey (ed.), *Birth to Old Age: Health in Transition* (Buckingham: Open University Press)

Sugarman, L. (1986) *Life-Span Development: Concepts, Theories and Interventions* (London: Routledge)

Suzman, R.M., Harris, T., Hadley, E.C., Kovar, M.G. and Weindruch, R. (1992) 'The robust oldest old: optimistic perspectives for increasing healthy life expectancy', in R.M. Suzman, D.P. Willis and K.G. Manton (eds), *The Oldest Old*, pp. 341–58 (New York: Oxford University Press)

Walker, A. (1993) 'Poverty and inequality in old age', in J. Bond, P. Coleman and S. Peace (eds), *Ageing in Society* (2nd Edition), pp. 280–303 (London: Sage)

Chapter 11

Ariès, P (1976) *Western Attitudes Towards Death* (London: Marion Boyars)

Bond, J., Coleman, P. and Peace, S. (eds) (1993) *Ageing in Society* (2nd Edition) (London: Sage)

Bowlby, J. (1946) *Forty-Four Juvenile Thieves: Their Characters and Home-Life* (London: Baillière, Tindall & Cox)

Channel 4 (1994) 'An interview with Dennis Potter' (London: Channel 4 TV)

Cumming, E. and Henry, W. (1961) *Growing Old: The Process of Disengagement* (New York: Basic Books)

Currer, C. (2001) *Responding to Grief: Dying, Bereavement and Social Care* (Basingstoke: Palgrave)

Davey, B. (ed.) (1995) *Birth to Old Age: Health in Transition* (Buckingham: Open University Press)

Davies, D. (1991) 'Cremation research project', *Pharos* 57(1): 22–9

Howe, D. (1995) *Attachment Theory for Social Work Practice* (London: Macmillan)

Kalish, R.A. (1985) 'The social context of death and dying', in R.H. Binstock and E. Shanas (eds), *Handbook of Ageing and the Social Sciences*, pp. 149–70 (New York: Van Nostrand Reinhold)

Kalish, R.A. and Reynolds, D.K. (1976) *Death and Ethnicity: A Psychocultural Study* (Los Angeles: University of Southern California Press)

Kastenbaum, R. and Alsenburg, R. (1976) *The Psychology of Death* (New York: Springer)

Kearl, M.C. (1989) *Endings: a Sociology of Death and Dying* (Oxford: Oxford University Press)

Kübler-Ross, E. (1970) *On Death and Dying* (London: Tavistock)

Murray Parkes, C. (1991) 'Attachment, bonding and psychiatric problems after bereavement in adult life', in Murray Parkes, C., Stevenson-Hinde, J. and Marris, P. (eds), *Attachment Across the Life Cycle*, pp. 268–92 (London and New York: Routledge)

Murray Parkes, C., Laungani, P. and Young, B. (1997) *Death and Bereavement Across Cultures* (London: Routledge)

NAHA/RoSPA Strategy Group (1990) *Action on Accidents* (Birmingham: NAHA/RoSPA)

Office of National Statistics (2000) *1998 Vital Statistics* (London: HMSO)

Sable, P. (1989) 'Attachment, anxiety and loss of husband', *American Journal of Orthopsychiatry* 59(4): 550–6

Schut, H., Stroebe, M., de Keijser, J. and van den Brout, J. (1997) 'Intervention for the bereaved: gender differences in the efficacy of grief counselling', British *Journal of Clinical Psychology* 36: 63–72

Seale, C. (1995) 'Dying', in B. Davey (ed.) *Birth to Old Age: Health in Transition*, pp. 178–87 (Buckingham: Open University Press)

Seale, C. (1998) *Constructing Death: The Sociology of Dying and Bereavement* (Cambridge: Cambridge University Press)

Sidell, M. (1993) 'Death, dying and bereavement', in J. Bond, P. Coleman and S. Peace (eds), *Ageing in Society* (2nd Edition), pp. 151–79 (London: Sage)

Stroebe, M. and Schut, H. (1999) 'The dual process model of coping with bereavement', *Death Studies* 23: 197–224

Thomas, Dylan, 'Do not go gentle into that good night' in *The Oxford Book of Twentieth Century English Verse*, edited by Philip Larkin (1973), p. 474 (Oxford: Clarendon Press)

Young, M. and Cullen, L. (1996) *A Good Death: Conversations with East Londoners* (London: Routledge)

Walter, T. (1994) *The Revival of Death* (London: Routledge)

Index